FAITH, NATIONALISM, AND THE FUTURE
OF LIBERAL DEMOCRACY

FAITH
NATIONALISM

and the Future of

LIBERAL
DEMOCRACY

DAVID M. ELCOTT

WITH
C. Colt Anderson, Tobias Cremer, and Volker Haarmann

University of Notre Dame Press
Notre Dame, Indiana

University of Notre Dame Press
Notre Dame, Indiana 46556
undpress.nd.edu

Published in the United States of America

Library of Congress Control Number: 2021931604

ISBN: 978-0-268-20060-2 (Hardback)
ISBN: 978-0-268-20062-6 (Webpdf)
ISBN: 978-0-268-20059-6 (Epub)

CONTENTS

Acknowledgments   vii

Introduction: Why We Write   1

ONE   Facing Liberal Democracy's Challenge: Why We   21
        Highlight the Role of Religious Identity in Populist
        Nationalist Movements

TWO   How to Understand the Populism of Europe   45

THREE   The Nationalist Assault on Liberal Democracy   65
        in the United States

FOUR   A Catholic Response to the Errors of Catholic   89
        Nationalism

FIVE   The Post-Holocaust Protestant Church as the   117
        Defender of Pluralistic Democracy

SIX   Each Human Being as an Image of God: A Jewish   135
        Response to Religious Nationalism

Epilogue: Religious Leadership, Civil Discourse,   157
and Democracy

Notes   165

Bibliography   181

About the Authors   215

Index   219

ACKNOWLEDGMENTS

Having peered into the deep abyss of populist nationalism and a president with autocratic instincts, the American people stood back from the brink. Barely. The 2020 election in the United States laid bare democracy's polarized fractures. A new president is inaugurated. Democracy prevails, for the moment. Yet, while Joe Biden won with a call for democratic decency, 74 million Americans voted to continue and expand Donald Trump's vision of America, assuring further assaults on its battered democratic processes. Similar elections around the world have shown that liberal democracy, embattled and threatened, can still triumph. But the road remains painful, fraught with anxiety and loss.

COVID-19 yet locks us up; the police murder of George Floyd in Summer 2020 sent us out to the streets; peaceful protesters were gassed and beaten. The November election in the United States promises further polarization and chaos. With the end of the Angela Merkel era, Germany's democratic future is uncharted. The Prime Minister of Israel is on trial, as is the nation's political outlook. Poland and Hungary continue their assaults on democratic norms even as the streets fill with protest and France's passionate secular laïcité furiously confronts radical Muslim assaults. Around the world, borders are closed to immigrants as societies fear their identities are imperiled. And dominant political movements from India to Myanmar, Indonesia to Brazil, threaten the rights of their minorities. In particular, the use of religious identity to fuel a vicious populist fervor is shaking the foundations of liberal democracy. The world this year seems to teeter on a dangerous precipice.

Although no historical moment is identical to another, it is easy to feel déjà vu. My mother fled Germany in spring 1939; her parents in August. The rest of my patriotic German family, with a thousand-year history in the Rhine Valley, perished under the populist nationalist fervor that swept so many countries, as did some eighty million people around the world. The two young coauthors of this book, Volker and Tobias, are Germans whose Protestant families lived through World War II, some family members fighting for Hitler. This painful legacy brought us together, along with Catholic historian and theologian C. Colt Anderson, with the shared purpose of reconciliation and mutual respect in passionate support of liberal democracy. It is no small feat in today's environment, where liberal democracy is increasingly threatened by those who seek its diminution or even its demise.

The memory of the past, the dangers of the present, and our faith in democracy are why we wrote this book.

We are an intergenerational team. I met Volker when he was a brilliant doctoral student at the University of Tübingen, long before he became a leader in the Protestant Church of the Rhineland. Together, as friends and colleagues, we have invested in Middle East peace and German Christian and Jewish relations. Colt became a cherished colleague and intellectual soulmate as we worked together imagining roles faith leaders could play in civic affairs. Tobias was a rare find, a young, erudite global scholar, studying in Paris, Harvard, and Cambridge, with professional stints in the German Bundestag. A deep friendship has blossomed alongside profound intellectual exchange. As much as we all are separated in age by decades, we are united across generations in our commitment to democracy.

Initially we planned to study major religions and nations around the world, calling on them to support human and civil rights and the democratic values that honor civic engagement. That far-reaching task proved too difficult to fulfill, so we ultimately focused on Europe and the United States even as we reference other political systems and religions. During this process, we turned for guidance and inspiration to a core of activist theologians and political scholars. Their eloquent voices are found throughout the book and, as friends and colleagues, have a place of honor here: Rajni Bakshi, Elan Ezrachi, Seth Farber, Katharine Henderson, Anantanand Rambachan, Tony Richie, Alissa Wahid, Jim Winkler, and Michelle Winowatan. We owe each of them a great debt for having participated in this undertaking, to defend liberal democracy as people of faith. This book would not exist without their insights and passion for goodness.

We are so grateful for the generous grant from the Ford Foundation, amplified with the support of Elaine Petschek, that launched this project, the nourishing encouragement of Eli Bortz and Matthew Dowd, the editors at the University of Notre Dame Press, and the careful, insistent editing of Mike Levine and Bob Banning that brought enhanced clarity to the story.

This moment of history tries the souls of even the deepest believers in human goodness. Sometimes the best way to fortify this belief is to experience the love of those who surround you. My children and grandchildren allow me to believe in hope, in a future in which fearless love and compassion thrive. My wife, Shira, embodies the gift of gratitude for the beauty of the world, and showers me with that gift of love and faith. From there, we can extend to the larger circles, family and friends and colleagues, until we embrace everything, for the whole universe emerged from the same pinpoint of energy and life. For those of faith, from one singularity, the divine source of all.

We write this—Colt and Tobias and Volker and I—during a global pandemic, a surreal time of deep uncertainty. We write because, in spite of the anxiety and fear, we join with you as believers that the arc of history so often invoked does bend toward justice and love and a future where democracy thrives and human dignity is honored. Together we can fortify the democratic institutions and values of our communities, our countries, and our world.

David M. Elcott
January 2021

Introduction

Why We Write

We write from a place of deep anxiety, with the awareness that one's personal biography in ways subtle and overt informs the choices and perspectives of even the most ivory-towered academic. We are easily brought to dark places watching young white Americans, with torches blazing, shouting "white power" and "Jews will not replace us," reminiscent of Nazi Brown Shirts in 1930. Similar demonstrations in Poland and Hungary call for a return to the traditions of Christian Europe. The populist and nationalist rhetoric of many political leaders grinds daily against our fundamental, if unduly hopeful, belief in the goodness and compassion of humanity. Across the planet, anger toward globe-trotting elites, austerity-minded politicians, and distant bureaucrats is igniting rebellious electoral upsets in nation after nation. And, these nationalist populists say, a deadly pandemic is fitting punishment for globalization, because foreigners bring death.

There is a story behind this rebellion. The Enlightenment led to the American and French Revolutions, the dawn of civil rights for citizens and democratic institutions that nurtured and sustained those rights. Increasingly, religious and civic affairs were disentangled, with a concomitant focus on enhancing individual rights.

While religious discrimination, as with other forms of prejudice, remained, secularism seemed ascendant and citizenship was decreasingly tethered to the majority religion. In many regions, personal autonomy and an expansion of freedom diminished the role of the "church." As the philosopher Elizabeth Anderson lightly explained: "If you look back at the origins of liberalism, it starts first with a certain settlement about religious difference. Catholics, Protestants—they are killing each other! Finally, Germany, England, all these places say, We're tired of these people killing each other, so we're going to make a peace settlement: religious toleration, live and let live."[1]

Following World War II, the idea that religion belongs at home and should be removed from the public square seemed to become the norm, a public value even if transgressed. Emerging nations, from India to Indonesia to Germany, refused to include the majority religion in their constitutions, while the United Nations declared freedom of religion a human right.

With the collapse of dominating empires, including the Soviet Union, and the diminished role of the United States in fostering democracy, religion-fueled nationalism has made a comeback, but now in the territory of liberal democracies. And so a spotlight on the role of religion is back in vogue, not merely a return to earlier epochs, but directing us to a very different and angry future.

In 1986, James Carse wrote about finite and infinite games.[2] As applied to Western liberal democratic systems, there is a tension—liberal democracy itself is an infinite game where one never "wins" permanently and the system has a range of checks and balances to keep the game going. It is hoped that regular and free elections, permanent bureaucracies, representative legislatures, local jurisdictions, independent courts, and unspoken norms and behaviors all help to keep the game alive and vital. Yet autocrats and autocratic political movements seek to permanently win, end the game with total victory and, in essence, shut down the game. These players, found around the world, have been given or have taken on names: the alt-right, populist nationalists, neo-Fascists, white supremacists, or other ethnic, racial, or religious supremacists.[3] While real differences may distinguish them, country by country, as a group we unite them in their commitment to illiberal democracy, the term we will use as we explore the ways religious identity is used to give them support.

Religion, too, has historically held the tension described by Carse—on one hand, religion can be an infinite game of change and growth. Religions also have had periods in which players sought to vanquish the other and end the game with a triumphant church.

This book is about the challenges to liberal democracies as some players, using religious identity as fuel, seek to make the game finite. Although no one election, legislative vote, or court decision alone signals apocalyptic catastrophe, in spite of what pundits may claim, liberal democracy can be weakened and its efficacy eroded by savvy players. These opponents hope to win by permanently destroying the competition, gutting democratic institutions by purging those seeking to uphold the historic standards and norms of those institutions. These opponents promote political violence as well as legislative and executive decisions that undermine the core institutions and processes of liberal democracies. They use all forms of media to damage faith in what is factual and true. They threaten dissent. This assault is occurring in the United States and Europe and in many vulnerable liberal democracies across Africa, Asia, and Latin America. This is what illiberal democracy is all about, ending the game with a final, outright victory. The success or failure of democracy's opponents may well determine how the "game" of democracy unfolds.

Political Revolt in the Name of the Majority

As we said, an unmistakable seething anger flows across the globe. This anger is symptomatic of two broader trends in many liberal Western democracies. One is a righteous populist uprising in many countries over the place of the nation, a perception that tyrannical globalism is undermining and subjugating national autonomy. In this sense, populism is a response to a perceived way-of-life economic and spiritual stress that threatens a significant segment, if not the majority, of the nation. And the nation, as viewed by these populists, is the reification of a romanticized mythic history and culture that binds believers and excludes those not welcome, who do not or are not allowed to share these beliefs. Nationalist fervor thus provides deep meaning for its adherents now and clear, often exclusionist, political and policy choices for the future. A second parallel trend supports populist nationalism by offering a fundamental reshaping of politics by the resurgence of religion as a national identity marker—over a century after Nietzsche declared that "God is dead."[4]

A revolt by citizens against their nation's institutions and leaders is not per se a new phenomenon. Only a century ago, it seemed to be the norm in much of Europe. As Jill Lapore notes, by the 1930s, the infant democracies were under siege, Mussolini could boast that the liberal states would fail, and Hitler declared that he had achieved a "beautiful democracy."[5] As democratic governments fell around the world, the victors fortified each other in the language and policies that othered the vulnerable and marginalized (and often murdered) those deemed threats to the nation. The institutions of democracy were gutted.

By 2005, as in the 1930s, the numbers of liberal democracies again began to fall. Once again, triumphalist populist nationalists today share ideology and policy, as globally interconnected as the cosmopolitan free-market globalism the populists repudiate. Explosive technological changes are employed to alter the social architecture of visibility, access, and community, challenging the democratic contours of the public sphere as well as the social norms and political structures.[6] The leaders of these movements adopt language and strategies they then apply to the unique character of their own polity. They find support in the nationalism of their neighbors, believing that a new world of illiberal democracy will bring them revolutionary power.[7]

This union of nationalism and populism cultivates a belief in divisions between "us" and "them," a belief in patriotic folk living in their own country and joining in fierce opposition to the globalist status quo. They are the people who see themselves as deeply patriotic, yet they are the forgotten, virtuous, struggling and hardworking majority against the corrupt, self-serving elite consumed with political correctness and indifferent to the suffering and humiliation of the common folk.[8] A second aspect of this union creates a polity of insider and outsider. There is the majority, "people like us," who share values and history, who are grounded in a specific and unique culture, and who defend national purity and protect it from institutions and foreign intruders that would rob them of their way of life: globalists, multinational companies, immigrants who take away jobs, Muslims, "foreign" ethnic groups, and cosmopolitan Jews.[9]

The "democracy" of illiberal democracies is defined by the pure expression of the general will of the people, the majority, who can determine collectively what is true and right for their community. It assumes a shared discourse and set of values and beliefs. If there are dissenters, they do not have a voice in the decisions made by the community, nor should they have the right to veto the will of the majority. It is certainly an expansion of democracy in which the interests and voices of the ordinary people feature far more prominently,[10] but at a cost. When a minority is perceived to be the threat, democracy can be remolded to limit rather than expand participation. True unfettered majority-rule demands constant vigilance against alien voices, values, and people. Even when elected, as in the United States, Israel, Hungary, and Poland, illiberal leaders willing to vilify opponents as enemies of the state, attack the press, and demonize immigrants continue to rally against these nefarious forces that threaten at the borders, both physical and psychological. They claim to speak in the name of the silent majority. And in the cases that most occupy our focus, they will invoke the majority's religion as the foundation of the state—as the religion sanctioned not only by the consent of the governed, but by God. It is in this sense that populism, nationalism, and religious identities converge as illiberal democracies.

That said, illiberal democracy is contextual, reflective of the unique culture and history of each particular nation. Nationalist policies could be promulgated in the name of protecting women and LGBTQ citizens in Holland and Denmark against perceived Muslim homophobia and misogyny, yet be antigay in Poland. Hungarian leaders laud Israel as a Jewish bulwark of civilization even as they promote anti-Semitic tropes in Hungary. In most cases, the religion of the majority is fused with these populist movements as a crucial historical identity marker, grounding its patriotic citizens in the hoary traditions of their nation that leave little room for the "Other."

The language of Viktor Orbán, dominating Hungarian politics in the second decade of the twenty-first century, exemplifies illiberal democracy. He contends, first, that "there is an alternative to liberal democracy: it is called Christian democracy." As he argues, Christian democracy "is not about defending religious articles of faith." Instead, it seeks to protect "the ways of life springing from Christian culture." And this, he adds, means defending "human dignity, the family and the nation." Orbán goes on to warn his listeners to avoid an "intellectual trap"—namely, "the claim that Christian democracy can also, in fact, be liberal." To accept this argument, he tells his partisans, is tantamount to surrendering in the battle of ideas. Therefore, he urges his listeners, "Let us confidently declare that Christian democracy is not liberal. Liberal democracy is liberal, while Christian democracy is, by definition, not liberal: it is, if you like, illiberal."[11] In Israel, Jews defend the Jewish nation. In India, it is Hindus, in Myanmar, Buddhists, and in Indonesia, Muslims. Each group, in its historical, cultural, and religious uniqueness, defends the "true" nation against perceived invaders, barbarians who would pollute its purity.

Roger Eatwell and Matthew Goodwin explain that these populist nationalist movements share a set of deeply rooted societal changes that propel them. They distrust the political elites who are distant and not representative of their interests, they feel attacked as inhumane when they challenge immigration as a threat to their culture, and these feelings combine to (a) undermine the political alignments which allowed liberal democracies to thrive and (b) engender a sense of deprivation and loss.[12]

This sense of loss and abandonment among supporters of illiberal democracy, this experience of *déclassement*, is little understood by their critics. As one conservative critic of poor whites in America wrote in 2016, reflecting on the election of Donald Trump as the forty-fifth president of the United States, "Morally, they [Trump supporters] are indefensible. . . . The white American underclass is in thrall to a vicious, selfish culture whose main products are misery and used heroin needles. Donald Trump's speeches make them feel good. So does OxyContin."[13] But as Arlie Hochschild explains, those who are rebelling against the established elites see themselves as dutifully standing in line, having patiently waited their turn for the benefits of a globalized world that have never materialized. African Americans and gays in the United States, Muslim immigrants in Germany, Jews in Hungary and Poland are convenient enemies. Hochschild describes Donald Trump supporters: "Many have become discouraged, others depressed. They yearn to feel pride but instead have felt shame. Their land is no longer their own. Joined (at a Trump rally) with others like themselves, they now feel hopeful, joyous, elated. . . . As if magically lifted, *they are no longer strangers in their own land.*"[14]

They are clearly in pain. The death rate among high school–educated white American men and women from what are described as "deaths of despair" rose precipitously over the first decades of the twenty-first century.[15] And across the world, they are voting and marching against the existing globalist, neoliberal order. In so many places, then, there is a sense that the social contract has been shattered. To those who feel disenfranchised, liberal democracy has robbed them of their dignity, values, and culture. As Yuli Tamir notes, "It is easier to be a globalist if you are likely to enjoy the benefits of an open market, or to support free immigration if you feel secure in your social status and do not fear that newcomers are going to take your job, or reduce the value of your property by renting the next-door apartment, forcing your neighborhood schools to face new challenges." Nationalist feelings, Tamir continues, are a sensible response rather than an uncontrolled outburst.[16]

She adds: "Globalism failed to replace nationalism because it couldn't offer a political agenda that meets the most basic needs of modern individuals: the desire to be autonomous and self-governing agents, the will to live a meaningful life that stretches beyond the self, the need to belong, the desire to be part of a creative community, to feel special, find a place in the chain of being, and to enjoy a sense (or the illusion) of stability and cross-generational continuity."[17]

In addition, as Alissa Wahid explains in describing the threats to liberal democracy in Muslim-majority Indonesia, nations are faced with the declining power of the state to address needs, the lack of effective law enforcement, weak education systems that fail to adequately promote democracy, huge economic and social gaps, and ethno-racial prejudice between different groups. All of this combines to threaten the secular political system that allowed for religious freedom to flourish.[18]

Ironically, established religions often exacerbate these tensions. Faith communities have much to say about life's meaning and the need to uphold valued traditions, providing an abiding sense of comfort and belonging. But faith communities also can challenge the norms of society, projecting a threat to those comforting traditions. Facing societal conflicts, the Catholic Church of Pope Francis, whether in Italy or the United States, became a powerful voice defending foreign undocumented migrants. The same high moral claim of compassion for wandering Muslims could be found in mainline churches such as the Evangelical Church in Germany. Episcopalians, Reform Jews, and the United Church of Christ opened their doors to LGBTQ congregants, sanctioning same-sex marriage with rainbow flags. Progressive religious leaders marched arm in arm with African Americans fighting to tear down beloved memorials to dead segregationist and Confederate leaders in the American South.

It is also true that liberal democracies became preoccupied with the subjugation of those who are marginalized, of the homeless, and of the various minorities whose oppression is real. For so many, the rights of these marginalized individuals seemed to triumph over the values and concerns of the majority. As Michael Walzer notes, the liberal democratic revolution, in providing the benefits of citizenship, democratic government, science education, and economic advance, required the defeat of people's religious leaders and customary way of life.[19] Liberal nation-states and the social activist liberal churches that support them were seen as ignoring a very powerful constituency that is dismayed by the unwillingness of liberal elites to acknowledge the many ways diversity, including migrants, is destabilizing.[20] Illiberal democratic political movements and their leaders do not turn to the progressive voices of their churches and synagogues to express their anger and hurt. They seek to reestablish the purity of their nation, grounded in what they view as a traditional national culture that weds the state and society with the dominant religion. As we will describe, this deep connection to national religious identity is effectively used by these leaders to fuel that anger and hurt.

The focus of this book is not the nation-state itself. The revolutions that swept the world, from the United States in 1776 and France in 1789 to post–World War II, established nations built on shared memories, contemporary political association and a belief in a shared destiny. As Shlomo Avineri explains, "This nationalism upheld universal values, and its clearest manifestation was a statement by the father of Italian nationalism, Giuseppe Mazzini, who said he achieved being a citizen of the world by being the son of his nation and his country. This is how nationalism—and support for the independence of Poland, Greece and Italy—became the cornerstone of the progressive political forces of the 19th century."[21]

In this construct, Marx was wrong. The universalism of united workers never quenched the thirst for a more local, particular identity—not in the 1880s, as nation-states were forming, not with the collapse of empires, the world wars, or the dismemberment of the Soviet Union. Even in more recent years, in the name of democracy and the rights of a people to self-govern, new states form and plebiscites take place, from Catalan to Scotland, South Sudan to Kosovo. Yet the standing of liberal democracy governance as an efficient political system capable of addressing the range of issues facing nations today certainly has been compromised; democratic governments often seem incapable of effective decision-making. When one looks at the polarization that paralyzes policy and politics in nations from Israel to Britain and Indonesia, from Chile and Bolivia to the United States, Australia, and even Canada, it is easy to despair. The democratic national enterprise is for sure messy, and the issues and markers that unite a community are often fraught as governments attempt to deal with internal tensions, from language to religion, geography to ethnicity, cultural norms to political values. That said, within this world of nation-states are many that protect the rights of all their citizens, liberal democracies that, while struggling to govern, fervently hold on to democratic principles that defend the civil liberties and human rights of all those who reside within their borders. Our focus, however, is on those nations where liberal democracy is most challenged and under assault.

The national populism that undergirds illiberal democratic movements is not a flash protest, nor is it the final resting place for old white men. It no doubt will remain a potent force whose concerns must be addressed.[22] Patriotism, a sense of community, with mutual obligations and shared values among citizens, should not be the sole domain of conservative or illiberal ideologies. If liberal democracies have failed to convey life's meaning to their citizens, they must move quickly and respectfully to remedy this cardinal failure.

Critique can be lovingly patriotic. "It's a paradox of democracy that the best way to defend it is to attack it, to ask more of it, by way of criticism, protest, and dissent."[23] We fervently hope that liberal democratic leaders will seek to better understand the anger of their constituents, listen to their grievances, and address the chasm of class difference separating successful globalists from the disillusioned average working-class citizens, thereby renewing the social contract. That said, there is an imminent danger that core values of liberal democracy, with a focus on equity and human and civil rights, will be lost. As Anantanand Rambachan writes: "The problem of attributing ultimate value to a finite nation takes a sinister turn, with violent consequences, when definitions of the nation and national identity are championed to exclude some communities and to privilege others," especially when God is the source and justification for the exclusion.[24] As we look at the detritus of populist nationalist movements over the past hundred years, the cliché rings true that liberal democracy is deeply flawed, yet better than its alternatives. The illiberal alternatives that have arisen these past decades are the concern that drives this study.

An additional caveat here is critical. Antidemocratic political parties and governments are not the monopoly of right-wing movements. In fact, attacks on democracy often sound quite similar, whether coming from the left or the right. Daniel Ortega came to power in Nicaragua as an impassioned leftist after overthrowing a vicious dictatorship. His "Marxist" policies and alliances were perceived as so threatening to the United States under Ronald Reagan that a covert campaign to oust Ortega was initiated by Washington. Ortega, the avowed leftist, soon began to undermine the newly minted democratic institutions and processes of Nicaragua, replete with assaulting a free press and free association, suppressing civil rights, and attacking the opposition as traitors. Decades later, when Ortega and his wife returned to power, they aligned with reactionary forces, including Christian religious reactionaries, and once again assaulted democracy, now from the right in a family-run kleptocracy. In no way does this study exonerate left-wing populist extremists from antidemocratic behavior. They, too, threaten imminent danger to the human and civil rights and shared values of a liberal democracy. That said, at this moment in history, the focus of this book is the rise of illiberal, nationalist regimes and political movements, sometimes called the alt-right in the United States, and the ways that religious identity can be manipulated to attack and undermine liberal democratic institutions and processes.

Religion and National Identity

The idea that religion can play a central role in national identity is certainly not new. In the Bible, Joshua is commanded, after conquering Canaan, to proscribe all the idolatrous nations that reside there, as they could lead Israelites away from the God of Israel. Greek and Roman rulers made themselves gods to stamp their empires with divine approval. The nations of Europe have never stopped fighting over which religion would identify them. Spain united under the very Catholic Ferdinand and Isabella. To this day, the four Nordic national flags as well as the flag of Switzerland are emblazed with a Protestant Christian cross, while the ruling monarch of England has headed the Church of England for centuries. Jill Lepore reminds us that in the United States, religion was enlisted to battle the godlessness of Communism, with congregation membership shortly after World War II well over one hundred million. The number of Southern Baptists doubled between 1941 and 1961. The evangelical superstar Billy Graham, who preached to millions, became the counselor of presidents.[25] Phyllis Schlafly and others awakened a Christian opposition to secularism to save America from eternal damnation: "Their foot soldiers marched from the nation's Evangelical churches."[26]

Seeking a Different Path

For liberal democracy to flourish, its advocates will need to imagine and express effective responses that challenge the use of religious identity to fuel those who seek its demise. This is no easy task, for there is no neutral test of religious authenticity, and faith is complex and contradictory.[27] The same Bible used to excoriate homosexuals, condemning them to an eternal damnation, also proclaims all individuals, regardless of their sexual identity, as beloved images of God. Standing against religiously inflamed Hindu zealots destroying a mosque are devout Hindu leaders calling for respect across religions. Jewish religious fanatics may write on the doors of Palestinian shops, "Death to Arabs," while no less passionate Jews arrive the next morning to clean the defaced doors. If we see political leaders using religion as a cudgel to foment hatred and violence, how do we distinguish their faith from that of Martin Luther King Jr.,

Gandhi, or Pope John Paul II (who "shaped the politics of east central Europe in the 1980s as a pastor, evangelist, and witness to basic human rights")?[28] When faith is inextricably wedded to the political realm, determining what is true and pure is enigmatic.

No doubt, there have been and continue to be deeply believing religious, pious actors who see this illiberal form of state building as the perfect vehicle to promote exclusive religious conformity. An excellent example would be the ultra-Orthodox Haredi parties in Israel, who fervently believe that divine law supersedes any parliamentary decision but who participate in democratic elections to protect their own interests and promote their religious values as they attempt to force religious conformity across the country. The same could perhaps be said for the roles of the Russian Orthodox Church in using government to attack LGBTQ Russians or the Muslim Brotherhoods, with their fundamentalist agendas in Egypt and Jordan. As Scott Appleby aptly explains: "Most religious societies, in fact, have interpreted their experience of the sacred in such a way as to give religion a paradoxical role in human affairs—as the bearer of peace and sword. These apparently contradictory orientations reflect a continuing struggle within religion—and within the heart of each believer—over the meaning and character of the power encountered in the sacred and its coercive force or violence."[29]

The Religion of Liberal Democracy

Ours is a pragmatic and, knowingly, a modernist exploration of how religion engages in the public square. What perhaps was once organic in traditional societies—where believing and belonging merged with a culture of tradition and memory, where faith was singular and universal—seems impossible to find today in the regions we examined. No place in Western society, frustrating as it may be, is removed from the overwhelming multiple perspectives blasted at us about life's meaning. No one is immune from ruptures that discomfort organic traditions melding faith and society.

Along with Khalilah Brown-Dean, we are concerned about the ways religious identity can be used to foster the exclusion of individuals and communities from citizenship, political representation, and a role in determining public policy.[30] There is, for us, a litmus test concerning religion today that underlies the structure and analysis found in this volume: religion can foster patriotism, but should resist a populist nationalism built on exclusion—"othering" those who are different—in the name of God. No doubt, the universal and monotheist claims of (in particular) Western religious traditions, in theory and practice, have historically proven dangerous to liberal democracies. The trinity of monarch, the military, and the church, for example, roiled France for a century and still remains potent. Both distant and recent historical experience tells us that intolerance and violence can be the product of God-infused deep believers. And much has been written over the centuries about the religious zealotry of the faithful. Our focus, as we will explain below, is on the less studied role of religious identity independent even of traditional religious institutions and their leaders. We also stake a claim about what religious beliefs and practices are critical to nurture liberal democratic political systems that value diversity and constitutionally protected rights.

There are powerful religious voices that challenge those who, in the name of God, endorse illiberal rebellion against democratic political systems. Katharine Henderson writes of what for her is the core of Christianity, words that ground an alternative definition of religious authenticity:

As it must have been for Dietrich Bonhoeffer and Martin Luther King, Jr., the use of Christianity to bolster the agenda of a white supremacist, nationalist alt-right in both its extreme and mainstream forms is a "come to Jesus" moment. In their day and ours some Christians rise up to call out falsity, to lay bare the lie and to articulate a counter narrative. As then, so today some Christians hear the call "for such a moment as this" to do whatever it takes not only to redeem the Christian faith, but to build a more just and generous nation that has never yet been but yet could be.[31]

A similar and, for us, compelling claim is made of Judaism by David Saperstein, a contemporary rabbi, who amplifies this understanding of the role religion must play in a democratic state:

I side with those theologians who suggest that when creating the universe, God left one small part of creation undone. That part was social justice. Then God gave to us that which was given to nothing else in creation: the ability to understand and choose between wrong and right. In allowing us to be partners with God in completing creation, God ennobled humanity, raised us above mere biological existence . . . and gave to our lives destiny, meaning, and purpose. The work of repairing the world is holy work. And that is the work to which we are called.[32]

The religious person and the faith community in a liberal democracy define themselves by a biblical principle: "[God] has told you, O mortal, what is good; and what does the LORD require of you, but to do justice, and to love kindness, and to walk humbly with your God" (Micah 6:8 NRSV).

Our task is to explore what constitutes a constructive religious voice in the political arena, even in nurturing patriotism and democracy, and what undermines and threatens liberal democracies. Our examples will be drawn mainly from Europe and the United States. Although the United States is held as a model of the high wall separating church and state, its foundations and maturation always included religious engagement in civic affairs. If God was invoked to justify inhumane slavery or a genocidal western expansion, religion also infused the soaring rhetoric that brought the end of slavery and, a century later, galvanized Americans to fight for a wide range of civil rights and economic supports—for African Americans, Native Americans, the poor, for LGBTQ Americans, Muslim

Americans and immigrants, and other oppressed and marginalized individuals. We see religious leaders and faithful congregants speaking out for enhanced human and civil rights, marching for justice and freedom, putting their reputations or even their lives on the line, serving witness across the globe, eschewing divisive attacks and calling for reconciliation. It is not just the witness of Pope Francis to reject centuries of Catholic imperialism and call on all to care for the widow, the orphan, and the alien stranger, but deeply engaged Catholics in Europe and the United States who open churches and homes to refugee asylum seekers. And the very German Evangelical Church of Volker and Tobias, which once endorsed Hitler, also has become a voice of reconciliation and compassion.

We are well aware of the hesitation within the academy to credit these religious leaders and faithful congregants for mobilizing and affecting policy decisions and elections.[33] With a liberal commitment to raise ever higher the wall separating church and state, religious proclamations in the public square are often viewed as an automatic threat to democracy, dangerously replacing the will of the people with that of God. This is true in the United States and even more so in Europe, where religious affiliation has rapidly diminished. Given the painful history of religious intrusion over millennia, the concern is of course warranted. But political analysts and scholars are not generally the arbiters of the choices that citizens make. If we are honest analysts and committed to a deeper understanding of what is happening in the political realm around the world, the study of the use of religious identity in politics, governance, and policy making must be high on the academic agenda. That is why we are writing this book.

Here is the understanding of religious identity—not religion itself—that frames and organizes this study: In spite of how most of us think about religion, religious identity is not necessarily about deeply held belief in God or ritual observance and church attendance. In fact, we know that "none" is the growing cohort in surveys of religious affiliation in many countries. One could assume that religion is waning in many societies. In terms of attendance at services or adherence to religious law and custom, that may well be the case. Such a conclusion would be misleading, however. Our narrower focus on religious identity is much subtler, examining how it is being used to endorse and give credibility to illiberal democratic forces.

On Becoming Citizens

We are all socialized into a culture that has both explicit and hidden images of authenticity that inform us as to who is a "real" American or German, Pole, or Hungarian. One need not go to church to expect that a true German is one whose culture and lineage can be traced back to a time when "real" Germans were Christian—it is like a genetic inheritance that can lie low in consciousness but is somehow always present and impactful.[34] As Talal Asad reminded us years ago, "It is not simply worship but social, political, and economic institutions in general, within which individual biographies are lived out, that lend a stable character to the flow of a Christian's activity and to the quality of her experience."[35] In fact, Klara Plecita shows that the salience of Christianity as an identity marker has increased throughout Europe, but more in the secular countries than in those more pious, and that the more secularized the country, the greater the role of Christian customs and traditions as identity markers.[36]

It is in that sense that this book seeks to understand the ways religious identity is being weaponized to fuel revolts against a political, social, and economic order that values democracy in a global, human-rights-oriented, financially intertwined, and strikingly diverse world. In terms of its political meaning, it is not about one's belief or one's faithfulness to church, synagogue, temple, or mosque.[37] It is more about a secularized, faith-as-culture, civilizational and identitarian religion of belonging rather than believing, a way of defining the "we" of authentic citizens against the "they" who are alien and dangerous. In the end, such use of religion has little or even nothing to do with religious belief or practice.[38] One may be a passionate believer or reject the divine and yet believe deeply that citizens must share the legacy of religious identity upon which the nation was conceived. For these reasons, whether one is religious in the traditional sense of observance and faith is not our concern.

What we do see is that for these movements—some already in power and others vying for control—religious identity plays on core values of loyalty, authority, and purity to further inflame religious polarization and violent rhetoric that are being used to undermine liberal democracy. This certainly jeopardizes the democratic character of nations across the globe and the secure civil and human rights these nations are mandated to provide. In so doing, it simultaneously undercuts efforts in a range of arenas—the protection of certain minority groups, ameliorating poverty, integrating immigrants, or defending the rights and lives of women and oppressed groups, all in the name of upholding tradition and protecting the nation from contamination.

Theologians Can Help Rescue Liberal Democracy

Our faiths are quite varied, yet we come together with a deep history of civic engagement and concerns about the future of our faith communities and fear for the democratic systems they support. In a range of ways, we are deeply engaged in the political arena and well versed in religions and religious communities. Our goal is to offer a cogent historical and political analysis of what is happening in Europe and the United States, the central players of Western democracy, in terms of the revival of religious identity as a prerequisite for national membership. And if religion can play a central role in shaping the narratives of national identity, then we want to provide theological alternatives to support the very liberal democracies we have discussed.

This antidote, little discussed in political analyses, will highlight religious language that can speak in the public political and policy arenas with authority to counter antidemocratic forces. We also hope to encourage other religious leaders who are concerned about nativist, nationalist politics and who may have removed themselves from the public square in the name of church-state separation to now reenter forcefully to preserve the liberal democratic political systems that are so threatened. We seek to encourage people of faith to promote foundational support for the institutions and values of the democratic enterprise from within their own religious traditions and to stand passionately and resolutely against the hostility and cruelty that historically have resulted when religious zealotry and state power combine. We also offer a warning to faith communities that endorsing antidemocratic movements and politicians for narrow political gains is a Faustian bargain that will ultimately wreak havoc on everyone who believes the path to God is to care for the "other" in society: the needy, the widow and orphan, the stranger and marginalized.

Chapter 1 lays out a theoretical and socio-psychological framework for understanding the role of religious identity that supports the rise of illiberal democratic movements. The next two chapters provide a history and political analysis of religion, politics, and policies in Europe and the United States that foster this illiberal rebellion. We think it is important for both religious and secular citizens to understand and resist the abuse of religion for political gain. To lay the groundwork for a religious response to this development, we offer a chapter each on Catholicism, Protestantism, and Judaism, showing how they can nourish liberal democracy.

How to Move Forward

For us, violence does not sanctify God's name. The world has been here before as many faithful Christians in Europe heartily endorsed or passively stood by acts of persecution, violence, and genocide. Christians and Jews in America accepted a century of vicious segregation. With the violent rhetoric trumpeted daily in so many places, one could sadly begin to believe that the last decades of increased democracy and a courageous global commitment to human and civil rights for a very diverse world population are aberrant, a small blip in human history. It is easy to imagine that liberal democracy is like a beautiful garden that flourished briefly but now is increasingly infected with weeds and blight that may well overwhelm and consume the entire landscape.

The faith expressed in this book has hope at its core, a fundamental belief that the universe itself is on an imperfect, but positive, trajectory toward greater goodness, compassion, justice, equity, and humanity. There is a mystical belief that in the creation of the world, God's presence was shattered and that the task of human beings is to gather the shards of divine presence until the brokenness will be repaired and the painful hemorrhaging healed.

It is toward that vision and goal that, together, we write.

CHAPTER ONE

Facing Liberal Democracy's Challenge

*Why We Highlight the Role of Religious
Identity in Populist Nationalist Movements*

Across the globe, appeals to tribalism and xenophobia are gaining strength.

In 2008, before antidemocratic forces came to the fore, Miriam Elman could write about the tempering effect of democracy on religious parties in Israeli politics: "Ideology, however, is not determinative—regular participation in the electoral process and access to government resources has over time also worked to moderate initially hardline party positions. The fact that religious political parties typically serve as pivotal parties in Israel's governing coalitions accounts for why these parties, and their constituents, have largely avoided extremism. As a result of the integration of religious political parties into Israel's proportional representation, multi-party system, extremist violence in Israel has tended to be extra-parliamentary."[1]

Such moderation has faded from the political systems we are studying (and in contemporary Israel, the only example of a Jewish-majority democracy). There is a serious diminution of trust in democratic institutions to address the challenges of this century and a corresponding willingness to support alternative political systems. As a 2017 Pew survey reveals, "Large numbers in many nations would entertain political systems that are inconsistent with liberal democracy."[2]

Some posit the cause to be an exacerbated Durkheimian anomie, as individuals and even nations feel marginalized by globalization. Others cite a fatigue with liberalism, or the economic disparities that produce middle-class *déclassement*, or ruthless international corporations that act independently of any government. There are those who argue that the commitment of citizens to democracy may be vibrant enough to withstand this trend, but autocratic strongmen and weak traditional political parties undermine democratic institutions. Studies of this dynamic focus mainly on economic or social *déclassement*, the authoritarian personality, or the charismatic demagogue. Religion is usually ignored completely or given cursory treatment. Yet religious identity is a vital talisman of national identity found at the core of most self-defined illiberal movements, such as Catholic Law and Justice in Poland or the Christian Coalition in the United States.[3]

Religion Is *Not*, in the First Instance, a Matter of Belief

It seems that there are those who write about politics and those who write about religion while few analysts deal with both. Politics is about ideology, political parties, charismatic leaders, and, often, race and ethnicity. Religion is about churches and mosques and synagogues, doctrinal creed, belief in the supernatural, observance, and, often, religious conflict. For this work, we find the dichotomy unhelpful. "I want to persuade you," Kwame Appiah has written, "that religion is *not*, in the first instance, a matter of belief." He goes on to describe Jews and Hindus (among others) for whom belief in God is irrelevant to their religious identity. Atheists can still "believe" in their connections to a religious tradition. Christmas trees and Easter egg hunts are not catechisms, but practices that seem natural to those living within that community.[4] Rajni Bakshi adds: "Faith as a pathfinder through the maze of life and after-life has a tenuous connection to faith as the basis of an 'identity' that gives people both a sense of belonging-in-community and marks out who are the 'other.'"[5] Religious identity is about belonging, not necessarily believing.

Some scholars and journalists who until recently defined the ideal society as secular are beginning to understand that religion plays a serious role in the politics and policies of the public square.

If we consider past decades, however, recent developments, such as increased globalization and multiculturalization in Europe, have challenged these ideals on multiple levels. To give some examples, news media in Europe regularly follow public debates on the use of religious symbols in a public space, religious methods of animal slaughter, and child abuse scandals in different religious institutions. Furthermore, in academia, there is a rising call to revisit the role and place of religion in the contemporary European public sphere.[6]

However much we may wish the world to be, when people speak of being a "real" German or Pole, they are not describing a native-born, third-generation, college-educated, light-skinned Muslim. The concepts of "Germanness" and "Polishness" are inseparable from religion but, we reiterate, may have nothing to do with religious practice and belief. Clearly, the resistance to Communism that helped bring its downfall in Poland included many faithful, traditional, and believing Catholics. Yet beyond the religious choices of individuals, if one speaks of Polish culture, it is impossible to remove Catholicism from the picture, regardless of how many Poles still go to church.

Three cases are descriptive of a more analytically constructive way to understand the rising significance of using religion as a talisman of traditional culture. The first concerns debates that have taken place in Bavaria as the Christian Democratic Union struggled to maintain its political base against the rising tide of right-wing nationalist forces. The staff of the German media giant Der Spiegel, in an article entitled "Culture War over German Identity: Religious Symbols Take Center Stage," writes: "Religion, something that had long since seemed to have lost its importance in Germany, is at the forefront. Once again, religions are playing a powerful role in the world—and it is a development that is making itself felt in even the most bucolic of German neighborhoods."

The article adds that the cross is to hold a status in government buildings similar to that of the blue and white Bavarian state flag. The cabinet decision declares that it is an expression of Bavaria's historical and cultural identity, the "fundamental symbol of Christian-Occidental heritage." It is not a "religious symbol" and has more to do with the "people's desire to have their identity assured."[7]

The second case comes from an article in the *New York Times* by Steven Erlanger that describes the rise of the anti-immigrant, anti-Europe Sweden Democrat party and observes: "What they are selling, most people agree, is nostalgia for a mythic Sweden of the 1950s—safe, prosperous and white."[8] Another significant marker of Swedish identity in that earlier time, along with race and economic equality, was a national Lutheran Church to which almost all Swedish citizens belonged. To be Swedish meant carrying a Christian identity, whether or not one was a faithful, church-attending believer. The article missed the obvious because it presumed that since few Swedes go to church today, religious identity no longer resonates. What Erlanger failed to understand is that *jul*—Swedish Christmas and a secular but well-celebrated Easter—are ingrained in Swedish culture even for those who do not believe in the Immaculate Conception or Jesus as the son of God.[9]

And in Charleston, West Virginia, the mayor assumed innocuously that changing the traditional Christmas Parade to a Winter Parade would encourage respect for the increased diversity in town. Although only just over a third of its residents are church-attending Christians,[10] the response to renaming the venerable event was immediate and furious. As the reporter noted, the change from "Christmas" to "Winter" hit at something deeper, a shot against a way of life "that had already changed so much in recent decades as the coal industry in the region collapsed, jobs in chemical manufacturing disappeared, shops closed and large numbers of people moved out of town altogether, leaving a place so different from the

Charleston longtime residents remember from their youth." The resulting firestorm shocked the mayor; the Christmas parade was quickly reinstated.[11]

Titus Hjelm, speaking of those whose Christianity is expressed through their nationalist fervor, says it well: "Finally, is God back? The blunt answer is 'no.' To put it differently: religion, not God, is back. There is an internal secularization of discourse, if you will, at work in the new visibility of religion. . . . It is their public activity which is its focus, not the interior life of faith itself, nor the religious reasons or goals which motivate it. Religion is visible because it can be good or bad, but God has little to do with it."[12]

The religion Hjelm describes is about identity, nostalgic symbols, an incarnated sensibility in which God is manifest in land and flags, history and tradition. It is about the symbolism of head scarves in Germany and cross wearing in France, about what venerating Catholic icons means for Spanish towns or about forbidding male circumcision that offends Danish sensibilities. We often mistake the absence of God for a secularized world. Religious identity as a source of conflict, violence, and xenophobia is healthy and well.

Societies, in ways subtle and overt, establish identities that become normative models of who belongs. Appiah gives us language to describe this, *habitus* and *essentialism*. He explains these terms by describing human beings as programmed to take "a label and a picture of how to apply it that entertains norms about how people who have the label should behave and how they should be treated."[13] There are markers that, whether conscious or not, describe authenticity. In the United States, a white, tall, Christian, heterosexual male who is a native English speaker holds the "unmarked" position—his is the image that would come to mind when certain leaders and nationalist pundits talk about "real" Americans. Those who do not conform to that image—black, Muslim, Latino with an accent, transgender, wheelchair bound—hold a "marked" position. They do not fit the normative image of an American in spite of our ethical wish that they did. Or, as one news commentator explained to children, "Santa is just white. . . . He is what he is."[14]

We live within a culture and inherit its norms, values, and behaviors—what Appiah calls habitus—in ways that are so natural, they are unconscious. Appiah continues: "Habitus and identity are connected by the fact that we recognize certain forms of behavior . . . as the signs of certain forms of identity and that our identities shape our habitus unconsciously. I've said that identities matter because they give us reasons to do things, reasons we think about consciously."[15]

One does not need to be a believing Christian or a descendant of the original Mayflower colonists to fit the normative model of a "true" American. But a Black Muslim whose family was captured and forcibly transported to America and slavery in the 1600s will never qualify as a "real" American as long as the combination of one's race, ethnicity, and religious identity are used to determine authenticity. When Poles march through the street chanting "Poland is Catholic" or white supremacists shout "Jews will not replace us" in Charlottesville, they are not declaring their obedience to the "church" or even to God. They are proclaiming who they believe to be "real Poles" and "real Americans."

Susan Gelman deepens our understanding of the ways we "see" the world. She describes the ways we categorize and utilize identity to make sense of the world, to bring together what may seem like disparate identities into a coherent view of who belongs and who does not, a view that certain categories have an underlying reality or true nature that one cannot observe directly but that gives an object its identity and is responsible for other similarities that that category of members share.[16]

Essentialists and Communitarians

Children become essentialists early on, long before they can consciously explain what differentiates them from the "other," and they are communitarian in their sense of belonging. These orientations are safety mechanisms that probably evolved before we became Homo sapiens, a way to separate friend from foe and help from danger. And we all carry a clear image of who belongs and who does not for the rest of our lives, so that even when one becomes conscious of racism or misogyny or religious pluralism, one must overcome the stereotypes that first come to mind.[17]

There is always the hope that we moderns, immersed in this media-savvy, interconnected world, are personally capable of transcending these parochial, even primitive, ways of differentiating human beings, especially when it comes to religious identities. Religion is a particularly contentious issue when applied to the political sphere since academics have long claimed that religion is on the wane. Yet the doyen of the decreased place of religion, Peter Berger, admitted late in life that he was misguided, claiming that "the place people should look for secularization is in the common rooms of elite universities rather than in the world at large."[18] That is, perhaps, one reason why few scholars anticipated the use of religious identities to so effectively fuel the "Send Them Back" rage that was experienced at Trump rallies against Muslim Congresswomen or Hungarian hatred of a demonized George Soros, the Hungarian-born Jew, who built a European liberal university. Both Trump's and Orbán's definition of Christian democracy was an illiberal form of political organization calling on religious identity to define who is an authentic member of the tribe.[19] We are told that Germans don't attend church or even believe in God and that religion itself is not a force in politics or determining social norms. In fact, the acceptance of self-identity that aligns with and is inspired by the majority religion, not church attendance per se, is quite robust in Germany, as it is across the European Union, especially among the young.[20]

That is not to say that in each case we examine, there are not those who immerse themselves in the rituals and practices of their religion. While it is certainly true that, while religion can be used as a source of and motivation for national purification and marginalization of "others," this is not a necessary outcome of faith. Faith can be compelling as a way to create deep relationships, a communitarian spirit. Religion, beyond its theology, is about belonging, finding a sense of meaning within a community. Identifying in something beyond oneself reinforces that "belief in belonging," locating a kinship with a specific group of people, finding common cause with a community to whom one gives loyalty, especially to those recognized as having legitimate authority. Religion and its deep sense of belonging foster and often inspire fealty to its sacred symbols and acts that give people meaning.

What we now surmise is that national identity, with its own patriotism, symbols, and beliefs, can create a communitarian-inspired civil religion whereby the state itself is seen as sacred.[21] This civil religion has rituals to perform and a community that can sustain and nourish social identities—I am Polish, I am Latino. As Anne Koch notes, "This understanding of civil religion is a religion based on the state, which is said to need the individual's moral substance and the religion's founding beliefs for its own legitimization."[22] These identities often cross boundaries and combine, incorporating values and behaviors that deepen one's identity: I am a white Christian American male or I am a Catholic Austrian woman. When we want to understand the impact of religious identity in one's life, it is crucial to recognize that "belief needs to be situated in place and time and analyzed as not just religious but also as a political force."[23]

An essential element shared by illiberal democracies is that they seek to purify the nation, which they see as tainted or even poisoned by alien forces, often in a combination of race, ethnicity, and religious identity. Corruption is not about unethical politics or money. It is about the purpose of this form of nationalism, which, in each of our cases as it is in much of the world, fuses religious identity with the state. Jason Stanley notes, in a statement that to some would seem a hyperbolic use of *fascist* but that does reflect the assaults by extreme nationalists who use *tradition* as a code word for the "real" nation that shares religious history along with race and ethnicity: "Corruption, to the fascist politician, is really about the corruption of purity rather than the law. Officially, the fascist politician's denunciation of corruption sounds like a denunciation of political corruption. But such talk is intended to evoke corruption in the sense of the usurpation of traditional order."[24]

One hears this from Buddhist monks in Myanmar, Jews in settlements on the West Bank, and ISIS preachers. Donald Trump, stoking fear of corruption, falsely decried the impurity of a Black Muslim as president of the United States. As José Casanova presciently argued, religion has returned to the realm of politics as a medium for ethnic and social conflicts.[25]

Faith and Democratic Discourse

It is critical that this volume models respect for religious and political diversity and for constructive and respectful civil discourse. It is possible to imagine a debate over the sanctity of life and family that could include those who support and oppose abortion or same-sex marriage, while not using dismissive or even demonizing language to describe those with whom we disagree. One could pragmatically oppose the German government's decision to allow a million refugees to enter the country, yet eschew xenophobic, racist attacks. A church member could seek the expansion of religious liberty while passionately protesting discrimination of any sort against other human beings. One can challenge the policy focus on seeking diversity through affirmative action in schools or the workplace, yet fight for an equal and just society. A democracy that recognizes and supports human diversity can contain a great deal of argument and dissent, from the left or the right, if there is a culture of respect for both majority rule and individual rights. A vibrant democracy that promotes trust in the processes and institutions of democratic rule and brings to office politicians committed to the values and norms of democracy should be capable of addressing difficult policy debates that respect the validity of a decision (whether by majority vote, legislative action, or court decisions) and yet advocate and fight to have it changed. This is as true for liberals as it is for conservatives.

Fundamental to liberal democracy is that no one owns the truth. But it is not religious or secular truths that the populist nationalists are seeking. In fact, "Western right-wing populists are using Christianity as an identity marker between 'us' and 'them'— while remaining distanced from Christian values and beliefs in practice."[26] And such demonizing of the "other" is descriptive of the ways religions are used by many of their adherents across the globe.

How, then, can deep religious belief unite with pluralist, democratic values that allow for individual liberties and rights? We offer understandings of God and deep religious commitment that eschew absolute knowledge by explaining that God is ultimately unknowable—claims to the contrary border on idolatry.[27] Such views do not depend on liberal or progressive theological claims. Tony Richie, a Pentecostal evangelical leader, may well agree with many policy decisions of the Trump administration, even as he defends democratic values in principle and practice. As he notes, speaking to his own community: "For me the word 'narrow' suggests a self-centered psychosis that alienates itself from any realities of divine presence beyond its own borders. Often it ostracizes itself even as it demonizes others. Much so-called religious Fundamentalism sallies forth under this garbled guise. . . . A valid, vibrant Pentecostal theology of religions that does not compromise biblical, historic Christianity or act condescendingly or contemptuously toward other world religions is both possible and desirable for Pentecostals and for our friends in the interfaith venture."[28]

The value and goal of this analysis is to shine a focused light on the move from personal religious belief to doctrinal catechism to the nation as an embodiment and expression of the majority's religious identity. That path is at the core of most, if not all, illiberal nationalist political movements. Those movements are challenging the constitutional democratic norms and values adopted or reaffirmed in Western Europe and the United States following World War II as well as post-Soviet Eastern Europe. These values, embodied in the Universal Declaration of Human Rights, include, among others, some form of representative democracy, free elections, and the protection of individual human and civil rights, asylum seekers, and refugees.

In the political movements that have arisen to challenge some if not all of these norms and values in the countries of this study, national exceptionalism flows from some form of religious sanction or cultural identity and the community's commitment to uphold its perceived "traditional" norms and values of purity.[29] *Tradition* then overflows as a catchall term to justify age-old oppressions, such as slavery or the suppression of women's equality, and ancient battles such as that between Serbian Christians and the Ottoman Empire in 1389, which was replayed in Kosovo in the 1990s. The leaders and members of such nationalist-religious movements are encouraged to perceive themselves under threat in a battle to protect the nation from what they see as the potential pollution of society (the intrusion of the "other" into their domain). The battle against such pollution is now fundamental to their religious—and their political—worldviews.[30]

Again, a vibrant democracy can handle deep political disagreement if its leaders and institutions commit to the democratic rules of the game, accept the political legitimacy of opponents, eschew violence as a force for change, and protect the civil liberties of opponents, media, and vulnerable populations.[31]

What Do We Mean by a Religious-Nationalist Revival?

We now acknowledge that religion as an aspect of national identity never went away and the global spread of illiberal democracies fueled by religious zealotry is not limited to majority-Christian nations. For example, Rajni Bakshi describes the challenges to the secular Indian state: "Since 2013, there have been four assassinations of intellectual activists who actively opposed the Hindutva project. Government investigators have found links between these murders and identified the culprits as people mobilized by Hindu terrorist groups. These investigations have also unearthed a 'hit-list' of other public figures who are in danger because of their vocal opposition to Hindutva."[32]

But by 2020, the Indian government, led by Prime Minister Modi, embarked on a Hindutva project that so challenged India's democracy that the United Nations High Commissioner for Human Rights petitioned India's High Court to overturn a citizenship amendment potentially threatening the rights of over 170 million Muslims.[33]

From Israel, where a Jewish-majority Knesset felt the need to fortify Israel as a Jewish nation, to Indonesia, which imprisoned the Christian mayor of Jakarta for blasphemy, to Uganda, where the born-again Christian president endorsed death to homosexuals, nationalists have fused their patriotism with the majority's religious identity. And, as Ruth Braunstein and Malaena Taylor note, the United States is not exempt from this upheaval. In discussing America and the core nationalist populist constituency that helped elect Donald Trump, they note that "white Christians (including those who are only nominally Christian) align Christian and national identities as one means of marginalizing ethnic and religious 'others.'"[34] The same can be said of many political movements across Europe. What we seek to show is that the perceived threat (by what are deemed "foreign" or "liberal" as opposed to "traditional" forces) to their faith-based national identity leads illiberal democracies to use religious identity to support policies and practices that challenge democratic norms, forcefully demonizing and pushing out those who do not share that identity.

In 1990, with the fall of Communism, it was possible to imagine that the world had fundamentally changed. In the course of fewer than fifty years, the totalitarian forces of Fascism and Communism had fallen, while colonial empires faded to allow nations the autonomy of their own identity within the orbit of an increasingly interlinked global society. Francis Fukuyama could write: "What we may be witnessing is not just the end of the Cold War, or the passing of a particular period of post-war history, but the end of history as such: that is, the end point of mankind's ideological evolution and the universalization of Western liberal democracy as the final form of human government."[35]

The course of history now seemed determined. In particular, the secular state grounded in neoliberal market values had successfully and finally relegated religion to its appropriate place—in the home, in the church, an artifact of one's personal life. Whatever nominal residual interaction existed between church and state was incidental; the diminution of religion's ability to dictate government policy or determine elections was the obvious by-product of the collapse and irrelevance of ideology as a driving force in global or domestic affairs. This seemed true not only in Europe, where little seemed to remain of the Christian in the Christian Democratic parties, but even in fundamentally secular constitutions from Indonesia to Nigeria, from Brazil to India.

In retrospect, it is clear that religion continued to provide a powerful identity, even in those nations where its expression had diminished in importance or was suppressed. Yet political analysts misunderstood the fealty to a national religious identity even of those deemed unfaithful or unchurched. With the collapse of dominating empires and the increased globalization that seemed to undermine the unique regional, ethnic, religious, and historical experiences of local communities, social identities that had been either suppressed or pushed aside in the name of colonialism, economic gain, and nation building began to reassert themselves. The backlash was, for many, unanticipated. Why would people choose narrow parochial values over the opportunities and obvious economic gains of globalization? What could motivate an increasingly literate and linked community to return to what were seen as premodern religious nationalist identities? While economists and political scientists continued to preach of a tide that would raise the living standards of everyone in a global society, they ignored the resurgence of a religiously identified nationalism.

In 1991, shortly after Fukuyama wrote, the seemingly secular and liberated European nation of Yugoslavia broke apart, a harbinger that as central powers collapsed, identity politics would reassert itself. In hiding for decades under Soviet, imperial European, and American hegemonic rule, religious and ethnic conflicts were suppressed. Now they could emerge, with devastating force. And they did. The civil war that ensued pitted Orthodox Serbs, Catholic Croats, and Muslim Bosnians against each other. Neighbors who essentially were indistinguishable in terms of language, dress, and education became mortal enemies. The horror begat the greatest loss of life and most ferocious examples of human brutality on the

European continent since World War II. As regions became further inflamed in group violence—the Caucasus regions of the former Soviet Union, Nigeria's Muslims and Christians, Sri Lanka's Tamils and Buddhists, Muslim Azerbaijan and Orthodox Christian Armenia, Iraqi Shiite and Sunni Muslims, and al-Qaeda and ISIS as jihadi movements—the earlier Irish Troubles, the Muslim-Hindu battles of 1948, and conflicts between the Jewish Israelis and Muslim and Christian Palestinians and between Lebanese Sunni, Shiite, Christian, and Druze now seemed like portents describing the future rather than anachronistic residues of premodern times. While theology may not have been the rationale for conflict, religious identity seems to be consistently wedded to the ethnic or national battles that rage across Africa, Asia, Europe, and the Americas.

Even then, political analysts in general tended to see religious identity and faith claims as incidental to conflict. Most studies assume that real issues of economic disparity, raw political power grabs, regional rivalry, historic ethnic conflicts, coalition battles and personality conflicts would explain why so many democracies and nascent democracies seem to be unstable.[36] Perhaps the rise of al-Qaeda and ISIS opened analysts to the power of religious identity as a mobilization tool. Indeed, in the last decade, the assaults on liberal democracy around the world have inevitably been paired with a reassertion of religion at the core of national or regional identity.

As a 2017 Pew study notes, "Religion has reasserted itself as an important part of individual and national identity in many of the Central and Eastern European countries where communist regimes once repressed religious worship and promoted atheism."[37] In some nations, such as Poland, Hungary, Austria, and Italy, the governments already reflected this reassertion of religion to mobilize their majorities. Even in liberal Germany, Holland, and Denmark, authoritarian-minded political parties became reminders that one's religious identity, far from being relegated to the home and church, roared back as a major factor in defining the nation and in political conflict. For these political parties, the coherence that comes from religious identity and tradition linked to one's national identity often seems to offer more meaning than universal democratic values. And with this reality, the inability of globalized, liberal political leaders to speak meaningfully to religiously identified folk undermines their ability to counter the rise of religious nationalism that threatens the fabric and stability of their liberal democracies.

For the populist nationalists who challenge liberal democracy, membership in a national community is not merely a function of birth. Rather, it derives from an indigenous, inherently impermeable boundary that clusters a vision of what is authentic to that culture and its traditions.[38] This is evident even in immigrant countries such as the United States where almost 30 percent of the population is first or second generation, yet presidential candidate Donald Trump could state, "Why do we want all these people from 'shithole countries' coming here?" while endorsing the few immigrants from Scandinavia as desirables. Whether it is Viktor Orbán decrying the Muslim invasion, France's Le Pen, Italy's Salvini, or Austria's Heinz Christian Strache predicting that immigration will end European civilization or that, as Holland's Geert Wider declares, Europe will cease to exist, the threat of cultural annihilation is central to the attacks on liberal democracies and their adherents.[39] A Law and Justice Polish manifesto declared: "We do not treat belonging to the Polish nation as a value just because it was given by birth and cultural inheritance, but also because it results from a characteristic of our tradition. It is related in an inextricable way with Christianity and has an exceptionally strong connection to freedom and equality."[40]

The authoritarian-minded party platform of the Alternatives for Germany (Alternative für Deutschland [AfD]) is as clear about who is allowed into Germany and what is a traditional, and therefore exclusionary, German identity:

The AfD is committed to German as the predominant culture. This culture is derived from three sources: firstly, the religious traditions of Christianity; secondly, the scientific and humanistic heritage, whose ancient roots were renewed during the period of Renaissance and the Age of Enlightenment; and thirdly, Roman law, upon which our constitutional state is founded. Together, these traditions are the foundation of our free and democratic society, and they determine daily patterns of social interaction in society, and shape the relationship between the sexes as well as the conduct of parents towards their children. The ideology of multiculturalism is blind to history and puts on a par imported cultural trends with the indigenous culture, thereby degrading the value system of the latter. The AfD views this as a serious threat to social peace and the survival of the nation state as a cultural unit. It is the duty of the government and civil society to confidently protect German cultural identity as the predominant culture.[41]

One sees such assaults on pluralist, multiculture democracies—and in this age all nations have diverse populations—stretching around the globe. As Anantanand Rambachan explains: "The glorification of the nation is often, in actuality, the exaltation of a particular ethnic or religious community above other groups considered to have lesser worth. The spiritual obstacles of egocentrism, however, highlighted in the Hindu tradition, do not disappear when these are projected and transferred onto the nation and when we exalt ourselves in the name of our nations. In fact, these become more dangerous when professed in the name of the nation since there is a self-deception that conceals the betrayal of religious values."[42]

What Do We Consider as Assaults on Democracy?

There must be key indicators that testify to assaults on democracy. Steven Levitsky and Daniel Ziblatt[43] offer a core of four. We will amplify their list. In highlighting the shifts in values and behavior that undermine democratic systems, Levitsky and Ziblatt certainly rely heavily on twentieth-century secular examples, from Nazism and Italian Fascism to Soviet Communism. The unexpected additional fervor of religious nationalism, often imbued with apocalyptic messianic visions, only increases the dangers that Levitsky and Ziblatt fear. The list shows how, without a revolution or coup d'état, a nation's democratic institutions, political processes, and pluralist values can be corroded and ultimately undermined, leaving the shell of what once was a democracy dedicated to protect human and civil rights.

First, we look for a rejection of or weak commitment to the rules of the game. Does a leader or the political party reject or state a willingness to violate the core constitutional principles of the nation, calling for populist democratic measures and restricting basic civil rights or rejecting credible electoral results?

Many examples from recent years of attacks against the rule of law and the electoral process can be cited. Israel proclaimed itself a Jewish nation, saying the government's role is to protect and enhance only the Jewish nature of the state as preeminent and, therefore, to diminish the status of non-Jews. The country has thereby discredited its claim to be a pluralist democracy. In Hungary and Poland, the successful attempts to undercut the judiciary's independent role as a check on the majority's power were actions that undermined the rule of law. In the United States, assertions that the threat of terrorism trumps the protection of basic civil rights, or that the judicial processes and judges cannot be trusted, challenge faith in the constitutional separation of powers. When the president says he may not accept election results and claims fraud even before the election takes place, the very foundation of democracy as the expression of the people's vote is undermined. In Indonesia religious law is used to override secular constitutions and promote violence against Christians. Using the power of the presidency over foreign policy to undermine an opposition candidate for political gain is exactly what concerned the authors of the United States Constitution about a monarchical autocrat.

Second, we look at ways political actors deny the legitimacy of the opposition. In a prior age, Senator Joseph McCarthy would accuse opponents of being Communists, while the Soviets would denounce the opposition as sordid capitalists. In the past decade President Trump allowed supporters at his rallies to chant "Send them back," in reference to elected members of Congress who are women of color. A more ominous example occurred in 2019, when he publicly attacked the media as "enemy of the people" nineteen times, the exact phrase used by Stalin, Hitler's *Der Stürmer*, and Mao Zedong to describe perceived enemies who were eventually murdered or incarcerated.[44] In Hungary, a "Stop Soros" law criminalized the support of democratic institutions undertaken by George Soros. Such accusations, portraying political opponents as enemies of the state, subversive agents, and existential threats, undermine the health and vitality of any democracy. Although factionalism deeply concerned him, Madison notes in Federalist Paper No. 10: "The diversity in the faculties of men, from which the rights of property originate, is not less an insuperable obstacle to a uniformity of interests. The protection of these faculties is the first object of government."[45] Attempting to silence the opposition or paint it as a threat to the nation are a significant step toward undemocratic political systems.

Equally concerning is the third indicator, a threat to use violence to address political conflict. A democracy does not need paramilitary forces or armed gangs to inject violence into the political process. Weaponizing mobs through political rhetoric, which enables leaders of extremists to proclaim their innocence, has proven a highly successful tactic of demagogues and antidemocratic movements. In Germany, where an AfD "victory" rally did lead to violence, the party benefited at the polls.[46]

In the United States, Trump called for violence at rallies against those who opposed him, using phrases such as "Knock the crap out of him, would you? I promise I will pay your legal fees," and (as a member of the audience was being pushed out), "Maybe he should have been roughed up more," and, "I'd like to punch him in the face." It is not difficult to surmise that the rise in rhetorical violence is correlated with physical violence in the political realm.

Such examples of violent rhetoric can be heard around the world from Brazil, where a journalist was assaulted by a far-right supporter of President Bolsonaro at a television and radio studio in São Paulo while live on the air,[47] to Germany, where pro-immigrant mayor Walter Lübcke was murdered by a right-wing nationalist who opposed Germany's immigration policies,[48] or in Duarte's Philippines, Putin's Russia, or el Sisi's Egypt. Seth Farber sees the danger of this antidemocratic violence in the assassination of Israel's Prime Minister Yitzhak Rabin: "The Talmudic tradition allows someone whose life is threatened to kill the rodef (a 'pursuer'). The argument advanced by ultra-nationalists and a small cluster of rabbis claimed that anyone engaging in peace negotiations of the sort in which Prime Minister Rabin was involved was directly threatening the lives of Jews in Israel, and thus, was deserving of death. . . . This is a painful example of religious tradition being hijacked and mobilized to justify ultra-nationalist aims."[49]

These threats to democracy all contribute to the curtailing of civil liberties, but extremists also take more direct measures in this regard. Dutch populist radical-right parties seek to ban head scarves worn by Muslim females, and the Swiss People's Party (SVP) wants to prohibit the building of minarets.[50] In the United States, efforts to suppress voter turnout or disenfranchise particular groups have been actively endorsed by politicians and ignored by the Supreme Court. The language of Donald Trump altered political discourse as he threatened "to kick Muslims out of the country," "smash" the United States Court of Appeals for the Ninth Circuit, attack federal workers in the Justice Department, and use federal tax laws against National Football League players. He promoted policies that illegally separated asylum-seeking parents from their children. In such cases, the unwillingness of other branches of government to protect civil liberties is a reminder of how fragile the institutions of government can be when faced with a concerted assault by a powerful opponent.

A final sign of assault on liberal democracy is a willingness to use "the big lie" to undermine confidence in the media and all who voice disagreement. The psychology behind these assertions is supported by research that explains how, without experientially tested anchors, conventional personal opinions are relatively weak and, therefore, can more easily be altered, and large discrepancies have more influence than smaller ones.[51]

Trump supporters, for example, stoked by Trump's hostile rhetoric at rallies, were seen lashing out at reporters, who needed protection to cover his events. By mid-2018, a majority of Republicans considered the independent media "the enemy of the people."[52] In cases where the government was controlled by the nationalist party, as in Poland and Hungary and the United States, such attacks not only undermine the civility of political discourse but, fortified with religious language and symbols, create an alternative world in which undemocratic behavior and values can flourish. All critical news becomes "fake" news, and truth and fact lose credibility and significance.[53]

Why Offer Theological Responses?

There are many ways to address these threats to the processes and institutions of democracy. A focus on religious identity as a core element of illiberal nationalism adds to our understanding of root causes, of the ways in which the loss of meaning and community in a globalized world demands a remedy. If religion is useful as a tool to support the cause of extremists, it also can provide the very sense of purpose and community that many cannot find in a globalized world. This loss often leads to a retraction from civic life or, worse, a radicalization that rejects the political pluralism and civil discourse necessary for democracy to thrive. As religious activist scholar Katharine Henderson states: "We know the power spirituality holds to inspire compassion, to help us love our neighbor as well as the stranger and to bring people together for the common good. Yet, as we also know all too well, religion, when weaponized and misused, can be a force that divides us by promoting mistrust, bigotry and discrimination."[54]

We believe that religious leaders and their unique faith communities could be a huge asset—if not the most important one—in healing ruptures and in restoring faith in political institutions and processes. For every faith claim that endorses violence, discrimination, and demonization of the other in the name of God, there are religious voices that can offer authentic theological principles from within their own traditions of respect for the other, engagement with those with whom we differ, and the idea that one's own religious commitments and beliefs need not deny the faith of others.

A religious leader can be a patriot, deeply committed to the health and success of the national enterprise, yet reject destructive nationalism, which creates an artificial world of "them" and "us." Because nationalist movements use terms that have religious roots—*pollution*, *impurity*, and *contamination*—to justify and advance their cause, religious leaders need to provide an alternative.[55] Jim Winkler, as president of the National Council of Churches, speaks to the challenge of religious leaders committed to democracy:

> Alt-right, white nationalist and supremacist movements reflect deep fears that require deep answers that can be found in biblical and theological study. After all, the fear of others and how to respond to that fear can be found throughout scripture. It pains me as a faithful Christian when I see the church reflect these same societal illnesses and must therefore confront fears and anxieties with humility. To refuse to recognize the other as anything less than fully human is heretical and must be named as contrary to our identity as Christians. The most repeated command in the Bible calls on us to overcome our fears and care for the widow, the orphan and stranger in our midst, exactly because we are so vulnerable to become like those who oppressed us. It is the role of our churches to work hard to heal the sicknesses of hatred and xenophobia in society and equip our followers to address both the concrete situations that abound each day and larger structural forces.[56]

Where authoritarian governments or nationalist movements have attempted to undermine the human and civil rights of their fellow citizens, it is precisely the voices of religious leaders that have the authority to challenge, especially when those individuals are of the majority religion. On this issue, Pope Francis could be an exemplary model. He did not deny, as extremists claim, that there is sin, or that there is a judge, or that people need to embrace a life of ongoing conversion. All he has denied is that it is our role to judge people. As Pope Francis declared:

> An authentic faith—which is never comfortable or completely personal—always involves a deep desire to change the world, to transmit values, to leave this earth somehow better that we found it. We love this magnificent planet on which God has put us, and we love the human family which dwells here, with all its tragedies and struggles, its hopes and aspirations, its strengths and weaknesses. The earth is our common home and all of us are brothers and sisters. If indeed "the just ordering of society and of the state is a central responsibility of politics," the Church "cannot and must not remain on the sidelines in the fight for justice."[57]

Our hope is to provide models of religious language that are authentic to three faith communities, with particular scriptural and historical references, which can give meaning to the faithful. Our goal is to make these models valuably competitive to undermine the credibility of religious attacks on a pluralist view that endorses diversity.

Righteousness and justice in the name of God rather than calls for violence and divine wrath on those who do not believe; calling for all peoples to join and come together to the mountain of God rather than teaching theologies that claim the nation only for Muslims or Jews, Christians, Buddhists, or Hindus; seeking and seeing God in the face of the other and relationship building that leads to respect and a desire to do good expressed well in the Qur'anic verse "So compete with each other in doing good" rather than finding reasons to marginalize and oppress others, all offer a positive alternative religious identity that upholds and sustains the values of liberal democracies. These traditions can be found in each religious community, and they are preached by significant faith leaders in the authentic idiom of their religions. It may be unusual for a political analysis that examines the rise of nationalist fervor to quote holy scriptures. But if leaders kidnap and manipulate religious identity to fuel nationalist attacks on democracy, to "other" minorities within the nation, to justify threats and intimidation of refugees and immigrants and taunt and demonize political opponents and public media, then we will need brave religious leaders and powerful theologies to counter the threats. It is not enough to provide an analysis and expose the dangers—we also offer a call for action by those whose voices can provide a remedy that will heal the hemorrhaging of democracy.

CHAPTER TWO

How to Understand the Populism of Europe

Several thousand people had gathered around Dresden's beautifully lit Frauenkirche on a cold February evening in 2015. Many were holding candles or oversized crosses. Together they sang "Silent Night," "Rejoice, the Christ Child Comes Soon!," and other traditional Christian hymns as they began to march through Germany's capital of Baroque. Their mission was to send a powerful signal for the preservation and defense of the Christian occident and is reflective of a resurgent nationalist political wind sweeping across Europe. Or so at least suggested their name: The Patriotic Europeans Against the Islamisation of the Christian Occident, or simply PEGIDA.[1] And this wind comes with explicitly religious overtones. PEGIDA's conspicuous use of Christian language and symbols is representative of the use of religious themes by similar movements in other European countries. While PEGIDA carried oversized crosses through Dresden, the Alternative for Germany (AfD) claimed to defend Germany's "Christian traditions"; Hungary's president, Viktor Orbán, called for a re-Christianization of Europe; and the French Rassemblement National (formerly Front National) marched through Paris in veneration of a Catholic saint. Ironically, even a professed atheist, like the leader of the right-wing populist Dutch Freedom Party, Geert Wilders, claims to defend the Netherlands' "Judeo-Christian identity."[2] In sum, religion, it seems, has made a powerful comeback in secular European politics in the form of an ethno-culturalist nationalism that is revolting against liberal democracy.

Many observers are quick to take right-wing populists' religious references at face value and interpret them as expressions of a reactionary alliance between the new right and orthodox Christianity, standing against the forces of secularization, liberalization, and globalization.[3] However, a number of indicators suggest that the reality is more complicated. There is, for instance, the empirical finding that the resurgence of references to Europe's religio-cultural identity appears to develop independently from, or even in a negative correlation with, the development of individual religious belief and practice.[4] Moreover, studies have shown that, in spite of right-wing populists' aggressive use of religious themes, their supporters are actually disproportionately irreligious, and that church attendance is one of the strongest empirical predictors for not voting a right-wing populist ticket.[5] Finally, European church leaders have unequivocally spoken out against right-wing movements, with some going as far as the former president of the Lutheran World Federation, Bishop Christian Krause, who called the use of religious symbols by right-wing advocates of illiberal democracy "perverted."[6]

In our effort to better understand the use of religion in this right-wing populist challenge to liberal democracy, this chapter investigates the relationship between the political forces that challenge liberal norms and values and a resurgent reference to Europe's Judeo-Christian heritage and identity. It focuses specifically on the case of Germany, where the paradoxes appear particularly strong. Thus in Germany PEGIDA and the AfD have made significant use of Christian themes in their rhetoric, while the formal German churches have been particularly outspoken against this use of religion. Moreover, it is here that the empirical "God gap" between religious and irreligious voters' support for the AfD is especially striking.[7] It appears that while religion as a form of cultural identity marker may work as fuel for right-wing populism, religion as a theological faith and social institution has the potential to work as a bulwark against it. This dynamic might not be limited to Germany, but extend to Europe and beyond.

This chapter follows a straightforward structure. We will begin with a brief review of the historical development of the relationship between religion and democracy in Germany after the Second World War, paying particular attention to the relatively "happy marriage of convenience" between politics and religion in the context of German Christian Democracy. The next section will focus on how the emergence of a new social cleavage in German identity has put this marriage into question. We will concentrate on how Germany's AfD seeks to employ Christian themes as a cultural identity marker against Islam, while often remaining distanced from Christian beliefs, values, and institutions. Then we will turn to the reaction of Christian voters, parties, and churches to these co-optation attempts. In considering the empirical finding that the AfD does best among irreligious voters, while practicing Christians remain comparatively "immune" to the rhetoric of illiberal nationalist leaders, we will review several potential explanations, ranging from differences in individual attitudes between religious and irreligious voters, to the role of the mainstream political parties in providing electoral alternatives to Christians, as well as to the relevance of the public interventions of the institutional churches. As we emphasize throughout the book, the exhortations of religious leaders to support the principles and values of liberal democracy can have significant impact by legitimizing or debunking right-wing political use of religion.

A (Happy) Marriage of Convenience: Christianity and Democracy in Germany after WWII

Politics and institutional religion are tightly intertwined in today's Germany. In October 2017, Germany's chancellor, Angela Merkel, the daughter of a Protestant pastor, was sworn in to her fourth term in office by Federal President Frank-Walter Steinmeier. President Steinmeier himself had been poised to become the president of the

German Protestant Reformation Church Day, celebrating the five-hundredth anniversary of the Protestant Reformation, prior to taking over the federal presidency from his predecessor, Joachim Gauck, who himself was a Protestant pastor. Of the members of the new cabinet sworn in, three-quarters were active members of one of the great German churches—compared with 62 percent of the members of the German Parliament (Bundestag) and just about 54 percent in the general population.[8] Similarly, many German Catholic bishops are members of Merkel's Christian Democratic Union (CDU/CSU), while a large number of their Protestant counterparts are card-carrying Social Democrats (SPD). This personal proximity among the churches and mainstream parties is mirrored on the content level, where preaching and public ecclesiastical statements by church leaders—in particular those written in response to the rise of illiberal forces—read like fierce defenses of Germany's liberal order. Conversely, there is almost no anticlericalism in the mainstream parties.[9] Indeed the amicability between the churches and Germany's traditional liberal political order goes so far as to incite the right-wing populist AfD to speak of an "unholy alliance" between the political establishment and Germany's main Protestant and Catholic churches, whom they decry as "system churches" and whose bishops they call "government spokesmen."[10]

Yet this cordial relationship between liberal democracy and religion in Germany was not easily established. On the Protestant side, prior to 1945 a century-old alliance between throne and altar landed the majority of the Protestant electorate and clergy in the antidemocratic camp of early-twentieth-century Weimar politics.[11] And although most of the Protestant establishment would have preferred the old Kaiser over a new Führer, most still opted for the Nazis over the Catholic Zentrum party or "godless" socialism.[12] Catholics voted NSDAP[13] at much lower rates than Protestants, and Catholic authorities remained much more critical of the Nazi ideal of a racially defined "Positive Christianity," which would purge Christianity from all "Jewish influences" (including the Old Testament and many of the apostles).[14] Yet throughout Europe the majority of Catholics were no democratic enthusiasts either. Although Catholics did support democracy in countries like Germany, where the Catholic minority had been discriminated against for decades, the position of the church was very different in countries where it had its own alliance with the throne, as in Franco's Spain, Salazar's Portugal, or Pétain's France.[15] It was only after 1945, once Nazism had shown its true horrors and revealed its plans for an atheist "final solution of the Church question," that the majority of German Christians and their spiritual leaders made a full conversion to democracy.[16] This conversion certainly was spurred by the realization that the Communist alternative—promoting state atheism, demolishing churches, and systematically persecuting believers—was scarcely more appealing than Nazism.

The Protestant church, which had amassed greater guilt under Nazism, felt the need to repent most urgently. In October 1945, in the Stuttgart Declaration of Guilt, the Council of the Evangelical Church in Germany professed: "Through us, infinite wrong was brought over many peoples and countries. . . . We accuse ourselves for not standing up with our beliefs more courageously, for not praying more faithfully, for not believing more joyously, and for not loving more ardently." The newly founded German Evangelical Church (EKD) fundamentally transformed German Protestantism: internal democracy was strengthened; former protagonists of the minority "confessing Church," which had opposed the Nazis, took up leadership positions.[17]

The Catholic Church of 1945 felt in less immediate need to seek a radical reversal. Yet many European Catholic activists and politicians were still inspired to reevaluate democracy as a lesser evil as a result of the persecution some experienced alongside democrats under the Nazis and the new Communist regimes in Eastern Europe.[18] As a result, a new political movement of Christian democracy gathered momentum in Europe. Consisting of laypersons rather than of the more skeptical institutional church, it set itself to the challenge of "how to reconcile Christianity and democracy; or failing a full reconciliation, how to render democracy safe for Christianity under modern conditions."[19]

Scholars like Ian Linden, Wolfram Kaiser, and Helmut Wohnout have shown the importance of this movement in establishing liberal democracies, legitimizing the market economy, endorsing the European project, and pressuring Rome toward opening itself up to democracy—a process ultimately crowned by the embrace of modernity and democracy at the second Vatican Council.[20] Christianity as a force for liberal democracy was perhaps most momentous in Germany. Under the leadership of Konrad Adenauer, the newly founded CDU/CSU brought together Protestants and Catholics in one prodemocratic party for the first time. This new "Union" party thereby not only gave Protestants a new democratic home but also provided a narrative and connection point to "another Germany" rooted in German history and civilization and held together by institutions untainted by Nazism.[21] This narrative attracted millions of disillusioned Germans back to the pews and the ranks of the new party, which quickly became Germany's largest political party. It also appealed to the allied powers, who, keenly on the lookout for a positive counternarrative to Nazism and for trustworthy politicians, seized the opportunity to entrust the Christian supporters of liberal democracy, alongside the more secular Social Democrats, with the creation of Germany's new basic law (*Grundgesetz*).[22]

The *Grundgesetz*, which took the form of Germany's constitution, bears a strong Christian signature that aligns with liberal democratic principles and became something of a "marriage contract" for the close postwar relationship between religion and the state. On a philosophical level, it mirrors Christian skepticism toward direct democracy and secular ideology, by constraining popular sovereignty through powerful courts and the establishment of several immutable foundational rights. As Jan-Werner Müller puts it, Christian democrats "sought to constrain the demos . . . internally through a revival of conservative forms of lay activism (hence a particular kind of 'Christian demos') and externally through institutions such as constitutional courts and (supranationally) the European Court of Human Rights."[23] On an institutional level, the *Grundgesetz* followed the line of the Catholic constitutional lawyer Ernst-Wolfgang Böckenförde, who wrote that "the liberal, secularized state lives off preconditions that it cannot itself guarantee" while establishing a relationship of affirmative "benevolent neutrality."[24] That is, the German state guarantees religious freedom and equal rights for different religious groups but recognizes its own dependency on such groups to frame debates, instill social cohesion, and foster shared values, virtues, and identity. It therefore endows religious institutions—and not just the Christian churches but also other faith communities—with a quasi-public status, collecting member contributions through taxes, subsidizing faith-run hospitals, schools, and welfare organizations, and enshrining religious education in schools and universities.

This close social, constitutional, and institutional association between church and state has proved to be a relatively happy alliance, with the churches enjoying their constitutional privileges and social status and the state relying on the churches to bridge public divides and fulfill social tasks. Among other things, the churches played an important role in mitigating the two traditional social cleavages in Western societies—the economic cleavage between workers and capitalists and the cultural cleavage between social conservatism and social liberalism—by anchoring themselves on both sides of each cleavage. They advocated welfare distribution in tune with Catholic social doctrine while acting as a bulwark against Communism.[25] They supported the social democratic chancellor Willy Brandt's new social and foreign policy without giving up their role as guarantors of what churches considered traditional values.[26] And they provided a platform for the peace and environmental movements of the 1980s without questioning the legitimacy of the German political system.[27] This is not to say that the churches' roles and positions were not highly contested at times, but their quasi-official mediator role saved them from being perceived as overly partisan and defused religion as a wedge issue and political identity marker in society.[28]

More recently, however, this conjugal settlement has been confronted with a serious marital crises as the economic and moral cleavages of the twentieth century are increasingly overshadowed by the rise of a new cleavage in national and cultural identity. In this context, the new force of the illiberal populist politics, in the form of the AfD, not only puts into question Germany's political system but also brings back religion as a wedge issue and exclusivist identity marker in German politics.

The Defenders of the Faith? The Advent of the AfD and Its References to Christian Identity

The AfD clearly rejects an Islamic practice of faith that is directed against the liberal-democratic basic order, our laws, and against the Judeo-Christian and humanistic foundations of our culture.[29]

We do not seek to defend Christianity in any religious sense, but as a traditional way of life in Germany, as a traditional sense of home ("Heimatgefühl"). Christianity is only a metaphor for the customs inherited from our Fathers.[30]

These AfD statements are emblematic not only of the fact that references to Europe's Judeo-Christian identity have returned as a politicized issue to Germany but also of the way in which such movements throughout Europe seek to employ Christianity in the new identity cleavage—not as an individual faith, but as a culturalized identity marker of the nation, directed primarily against Islam.

The AfD was initially not a typical candidate for bringing religious conformity back into the German political debate. When a few dozen "concerned citizens" came together on a snowy morning in February 2013 in the Christian community center of Oberursel, at the invitation of the economics professor Bernd Lucke, there was little talk of the defense of "German identity" or "the Christian Occident" against the dangers of "Islamisation" or "foreign infiltration."[31] Like Lucke, most participants were well-educated members of the Western-German middle class (among them a disproportionate number of university professors). They wanted the AfD to be a "party of a new type" appealing to "those middle-class and academic milieus that consider themselves through their status as high achievers."[32] Five years later, the same party had entered all sixteen German state parliaments, was the largest opposition party in the federal Bundestag, and trailed only the CDU as the strongest party in the polls in the fall of 2018.[33] In some states, there was even talk of it assuming government responsibilities. But the party had also been fundamentally transformed. It had ousted Lucke and most of his supporters from its ranks, had adopted an economic policy that few would consider fiscally conservative, had sourced its voters from the Eastern German working class, and was speaking of little else but the defense of "German identity" and "the Christian Occident" against the dangers of "Islamisation" and "foreign infiltration."[34]

What had happened? The AfD's path from the free market and "the professors' party" to the "precariat's party," focused on immigration and Islam, has been paved by political infighting, reactions to social exclusion, and ideological radicalization.[35] But its overall direction is most adequately explained through the emergence of a new identity cleavage in Germany and many other Western democracies that is increasingly replacing traditional economic issues with questions of national culture and identity.[36] As we noted, this new cleavage pits a vision of a clearly defined national group identity based on ethnicity, culture, and authority against the globalist ideas of universalism and diversity founded on individualist identities. David Goodhart speaks of a new divide between "Somewheres" and "Anywheres," Simon Bornschier of a rift between "demarcationists" and "integrationists," and Yuval Hariri of a conflict between "nationalists" and "globalists."[37] In Germany, J. M. Dostal shows that "immigration" became the new "wedge issue" in the 2017 federal elections, and Pieter De Wilde, Wolfgang Merkel, Ruud Koopmans, and others find that the cultural divide between "cosmopolitans" and "communitarians" now dominates the political debate.[38] They also show that this divide is not just a backlash against the 2015/2016 refugee crisis, but has emerged over decades, as traditional sources of identity such as religion, class, and nationality have been eroded by individualization, secularization, and immigration.

Traditional party systems seem ill-equipped to deal with this new political fault line. Since the end of the Cold War, the mainstream left has increasingly substituted old communitarian instincts of the working class with what Thomas Frank calls the individualist "liberalism of the rich."[39] And the mainstream right has replaced emphases on patriotism and national identity with a cosmopolitan conservatism, incarnated by figures such as Angela Merkel, whose Grand Coalition of Social Democrats and Christian Democrats is considered "perhaps the best example of this new mainstream pro-immigration consensus."[40]

The result is a vacuum of representation for traditionalist communitarians looking for collective forms of identity. Political entrepreneurs on the populist right have begun to fill this vacuum. Thus, most Western European right-wing populist parties made an "identitarian turn" in the 1990s and 2000s, and many Eastern European mainstream conservative parties took a similar path in the late 2000s.[41] In their attempt to resist what they perceive as a liberal overreach, undermining traditional forms of collective identity, these parties challenge globalist ideology and strongly oppose immigration.[42] But they often also question the institutions, rules, and norms of the political system itself. The examples of Poland's Law and Justice and Hungary's Fidesz movements are frequently cited as previews of what might happen to democracies with right-wing populists in power. In Poland, EU politician Guy Verhofstad accused the government of "purges of the intelligence services and police, searches in associations' headquarters, measures to weaken the Constitutional Tribunal and now the dismissal of public broadcasting" in the context of what Law and Justice calls an attempt to "cure" their country's "diseases" after "25 years of liberal indoctrination."[43] As we have noted, Viktor Orbán's government in Hungary went even further, systematically restricting media pluralism (about 90 percent of local media outlets are owned by the state), undermining the independence of the judiciary, and intimidating civil society, most notably George Soros (in often anti-Semitic tones) and his Central European University. While still far away from mounting such concerted attacks on Germany's democratic institutions, the AfD has similarly turned away from traditional (neo)liberal "professors' topics" like the Euro or fiscal conservatism, and has substituted for them the New Right's core topics of immigration and national identity.[44] As was the case for these parties in other European countries—the populist aspects of their agendas—the AfD has become increasingly aggressive in its criticism of Germany's "political system" and its institutions, including the "system parties," the "liars press," and the "chancellor-dictator," all of whom they claim are seeking to destroy the German people, culture, and identity. Some AfD representatives have even gone so far as to justify the violent anti-immigration riots and vigilantism in Chemnitz in 2018 as "normal" reactions to what they consider to be a state failure.[45] Other AfD leaders have defended far-right anti-coronavirus-measures demonstrators and conspiracy theorists, who illegally sought to storm the German Reichstag and waved Neo-Nazi flags at its gates, as "not a danger for Democracy."[46]

Interestingly, in the context of this identitarian turn, religion has become crucial in defining national identity and making the distinction between "us" and "them." Scholars like Eric Kaufmann, who have analyzed the new "identity politics" of the right, show that it is not equivalent to traditional racism based on a biological racial hierarchy, but that cultural identity, defined partly by religious conformity, is the key variable of distinction.[47] As we quoted in the beginning, Orbán, for instance, explained that Hungary's vision of an "illiberal democracy" was actually nothing other than real "Christian democracy," while Law and Justice seeks to justify their policies as a defense of Poland's "Catholic identity."[48] Yet scholars like Müller, Olivier Roy, Nadia Marzouki, and Duncan McDonnell have not only shown that being Christian "was purely about belonging, not about belief, let alone any concrete ethical conduct—a militant Christendom instead of a merciful Christianity"[49]—but also that it was primarily an identity marker *ex negativo* directed against the Islamic other.[50] In the triangular right-wing populist worldview based on "the claim that the homogenous 'good' people are suffering due to actions from above by elites, and from below by a variety of 'others,'" these "others" are increasingly redefined in religious terms.[51] As José Casanova observed: "Only a few decades ago, immigrants from Turkey in Germany were viewed as Turks and not as Muslims, immigrants from Pakistan in the UK were viewed as Pakistani and not as Muslims. . . . But today throughout Europe, immigrants from Muslim countries are not only classified as Muslims, but they have come to represent 'Islam' with all the baggage."[52] Especially in European secular societies, religion thus appears to be primarily a marker of "the other" and only secondarily a marker of the "us."

In Germany, this phenomenon is clearly visible in Germany's right-wing populist PEGIDA movement. PEGIDA and its spin-offs reference the (Christian) Occident (Abendland) in their name, select high-profile churches like the Dresden Frauenkirche or Cologne Cathedral as backdrops for their rallies, carry oversized crosses and candles, and intone Christian hymns. Yet a closer look reveals that the rallies are less about a positive appreciation of Christianity than a negative reaction to Islam. Speeches are dominated by warnings about Islamization, crosses bear Germany's national colors, and hymns are only hummed, as most of the unchurched participants do not know the lyrics (or in fact the melody).[53] A survey of right-wing demonstrators in Dresden even found that only a small minority of participants identified as Christians, while over three-quarters of them self-identified as irreligious.[54]

An analysis of Lothar Roos's "cultural-ethical triangle"—a tool to trace the Christian value orientation through parties' policies, personal virtues, or relations with religious institutions—provides a similar picture of AfD.[55] The AfD makes references to the Abendland, "Christian traditions," and Christian identity in its manifesto.[56] The "Christians in the AfD" (ChrAfD) was among the first party suborganizations, and its leadership claims that "the AfD is the only Christian party that still exists."[57] Yet, when we look at policies, traditional Christian values of personal virtue, and institutional relations, the AfD's "Christian credentials" appear scarcely more persuasive than those of PEGIDA. Marianne Heimbach-

Steins's research team at Münster University, for instance, conducted an extensive comparison of AfD positions with those postulated by Christian social ethics and found that "almost all of the topics considered in our analysis revealed profound differences between the program of the Alternative for Germany party and the Catholic Social Doctrine."[58] Many leaders of the AfD, such as Alexander Gauland and Björn Höcke, identified as irreligious or atheist—as did the majority of the AfD's MPs, who in 2017 were among the least religious in Parliament, with only one in three identifying as Christian (compared with 93 percent of Christian Democrats and 63 percent of liberals).[59] And even among those AfD leaders who do identify as Christian, many do not necessarily conform with the very traditional Christian-conservative lifestyle ideals they seem to endorse. For instance, parliamentary group president Alice Weidel conceived a child using artificial insemination, whom she is now raising with her female partner, while party president Jörg Meuten and former party president Frauke Petry left their families for new partners while in office.

While such personal lifestyle choices need not preclude a political or indeed personal embrace of Christianity, the AfD's increasingly contentious attitude toward religious institutions, themselves, suggests a more serious disconnect. In fact, the AfD is increasingly hostile toward religious institutions. It is the party that most radically questions the system of "benevolent neutrality" in favor of a French-style secularist system. And although this hostility toward public religion was initially directed against Islam, it has more recently expanded to the Christian churches. Several state affiliates have hence demanded abolishing the collection of church taxes through the state, cutting church privileges in education, severing the personal ties between church and state, and shutting down church officials' voices in politics.[60] Some officials, like Paul Armin Hampel, have even called for AfD members to leave the churches, whereas others refer to them as the "lobby groups," "profiteers of the asylum industry," and "Government spokesmen."[61]

This anticlericalism is partly a reaction to the church positions of what party leaders call the "established elite" and—as we will see in the next section—to their public attitude toward the AfD. Still, the failure of the AfD to see churches as independent actors further suggests that, like PEGIDA, the party is more interested in "Christendom" as a cultural identifier against Islam than in "Christianity" as a belief. However, more important than the question of whether or not the AfD should be considered a Christian party academically is whether it is perceived as such by other actors.

Explaining the God-Gap:
Voting Behavior and the Role of the Church

Voters are unpredictable. On the evening of October 14, 2018, as the results of the Bavarian state election arrived at the CSU's election party in Munich, the image of lederhosen, dirndls, and Augustiner beer was overshadowed by the gloom on the participants' faces. The CSU had just experienced its most traumatic defeat since 1950. In a deeply Catholic state, where it often scored between 50 percent and 60 percent of the vote, it had fallen to a mere 37 percent. At the same time, the AfD achieved a record score of over 11 percent. Many had long feared such a result, and in the months prior to the election, the CSU had begun copying some of the AfD's formulas, playing hard ball against immigration and placing crucifixes in public buildings, "not as a religious symbol," as Markus Söder, the minister-president of Bavaria, put it, but as a "profession of identity and Bavaria's cultural imprints."[62] While bishops condemned this culturalized use of the cross, CSU strategists haunted by the fear of losing their Catholic constituency to the AfD paid little heed to such details. The Sunday night results showed that the CSU's fear for their Catholic constituency was not unfounded: 54 percent of the 530,000 voters who had deserted the CSU said they did so because "the CSU had given up on its Christian convictions."[63] Yet most did not migrate in the expected direction. Instead of turning to the AfD, more voted for the left-wing liberal, promigration, old "bogey of the middle class," the Green party.

The Bavarian example is representative of many Christian voters', parties', and institutions' reaction to the New Right's identity politics. Scholars have found that in Europe, churchgoing, ritually observant religious voters appear empirically more "immune" to right-wing populists' religiously laden identity politics than unaffiliated and irreligious voters.[64] This trend can be seen in countries like the Netherlands, where secular voters are most likely to vote for Geert Wilders; in France and Italy, where church attendance has been one of the strongest predictors of voting against right-wing populists; and Denmark, where 98 percent of supporters of the right-wing populist Danish People's party report never or rarely attending church.[65] But it is particularly true in Germany, where the AfD has consistently scored almost twice as high among unaffiliated, irreligious voters as among Protestants or Catholics.[66] Some social scientists, such as Stijn Daenekindt, Willem de Koster, or Yann Raison du Cleuziou, even speak of a new schism within the right-wing electorate between a traditional religious right and a new secular right. The former consists primarily of the churchgoing, educated middle classes, more closely bound to church teachings and attached to mainstream conservative parties. The latter is mostly composed of working-class voters, who tend to combine secular values with cultural nativism and show less church allegiance but greater openness to right-wing populist parties.[67]

The existence and significance of this "God gap" appears to largely depend on the behavior of social organizations such as churches and mainstream parties and to a lesser degree on personal piety. To be sure, the latter might still play a role, either by keeping the faithful away from right-wing populist attitudes or by instilling in them an inner judge that prevents them from turning such attitudes into action. However, there is still only inconclusive empirical evidence for this claim.[68] Over the next years, the picture may become clearer. For now, note that religiously affiliated Christians tend to reject the populist attacks on their churches, along with some of the nationalist anti-immigrant messages of right-wing populists.

Although the jury is still out to evaluate the exact role of individual attitudes, scholars do have a clear picture of the role of religion in mainstream political parties. Kai Arzheimer and Elizabeth Carter, for instance, argue that in countries with strong Christian democratic parties like Germany or the Netherlands, Christian voters "are not 'available' to these [right-wing populist] parties because they [Christian voters] are still firmly attached to Christian Democratic or democratically committed conservative parties."[69] Roy contrasts this with the French presidential election of 2017. After the defeat of Francois Fillon in the first round, political Catholicism lost its political home. Consequently, Catholics' reservations vis-à-vis voting for Le Pen's National Front (FN) weakened during the second round.[70] Bornschier argues that center-left parties might be equally important in this context. One reason why the FN established itself in France in the 1970s, whereas the AfD only arose in Germany four decades later, is that "the Socialists in France pursued an 'adversarial strategy' regarding traditionalist-communitarian issues, making multiculturalism a central claim, while the SPD employed a 'dismissive strategy' by systematically downplaying the immigration question."[71] This strategy to oust (left-wing) identity politics from electoral politics helped counter the use of religion as an identity marker for the far right and kept the SPD (and the Green) open as parties for Christian voters and activists. As the Bavarian example illustrates, the existence of such Christian alternatives on the left also allowed Christian voters to "discipline" the CDU/CSU for drifting off to the right by shifting their vote to such alternatives.

The most important yet underestimated factor in explaining the God gap might be the institutional churches themselves. Andreas Püttmann, one of the most prolific commentators on the relationship between Christianity and the New Right in Germany, argues, for instance, that Germany's churches have been able to erect a powerful social taboo against voting AfD.[72] After their initial skepticism toward a new right-wing party, German churches came out strongly against PEGIDA and the AfD and condemned their use of religious themes once anti-immigration policies and nativist ideals had become their core issues. With measures ranging from public condemnations criticizing AfD rhetoric as "hate speech" (German Conference of Bishops 2016) to the exclusion of AfD activists from church positions and the National Church days, churches became one of the AfD's most avid public adversaries.[73] Association with this party came with significant social costs among congregants.

Since Germany's system of benevolent neutrality allows churches to maintain a certain stature not only within their practicing flock but throughout German society, such condemnations matter beyond self-identified Christians, thus further increasing the God gap.[74] By contrast, in countries where the church institutions are less outspoken, such as Poland or Hungary, the God gap appears to be smaller among practicing Christians. In cases where the churches condemn the populist nationalists but occupy a less respected social and institutional position, such as in France or the de-Christianized lands of the former East Germany, the God gap remains large only among practicing Christians.[75]

As a result, Germany's churches have helped not only to erect a social firewall between "respectable society" and the new right but also to discourage the latter from using religious rhetoric and symbols in the first place. The AfD has recently distanced itself from earlier prochurch positions, denounced the "system-churches" as "red-green filth," accused them of being in an "unholy alliance" with the government and redefined itself as "not a Christian party" (Alexander Gauland).[76] To be sure, these reactions also show some of the risks of church-constructed social firewalls, as such barriers might contribute to the social exclusion and radicalization of moderate AfD supporters, as well as to a politicization of Christianity that might undermine its capacity to act as a social bridge-builder. How this will ultimately play out remains to be seen. Still, these circumstances are evidence of the tremendous potential of European churches in this context, suggesting that democratic Christian values combined with institutional action might become a formidable bulwark against the right-wing populist political parties' use of religious identity to energize and mobilize voters.

What Finally Can We Say about Church, State, and Identity?

Returning to that cold February night in Dresden, this analysis has shown although PEGIDA's demonstrators used religious symbols and language during their anti-Muslim rally, this was not based on a positive appreciation of Christianity, but rather on an ethno-cultural rejection of the Islamic "other." PEGIDA used "Christendom" as a cultural identity marker, but without necessarily subscribing to "Christianity" as a faith. The Dresden rally supports some broader conclusions about the role of religion in the nationalist populist assault on liberal democracy. We have seen that in Germany, churches (once converted to democracy) and a constitutional system of "benevolent neutrality" toward religion produced a relatively happy marriage of religion and democratic politics, where religion bridged social cleavages and stood as a defender of the liberal democratic order. Yet in the context of new identity cleavages in Western societies, religious cultural identity, in the absence of religious beliefs, values, and institutions, can be easily and efficiently used by movements and politicians as a cultural identifier to divide a society into "us" and "the other." But the churches, which combine religious faith with religious identity, "believing" with "belonging," might be the best-placed actors to expose political co-optation of religion and to erect an effective social firewall against the forces of a culturalized ethno-nationalism.

Interestingly, in the case of the Dresden demonstration, a keen observer could come to this conclusion even without surveys on the religious beliefs of participants and systematic analyses of speeches and policy positions, simply by looking more closely at the Dresden Frauenkirche itself. Shortly after the beginning of the gathering, the pastor turned off the lights of the church to keep it from being "instrumentalized as a backdrop for xenophobic rallies."[77] His colleagues in other German churches, like the Cologne Cathedral, soon did the same. But those who support the liberal democracies—and liberal democratic parties—of Europe must remain vigilant. With scenes such as the one in Dresden becoming more frequent around the world, the fight over the role of religion in Europe has only just begun.

CHAPTER THREE

The Nationalist Assault on Liberal Democracy in the United States

Whereas religious wars plagued Europe for centuries, the liberal democracies we have described in chapter 1 are mainly the product of late twentieth and early twenty-first centuries. Their religious history is important, but as we saw, their political systems underwent radical changes. The United States was different as even before independence in 1776, the colonies juggled religious conviction with religious freedom, the role of the church as independent from the political processes. It is no surprise that religious freedom found its place in the Constitution ratified shortly after independence from England even as religion played a powerful role in society. America was and remains a land of deep religious faith. Therefore, unlike our analysis of Europe, our analysis of the United States takes us back to the origins of this nation as a home for religious refugees seeking freedom to believe and act according to their faiths.

There are two parallel mythic histories of the role of religion in the United States that help to explain both the current rise of religion-infused illiberal democracy and its opposition by those who endorse a strict separation of church and state. Yet there is some convergence, a widespread agreement we can explore, on the development of religious expression in America. America was founded by religious folk. Among the motivations that brought Europeans to the New World, escape from religious persecution ranks high—these early immigrants included church reformist Puritans in Massachusetts, Quakers and Mennonites in Pennsylvania, Anglicans in Virginia, Catholics in Maryland and Georgia, and Baptists in Rhode Island. While not every community invited religious diversity, the possibilities of settlement allowed for religious havens far away from the religious warfare of Europe, allowing communities of faith to flourish. The freedom to believe and the safety of the believers were enshrined in the first amendment to the U.S. Constitution—"Congress shall make no law respecting an establishment of religion, or prohibiting the free exercise thereof." And George Washington's letter to the Jews of Newport, Rhode Island, stating in biblical language that "every one shall sit in safety under his own vine and fig tree and there shall be none to make him afraid," testified that even non-Christians would be protected. Most Americans, no matter their political differences, agree that American citizens are free to believe as they choose and establish their own faith communities (albeit post 9/11, with pressures and even attacks on Muslims).

The primary American story has been that there is a high wall of church-state separation that ensures a secular government in a country of many equal faiths, even if Christianity, in all its denominational forms, is the faith of the overwhelming majority of Americans. In this narrative, religion plays a civic role in support of democracy: it accepts the constitutional rules of the game and the legitimacy of political opponents; it supports civil disobedience; it rejects violence while promoting the expansion of civil liberties.[1] As Andrew Whitehead, Samuel Perry, and Joseph Baker note: "Civil religion, on the one hand, often refers to America's covenantal relationship with a divine Creator who promises blessings for the nation for fulfilling its responsibility to defend liberty and justice. While vaguely connected to Christianity, appeals to civil religion rarely refer to Jesus Christ or other explicitly Christian symbols."[2]

This narrative has heroes: the Quakers who opposed wars, the religious activists who ran the Underground Railroad to free slaves, the suffragettes who invoked God to enfranchise women, and the religious leaders of all faiths who marched for civil rights, against post–World War II armed conflicts, and against nuclear weapons. We could include those who, in the name of God, demonstrate within the law as an act of civic engagement to support or oppose abortion or same-sex marriage. It would be hard to imagine the expansion of social justice in America without religious individuals and their communities who acted as citizens committed to the rule of law and were willing to engage in nonviolent activism even those with whom they disagreed—the hallmarks of both responsible civic engagement and pluralism.

The alternative story describes a faithful and divinely blessed Christian nation that benevolently allows for limited religious freedom for minority groups. Race is an overlay on the latter story of the true America, which is white, with African Americans, like Native Americans, converted to save their souls, yet incapable of becoming true members of the unmarked white Christian society whose ancestors founded this country as free men. This is a narrative that concerns us. Again, as Whitehead, Perry, and Baker explain: "This brand of religious nationalism appears to be unmoored from traditional Christian ideals and morality, and also tends toward authoritarian figures and righteous indignation."[3]

The difference in these narratives stems in part from disagreement about the meaning of the First Amendment—whether it provides for freedom from religion as well as freedom to practice one's religion. Is the United States a secular state that protects religious freedom, with, perhaps, an honored role for religious voices in civic discourse, or a white Christian civilization that is threatened by immigrants, social or political movements that endanger the moral purity of the nation, and the invasion of violent infidels prepared to destroy it? In support of the latter is the use of Christian identity to mobilize political support, well expressed by a president who could proclaim at Oral Roberts University, "There is an assault on Christianity. . . . There is an assault on everything we stand for, and we're going to stop the assault."[4]

While it is true that "in the United States this relationship between government and religion can never be in a final sense 'settled,'"[5] our purpose is to demonstrate how a deeply embedded exclusivist religious narrative can be used to support the rise in America of a certain form of illiberal democracy that believes in white Christian supremacy and sees others not merely as less, but as a potentially polluting danger to the sacred American enterprise. This movement challenges the post–World War II liberal democratic values and institutions of the United States and raises fundamental questions about the relationship today between church and state. In the coded language of Donald Trump, "If I win the election for President, we are going to Make America Great Again."[6]

It is not that Christianity supports the rise of illiberal religiously infused nationalism. Rather, political leaders choose to use the mantle of Christian identity, tapping into a narrative that renders significant numbers of Americans as "other" while diminishing the democratic structures and ethos of the United States. It is ironic that, on the whole, when social scientists write about religion, they cite the United States as the archetype of a secular state that protects religious freedom.[7] This view accords with one reading of history. While the United States may eschew the laicism found, for example, in France, where laws restrict even how religious individuals can dress, the ethos of American governance is secular. This commitment to separation of the church—any church—from government even precedes the American Revolution. In 1769, John Dickinson, one of America's founding fathers, could write: "Religion and Government are certainly very different Things, instituted for different Ends; the design of one being to promote our temporal Happiness; the design of the other to procure the Favour of God, and thereby the Salvation of our Souls. While these are kept distinct and apart, the Peace and welfare of Society is preserved, and the Ends of both are answered. By mixing them together, feuds, animosities and persecutions have been raised, which have deluged the World in Blood, and disgraced human Nature."[8]

In the secular narrative, both in theory and practice, mixing religion and democratic government was considered a breach of the core freedoms promised by the Revolution and then the Constitution. Adherents of this view cite Thomas Jefferson, an architect of American democracy, whose claim that the First Amendment constructs a high wall separating personal religious beliefs and practices from government action, whether in support or in opposition, serves as the ground upon which the secular public square exists.[9] Fearful of the denominational conflicts that infected the nations of Europe and the official roles that specific Protestant and Catholic religious denominations played in those governments, the United States would follow an opposite path. According to this narrative, federal, state, and local governments would not provide in any way for the needs of churches and would remain neutral on all religious matters, while religious leaders would avoid overt engagement in the political affairs of the country, would not hold political office while holding church leadership roles, and would eschew political partisanship. Even a populist President Jackson, so admired by political conservatives, demurred from calling for a day of prayer and fasting, writing: "I could not do otherwise without transcending the limits prescribed by the Constitution for the president, without feeling that I might in some degree disturb the security which religion now enjoys in this country, in its complete separation from the political concerns of the General Government."[10]

Certainly, those who tell the secular narrative recognize that the relationship between church and state has been complicated. In many cases, the moral voice for increased freedom, human and civil rights, and a welcoming America came from religious communities. But it also is true that the First Amendment did not formally apply to states or local jurisdictions, so that a citizen's experience may have included state-sanctioned and religiously motivated regulations that determine which shops could open on Sunday, God-invoking sworn declarations in court, and the endorsement of and support for Christianity and its holidays. And, as we shall see, the rise of evangelism and the Great Awakenings converted a nation of sparse church attendance at its birth to much greater fidelity to

Christian faith. Yet the thrust of state agnosticism gained support and credence over the centuries, seemingly leading to a consensus supporting an ever-higher separation wall.

Although there were ample examples of state-sanctioned or state-supported anti-Catholic and anti-Jewish legal (and sometimes physical) assaults, something to be discussed further on, World War II deeply affected policy and politics vis-à-vis religious freedom and equality. When the United States entered the war, state-sanctioned discrimination—the hallmark of Nazi Germany—became anathema, at least in public settings. In the war's aftermath, the battle against godless international communism brought America into competition for support from nations around the world representing a wide range of religious belief. A language of respect for all religious traditions and races characterized American foreign policy. This led to significant shifts in internal politics and policies, from the integration of the military to Supreme Court rulings on religion.

In 1947, the Supreme Court drew a very bright line concerning the separation of church and state. States and local districts could no longer endorse specific religions in any fashion. Prayer and Bible reading in schools were forbidden. The language was dire and unequivocal: "No tax in any amount, large or small, can be levied to support any religious activities or institutions, whatever they may be called, or whatever form they may adopt to teach or practice religion. Neither a state nor the Federal Government can, openly or secretly, participate in the affairs of any religious organizations or groups and vice versa. In the words of Jefferson, the clause against establishment of religion by law was intended to erect 'a wall of separation between church and state.'"[11]

In 1963, the assurance that no child in any school would be forced to participate in, listen to, or ask to refrain from joining in prayer was clarified and confirmed once again,[12] and in 1971, all funding for parochial schools was forbidden since it fostered "excessive entanglement" between government and religion, thus violating the Establishment Clause.[13] In 1985, the court ruled against any form of prayer—sectarian, nonsectarian, or quiet meditation—stating that "the State's endorsement by enactment of . . . prayer activities at the beginning of each school day is not consistent with the established principle that the government must pursue a course of complete neutrality toward religion."[14]

It would seem, then, that by the end of the twentieth century, the United States could boast a long history of secular separation, providing protection to believers and their religious institutions while separating government from religious entanglement. The United States as the model of political secularism was confirmed.

But there is an alternative narrative which, in light of political conditions in the United States in the third decade of the twenty-first century, may seem closer to reality, suggesting a fifty-year, mid-twentieth-century pause in the centuries-old entanglement of church and state. This narrative does not lead inevitably to an exclusionary Christian nationalism, but it does delineate a path to our present polarization.

Religious persecution did not, as a cherished version of American history has it, lead to an absolute commitment by early settlers to religious freedom. While those settlers fleeing Europe were in fact seeking havens from religious persecution, most of the communities they and later immigrants founded placed religion at their cores, tightly regulating behavior and belief. Even those exiled from the Puritan-run Massachusetts Bay Colony established other faith communities in Rhode Island and Pennsylvania. Eight of the thirteen British colonies had legally established Christian denominations, and throughout the colonies, there were laws mandating church attendance and, in accordance with religious practices, store hours, while taxes were collected to pay the salaries of ministers.[15] Throughout the colonies, dissenters in belief and practice or proselytizers who offered an alternative version of Christianity were often persecuted. Religious freedom was not at the core of America's foundation.

The early republic struggled over how to reconcile religion with slavery, taxation, Indian affairs, and equality. Religious rhetoric, scriptural and historical, was often employed for partisan benefit. As Amanda Porterfield notes, "Religious invective fueled incivility in the early republic, establishing grooves for religion's role in public life that have continued to prove politically effective."[16] Decades later, Supreme Court justice Joseph Story's 1865 treatise on constitutional law could give judicial support for the role of Christianity in American society: "It is impossible for those who believe in the truth of Christianity as a divine revelation to doubt that it is the especial duty of government to foster and encourage it among all the citizens and subjects."[17]

In a 1963 dissent that anticipated a shift in U.S. attitudes toward the positive role of religion in society, Justice Potter Stewart stated: "If religious exercises are held to be an impermissible activity in schools, religion is placed in an artificial and state-created disadvantage. . . . And a refusal to permit religious exercises thus is seen, not as the realization of state neutrality, but rather as the establishment of a religion of secularism, or at least, as governmental support of the beliefs of those who think that religious exercises should be conducted only in private."[18]

The United States Congress passed, with almost unanimous consent, the Religious Freedom Restoration Act in 1993, essentially agreeing with Justice Potter that a religiously neutral law can burden a religion just as much as one that was intended to interfere with religion. This act helped to end the prior half-century-long legal consensus that the wall of separation must be strictly enforced and that religion is a private matter that belongs at home and in church. Legislators and the courts have continued to chisel away at the wall. Holding for the majority that a cross on public land is permissible, Justice Anthony Kennedy wrote in 2010, "The goal of avoiding governmental endorsement [of religion] does not require eradication of all religious symbols in the public realm." The cross "evokes far more than religion." (Justice Stevens rejected that view: "The cross is not a universal symbol of sacrifice. It is the symbol of one particular sacrifice, and that sacrifice carries deeply significant meaning for those who adhere to the Christian faith").[19]

On May 5, 2014, the U.S. Supreme Court ruled 5–4 in favor of the Town of Greece, New York, confirming that the town's practice of beginning official government sessions with a deeply sectarian Christian prayer invoking Jesus does not violate the Establishment

Clause of the First Amendment.[20] In the same year, ruling on whether a privately held corporation could restrict contraceptives as part of a woman's healthcare policy based on its owners' religious beliefs, a majority held that it could.[21] Freedom of religion, in 2018 rulings, meant that one can discriminate against an individual in the name of deeply held (biblical) faith.

Prior to these turns in the law, many Christians thought that the government, through Congress and the courts, was anti-Christian and consistently protecting secularism, as well as minority religious groups, at a cost to the Christian majority. A shift was occurring among many Christians, including aspiring political leaders and judges. They believed that a rebalancing after a fifty-year experiment in forced national secularism was necessary because Christianity had been under assault. In this view, Justice Kennedy's assertion that the cross is a universal symbol confirmed that Christianity, as the majority religion, should once again benefit from the privileged position it had held for centuries. The resentment of years of perceived oppression became fuel for a political movement, exemplified by the Christian Coalition.[22]

If the courts, following World War II, were thoroughly committed to fostering a secular state, the culture of America at that time was more complicated. John Foster Dulles, the future secretary of state, declared in 1950, "What we lack is a righteous and dynamic faith. Without it all else avails us little."[23] The words "under God" were added to the Pledge of Allegiance, recited daily in schools across the country, in 1954. An evangelical Christian awakening burst forth in the late 1970s that sought to bring Christian faith, mores, and laws back to America.[24] By 1982, the conservatives' political hero, Ronald Reagan, reminded America of its Christian mission, quoting from both the Gospels and the Hebrew Bible:

"For God so loved the world that he gave his only begotten son that whosoever believeth in Him should not perish but have everlasting life." We have God's promise that what we give will be given back many times over. And we also have His promise that we could take to heart with regard to our country—"That if My people who are called by My name humble themselves and pray and seek My face and turn from their wicked ways, then will I hear from heaven and will forgive their sins and heal their land."[25]

This Christian mission, as we shall see, called on the faithful to rise up to save America. It ignited a battle to support what were considered traditional values—heteronormative, male-dominated, white Christian values—and to block, for example, pro-LGBTQ legislation or the Equal Rights Amendment. The hope was that Christianity would dominate the public square even if the political leaders themselves, such as Presidents Reagan or Trump, were not known for religious piety.[26] The mission made its way into politics. Increasingly, the Republican Party called for a return to "traditional values," to a time when Christian faith dominated public and private life. The party called for the public display of the Ten Commandments as a reflection of our history and our country's Judeo-Christian heritage, while affirming the rights of religious students to engage in voluntary prayer at public school events and to have equal access to school facilities.[27] By 2017, President Trump was able to declare a moral equivalency between the Neo-Nazis, the Ku Klux Klan, and white Supremacist marchers in Charlottesville, on the one hand, and those opposing the march, on the other. Following the march, just under a third of Americans claimed that the country's white European (Christian) heritage must be preserved, while a similar percentage disagreed.[28] The former portion of the electorate provided the bedrock constituency for the Tea Party in 2010 and for Donald Trump in 2016, continuing through the end of the decade.[29]

In light of the latest elections and the language and policies on the federal and state levels challenging what seemed to be the accepted norms and values of American democracy and church-state separation, the narrative of America as an eternal beacon of religious freedom has begun to appear less credible. Many founders of what became the United States, and many of their spiritual descendants, held a very powerful and compelling faith that this new land was an inheritance blessed by God. One can see this in town biblical names—Providence, Goshen, Salem, Bethlehem, New Canaan, Bethany—of the early colonies. One can hear it in the spiritual awakenings we will discuss below that recurred over centuries, and in the policies, such as Manifest Destiny, that were informed by zealous religious Christian passion. What becomes evident is that the very purpose of settling America was to further God's plan to reestablish a new Israel that expressed God's love of His faithful adherents. If we seek a founding statement of purpose, we hear Puritan minister John Winthrop, who preached in 1630 of a land of biblical promise. As they departed from England on the ship Arabella, Rev. Winthrop exhorted his Christian followers to be faithful, citing a text from 2 Samuel 7:10 (King James Version): "Moreover I will appoint a place for my people Israel, and will plant them, that they may dwell in a place of their own, and move no more." And he declared with Deuteronomic confidence: "We shall be as a City upon a Hill, the eyes of all people are upon us; so that if we shall [behave badly] and so cause [God] to withdraw his present help from us, . . . we shall [invite] the mouths of enemies to speak evil of the ways of God. . . . We shall shame the faces of many of gods worthy servants, and cause their prayers to be turned into curses upon us. . . . Therefore, let us choose life, that we, and our [children], may live; by obeying His voice and cleaving to Him, for He is our life and our prosperity."[30]

There is a trinity of assertions here that we need to explore. The first is that America is the promised land, the reestablishment of biblical Israel. The second is that there is a covenantal relationship between God and the white Christian settlers whose descendants will go on to found the United States. The third is that human behavior will bring blessings or curses on the enterprise of nation building. In unpacking this narrative of America as the reincarnation of biblical Israel and its covenant with God, we can better understand the extreme passions that animate contemporary American authoritarian-minded populist nationalists.

For the early settlers and their progeny, to build a new society was a covenantal act, a fulfillment of the promise to Israel's descendants, the wanderers in the desert seeking the promised land. They read their experience through the lens of biblical prophecy, according to which God's people must conquer the land of God's promise, expelling or destroying the heathens as God commanded and abiding by God's laws to protect the redemptive purity of the land and to maintain the covenant with God.[31] The national liturgy shows the tremendous staying power of the analogy. It can be heard in the "Battle Hymn of the Republic," written in 1861, and "God Bless America, Land That I Love," written in 1918 (ironically by a Jew, Irving Berlin). Patriotic speeches carry the message of God's promise and blessings and a citizen's Christian obligations. Abraham Lincoln invoked God's gracious favor in announcing the Emancipation Proclamation in 1863. Mary Elizabeth Lease spoke to the Women's Christian Temperance Union, which succeeded in its efforts to prohibit alcohol consumption in the United States: "Let no one for a moment believe that this uprising and federation of the people is but a passing episode in politics. It is a religious as well as a political movement, for we seek to put into practical operation the teachings and precepts of Jesus of Nazareth."[32] In the twenty-first century, the language of the narrative uniting Christianity with governance could not be more pronounced. As one evangelical pastor declared: "There is a moral and spiritual war for the souls of Americans. And this war must be waged by preaching the Gospel, prayer, and obedience to God's Word."[33]

Aligned with historic political shifts, the colonies and then the United States experienced spiritual revivals, the Great Awakenings, that added intensity to the spiritual lives of believers while bringing into the Protestant fold millions of converts. These religious movements, while focused on personal piety and salvation, had national implications. Not only did they create a shared national experience as preachers crossed the country, county by county, but they also set the stage for political action. Religious ferment in the mid-1700s enlarged the bounds of liberty and inspired resistance to the High Church British monarchy and its authority in the colonies. As a result, old structures began to crumble.[34] The same could be said in the years preceding the Civil War, when evangelical religious revivalism converted more women and African slaves and abolition became a religious imperative for many.[35] It is no surprise that Union soldiers marched to war singing, "As He died to make men holy, let us die to make men free, as God goes marching on." Nor is it unexpected that Protestant ministers in the South declared slavery to be part of a God-ordained plan.[36] The leaders of and participants in the Great Awakening in the early decades of the nineteenth century saw themselves as patriots who believed that Christianity was the wellspring of the republic and that conversion was a sign of intense patriotism. As the American Home Ministry assured its supporters, "We are doing the work of patriotism no less than that of Christianity."[37]

These spiritual events, then, linked personal behavior—piety, beliefs, and acts—with citizenship and patriotism. As Protestant readers of the Bible, these Americans well understood the demands of being a blessed and sacred people. The Bible provides a very clear and commanding code of purity. It posits the existence of one supreme and omnipotent God against whom there can be no equal force. It isn't Satan who threatens the covenant, but evil people: "Only one creature remains with 'demonic' power—the human being. Endowed with free will, his power is greater than any attributed to him by pagan society. Not only can he defy God but . . . he can drive God out of the sanctuary. In this respect, humans have replaced the demons."[38]

Humans who pursue evil, whose practices, whether private or public, pollute the very ground, who defy God's covenantal plan for America as the new Israel, the true promised land, will not only exile God from the sanctuary, but have the demonic capacity to expel God and God's grace from America. Such is the penalty for choosing sin and endorsing contamination[39]—not only for the faith community but for the nation itself.

Believers in the idea of America as a Christian nation, in order to sustain the nation's covenant with God, reserve the right to invoke government power because the nation's fate is not a private affair. For these believers, the consequences of a sin are not limited to the sinners alone. As Jacob Milgrom explains: "When the evildoers are punished, they bring down the righteous with them. Those who perish with the wicked are not entirely blameless, however. They are inadvertent sinners who, by having allowed the wicked to flourish, have also contributed to the pollution of the sanctuary."[40]

In this reading of the Bible and the American story, *immorality* threatens the very existence of America, polluting the purity of the American enterprise initiated by the faithful Christian settlers. Added to the fuel of potential pollution is a doctrinal belief that the world is a dangerous place filled with sin and lurking evil.[41]

As we have noted, there is no external decision maker who can determine what constitutes authentic religious theology and practice, in spite of fundamental catechisms declared by any church body. So it is not Christianity per se that provides the core of this union of Christian identity and illiberal politics, but a very distinct read of biblical text and nostalgia for a past in which Christianity was the norm as was segregation (black churches and white churches) and a very clear heteronormative male-dominant society. For mainline Christians and Catholics today, one can surmise that sin and evil are less significant than a commitment to build a world of goodness and compassion. The same could be said for many evangelicals.[42] That is not the case for those committed to a Christian-dominated illiberal democracy. They see a battleground, a nation in need of protection from pollution and divine abandonment. As Whitehead, Perry, and Baker explain, using the term *Christian nationalism*: "Christian nationalism, however, draws its roots from 'Old Testament' parallels between America and Israel, who was commanded to maintain cultural and blood purity, often through war, conquest, and separatism. Unlike civil religion, historical and contemporary appeals to Christian nationalism are often quite explicitly evangelical, and consequently, imply the exclusion of other religious faiths or cultures. Also paralleling Old Testament Israel, Christian nationalism is often linked with racialist sentiments, equating cultural purity with racial or ethnic exclusion."[43]

The value of this analysis is that the move from personal religious belief to doctrinal catechism to the nation as an embodiment and expression of Christian (initially Protestant) religious identity is at the core of the illiberal political movements that are challenging the secular constitutional democratic norms and values adopted or reaffirmed in the United States following World War II. This, of course, complicates our picture since these political leaders and many followers may well be people of deep and abiding faith. That said, as we have noted, the call to rise and defend Christian America, such as the Tea Party Revolt and the Republican Party Donald Trump reframed, clearly appeal to something beyond religious fervor as they challenge some if not all of the norms and values of American liberal democracy. "Make America Great Again" taps into a nostalgic past when a very white and very male church was entrenched in the state. There is no subtlety in Vice President Mike Pence's 2017 speech in Indiana, when he declared: "We've come to a pivotal moment in the life of this country. . . . It's a good time to pray for America. If His people who are called by His name will humble themselves and pray, He'll hear from heaven, and He'll heal this land!"[44]

And in 2011, governor and then presidential candidate Rick Perry (later a Cabinet member in the Trump administration) called on Americans to join him for a prayer-and-fasting event to heal "a nation that has not honored God in our successes or humbly called on Him in our struggles. . . . According to the Bible, the answer to a nation in such crisis is to gather in humility and repentance and ask God to intervene. . . . The Response will be a historic gathering of people from across the nation to pray and fast for America."[45]

At the same time, many evangelical religious leaders have ratcheted up the church-state conflict in calling on Christians to act to save the country. In a challenge to the Congressional ban on political endorsements from the pulpit, hundreds of evangelical ministers did exactly that, with ministers such as Rev. Gus Booth declaring, "If you're a Christian, you cannot support a candidate like Barack Obama or Hillary Clinton."[46] The Decision America Tour, for example, was born in 2016 when Franklin Graham visited all fifty states, challenging Christians to lead lives rooted in biblical principles and to pray earnestly for America. The response of two hundred evangelical leaders attacking a Christian evangelical call for the impeachment of Donald Trump in 2019 affirmed the fealty many evangelicals have to the President's white nationalist agenda.[47] As evangelical Christian leader Jerry Falwell explained, "The idea of Church-State separation was invented by the Devil to keep Christians from running their own country."[48]

Such exhortations tap into the belief that America is both blessed and endangered by spiritual pollution. American national exceptionalism flows from biblical religious sanction and cultural identity and the community's commitment to uphold its unique norms and values of purity. Especially, the battle to protect the nation from what these believers see as the potential pollution of society (the intrusion of the "other" into their domain) is fundamental to their religious—and their political—worldviews. The fear of sin that undermines America is a powerful political driver, opening the door to more extreme views of who is truly American, what made America great, and the role of the "other" in American society.

How then does belief in the biblical promise of America as the new Israel mutate into a political extremism that combines white supremacy and Christian supersessionism with American authoritarian-minded nationalism? The connection can be traced to the post–Civil War period. The rise of the Ku Klux Klan, composed entirely of white, Anglo-Saxon, Christian citizens, both male and female, paralleled the emancipation of slaves and a growing fear that America was in danger of pollution by people of other colors and religions. The Klan was founded immediately following the collapse of the Confederacy and played a role in Southern politics during Reconstruction. Following the 1876 election and the end of Union occupation, the Ku Klux Klan became a prominent force of intimidation through violence, lynching, and cross burnings. Their presence was at least tacitly supported by white churches and political leaders as Jim Crow segregation spread across much of the country. In fact, the Ku Klux Klan emblem was the Christian cross. The parallel massive influx of immigrants from non-Protestant countries that began in the late 1800s only exacerbated the sense that America was under siege, that true patriots would soon be overwhelmed by an alien invasion (a fear echoed in nationalist rhetoric today). The perceived threat to America and its white Christian patriots is perhaps best expressed in the 1915 film *Birth of a Nation*, which was given the honor of a viewing in the White House by Woodrow Wilson (who gave the Klan his tacit support). In its dramatic ideal vision of a white Christian America, it helped to inspire a rebirth of the Ku Klux Klan at Stone Mountain, Georgia (the largest shrine to white supremacy in the world), along with the idea that segregation was a heroic effort to protect America from racial and religious mongrelization. For those who supported this view, America was endangered not only by assertive African Americans but by hordes of non-Protestant immigrants. Between 1880 and 1924, some twenty-five million immigrants came to America, the majority "papist" Catholics, Orthodox Christians, and Jews, most of whom were also not seen as white.

The reaction in the 1920s was to protect the integrity of American society and the vision of a white Christian homeland by shutting down immigration and creating formal and informal restrictions that segregated housing, education, and employment beyond the Jim Crow segregation of African Americans. By 1924, almost all immigration to the United States from countries not in northwest Europe ceased. Political leaders, including Wilson, either supported the agenda of white Christian patriotism or, like Franklin D. Roosevelt, were silent.

It is also essential, in understanding contemporary America, to reflect on the synergistic union of Christian supersessionism and racism. In the post–Civil War period, Southern churches responded to attempts to integrate society by claiming segregation as a Christian mandate. It was Protestant and white religious leaders, mainly in Southern and Midwest states, that translated their theology of Christian redemption into political party politics, igniting fears that laws demanding racial, religious, and ethnic equality would oust good white Christians from their position of primacy and engineer the cultural collapse of white Christian America. Until

World War II, there was very little opposition from the political elites to the view that "the United States of America was to be, beyond anything else, a Christian refuge from a fallen world. Those who wished to control its power were expected to follow those guidelines."[49]

While many religious leaders fought for an end to segregation and for equality in the name of God, the union of nationalism, patriotism, and segregation was nurtured by that ever-present strain of Christianity that saw a unique role for white Christian America. Alabama governor George Wallace sounded as much the preacher as the politician when he declared in 1963:

> Today I have stood, where once Jefferson Davis stood, and took an oath to my people. It is very appropriate then that from this Cradle of the Confederacy, this very Heart of the Great Anglo-Saxon Southland, that today we sound the drum for freedom as have our generations of forebears before us done, time and time again through history. . . . In the name of the greatest people that have ever trod this earth, I draw the line in the dust and toss the gauntlet before the feet of tyranny . . . and I say . . . segregation today . . . segregation tomorrow . . . segregation forever. . . . God has placed us here in this crisis. . . . Let us not fail in this . . . our most historical moment.[50]

In what seems complex and ironic, the positions of the two main political parties concerning religion and civil rights began to shift in the latter part of the twentieth century. Once the Democratic Party under Lyndon Johnson became the architect of laws that sought to end discrimination in voting, housing, education, and employment, faith in the vision of a white Christian America migrated to the Republican Party. The union of redemptive faithful purity and political engagement rapidly informed Republican Party strategy, turning the Democratic South into a solid bastion of Republican support. As Forbes commentator Chris Ladd notes,

Republicans discovered that they could preserve white nationalism through a proxy fight for Christian Nationalism. They came to recognize that a weak, largely empty Republican grassroots structure in the South was ripe for takeover and colonization. Southern churches, warped by generations of theological evolution necessary to accommodate slavery and segregation, were all too willing to offer their political assistance to a white nationalist program. Southern religious institutions would lead a wave of political activism that helped keep white nationalism alive inside an increasingly unfriendly national climate.[51]

The language of the two Trump political campaigns and even after his defeat, from public statements to party platforms, allows us to trace the trajectory of this white Christian support of illiberal democracy among some Christians that challenges clear demarcations separating religious belief from government policy and politics. Donald Trump's language throughout his campaigns and presidency liberated hateful religious rhetoric. He has called for banning Muslim immigrants, considered closing all mosques, claimed that Islam is a religion of violence and that Muslims are setting up training camps in the United States, and said that the families of Muslim terrorists should be "taken out." In late 2018, the president described a caravan of Central American refugees as a mix of "criminals and unknown Middle Easterners." He then added that he has "alerted Border Patrol and Military that this is a National Emergency. Must change laws!" This is the next stage of populist nationalism, the use of a lie to call for emergency powers in response to false threats to the nation. His words are still echoed by a significant segment of the American population.

As we have noted, the path that led America to Charlottesville, Virginia, in the summer of 2017 reflects a rising and empowered strain of American populist nationalism. Hundreds of white men and women, some garbed in Ku Klux Klan robes, waving Confederate, Nazi, and American flags, marched through the streets with torches ablaze, chanting, "Jews will not replace us," and, "White lives matter." And the president of the United States, noting that many of the marchers wanted to protect monuments to the memory of the Confederacy, asserted a moral equivalency: "We condemn in the strongest possible terms this egregious display of hatred, bigotry and violence, on many sides. On many sides. It's been going on for a long time in our country." And he added: "You had people that were very fine people on both sides." Confirming the appeal of such rhetoric, which is now embedded in the Republican Party, which controls much of American political institutions, two-thirds of Republican voters supported President Trump's response to the overtly racist Christian supremacist march.[52]

Katharine Henderson explains the challenges facing Christian leaders today engaged in the public arena:

> For many Christians today, the way of Jesus that governs our lives has been hijacked for political and partisan purposes over the last decades. So deeply intertwined are Christian conservative faith and politics, it's hard to distinguish one from the other. As a Presbyterian, the history of my denomination alone tells the story of breakups and reunions, schisms and heresy trials. Division is nothing new in the church. But the theological divisions over doctrine, theology, governance and "brand" that have historically plagued the followers of Jesus, even before they were called Christian, have been exploited to win votes, garner political power and divide people from one another. The theological rifts over public issues, especially slavery and enduring racism—never adequately excavated or exorcized—live on and are now joined by other ones such as abortion, same sex marriage and the role of women in the home, the church and public life.[53]

What we learn is that when Christianity becomes explicitly political, then, unlike civil religion, it can be unmoored from pluralist and democratic traditions, emphasizing only its notions of exclusion and apocalyptic war and conquest. It also seems often to be unmoored from fidelity to Christian traditions to care for the stranger, attend church, and emulate Jesus's humility and outreach to those most vulnerable and even despised. Trump and many who have followed represent a prime example of this trend in that they are not traditionally religious or recognized to be of high moral character, facts which ultimately do little to dissuade many religiously identified supporters from supporting Donald Trump and others who speak the same Christian populist language. In this way, the myth of a Christian nation can function as a symbolic boundary uniting both personally religious and irreligious members of authoritarian-minded groups: "As a form of boundary-work, the claim that America is a Christian nation not only defines Christians as 'true' or prototypical Americans; it also defines non-Christians as outsiders, interlopers or even enemies."[54] Clearly, while the Trump presidency exemplified such views, such discourse no doubt will continue to live on.

As we stated in the beginning, this is, of course, not necessarily about Christianity—its values or moral code—but about a particular read of America as a Christian nation. Christians hold a wide range of views, and many of the greatest Christian leaders were historically and are presently committed to egalitarianism, social justice, and even progressive policies that endorse and sustain democracy. Rather, this is about the use of a particular Christian identity to undergird an illiberal political movement that challenges the core tenets of American democracy. The word "traditional" is a substitute, at this juncture of American history, for a uniquely conservative nationalist Christianity that houses within it antidemocratic forces. Many of these views are in fact challenged by a majority of Americans. Almost two-thirds of Americans and a majority of Catholics, mainline Protestants, and Jews (and those of no faith) support same-sex marriage and some form of abortion. In addition, an overwhelming majority of Americans oppose discrimination based on sexual preference, including same-sex marriage. Those advocating these progressive views would no doubt express them as embodying traditional American values of pluralism and respect for human dignity. Many would say these progressive values are deeply Christian.

Yet the current holders of the institutions of U.S. governance—the Supreme Court's conservative Christian majority, the Republicans in Congress, and legislators in many states—actively or tacitly endorse the polarizing statements and policies promulgated during the Trump administration. The positions stated in the Republican platforms of the past decades mimic the demands of the most conservative Christian nationalist minority. Donald Trump, and his Republican Party's America that would be great again, are an America in which white Christian patriots would once again determine the law of the land. The triumph of Donald Trump and the political forces unleashed reflect a fundamental shift—perhaps a battle no less significant than the Civil War—that threatens to render asunder a consensus about and confidence in liberal democracy as the political system of the United States. And religious identity plays a central role in this conflict. The America espoused by Christian populist nationalists is a limited democracy, dedicated to retaining control by disenfranchising whole segments of the population, while actively discriminating against those of color, other religious groups, and anyone who does not conform to the white, Christian, heteronormative image of the authentic American. No single election will defeat this movement.

Though the Religion and State world survey that examines religious institutions and their adherents does not include the United States, it provides metrics to determine how a country treats its religious and secular citizens. The survey, clearly grounding itself in liberal democratic values, includes questions concerning the role of the dominant religion, support for religious institutions, restrictions imposed, and forms of discrimination. It also focuses on key policy questions such as abortion, LGBTQ rights and same-sex marriage, and religious requirements for citizenship and immigration.[55] By examining both political rhetoric and government policies in the United States shortly before and since the 2016 election and using these survey questions as hallmarks of liberal democracy, we see radical shifts from the approximately six decades following

World War II during which the wall of separation was perhaps at its highest. We can then note and analyze the rise of authoritarian-minded illiberal Christian nationalist movements under the umbrella of the dominant conservative white Christian minority. It is not a pretty sight.

It is worth taking to heart Porterfield's admonition, "While civil democracy requires freedom of religion, the reverse does not hold. Religion does not require civil democracy and may often threaten it. . . . Religious partisans have often wanted to suppress if not exterminate their enemies and make their own approach . . . the basis of America."[56]

Whitehead, Perry, and Baker conclude their study with strong evidence that Christian nationalism played an important role in predicting which Americans voted for Donald Trump and, we can anticipate, the core of supporters who endorse his challenge to democratic norms with an apocalyptic and redemptive vision of America that calls for a triumph of Christian nationalism as the sole source of its salvation.

Although support for Trump has been linked to a number of other potential factors, such as class-based anxieties, sexism, anti-black animus, xenophobia, and Islamophobia—all of which are empirically related to Christian nationalism—we find that the Christian nationalist vote for Trump is not synonymous with, reducible to, or epiphenomenal of any of these other ideologies. Christian nationalism is also not merely a proxy for evangelical Protestant affiliation, traditionalist religiosity, or political conservatism and affiliation with the Republican Party. Rather, Christian nationalism is a pervasive set of beliefs and ideals that merge American and Christian group memberships—along with their histories and futures—that helped shape the political actions of Americans who viewed a Trump presidency as a defense of the country's perceived Christian heritage and a step toward the restoration of a distinctly Christian future. Christian nationalism provides a metanarrative for a religiously distinct national identity, and Americans who embrace this narrative and perceive threats to that identity overwhelmingly voted for Trump.[57]

The founding credo of the United States is that all who reside in its borders are created equal and endowed with ever-expanding civil and human rights. At its democratic core is, as Lincoln reminded his fellow citizens, a government of the people, by the people, and for the people. To sustain this political system, members must play by the established rules of the game, respect the legitimacy of the opposition, defend the rights of those with whom they disagree, eschew violence, and protect the many voices that participate in the political process. These values, while certainly threatened over the centuries by demagogic politicians, discriminatory legislation, racist judicial fiat, and antidemocratic movements, remain fundamental principles that must be sustained and nurtured by the constructive civic engagement of the American citizenry. They have no independent existence save the actions of citizens and the health and vitality of their political institutions.

It is in moments such as these, when the core sustaining democratic values are challenged, that a counter force must speak out and mobilize a majority committed to democracy. Religious leaders in America are not exempt from this task if democracy is to triumph. Their place is on the side of tradition—the American democratic tradition—that defends the widow, the orphan, and the stranger in their midst and assures them that none shall make them afraid.

CHAPTER FOUR

A Catholic Response to the Errors of Catholic Nationalism

The use of religion by politicians and civic leaders, Catholic or otherwise, is not new. American history provides many examples. Religious rhetoric played a significant role in the abolitionist and civil rights movements, but it was also deployed in support of slavery and segregation. There is nothing wrong with connecting a political message to a religious tradition. However, when groups begin to claim that their political truths determine what it means to be a faithful member of a religious community, they reduce mystery to the mundane and eternity to the transitory. While one certainly may employ religious beliefs to consider policies and political choices, politics as a litmus test of faith introduces angry divisions into the community by presenting ideological positions as testimony for religious purity. These efforts to subordinate religious identity to political gain are a form of blasphemy that requires constant vigilance on the part of faith communities. In our case, this requires leaders in the faith community to teach its members how to identify illegitimate appropriations of their faith in the name of nationalist illiberal claims. The growth of political movements that use Catholicism to justify their illiberal stance in Europe and the United States, therefore, requires a clear response that lays bare the theological errors of such movements.

It is a Catholic axiom that in order to lead someone away from error, you must recognize the truth that gives power to the error.[1] Error has a parasitic relationship with truth. Those who expound an illiberal nationalism exploit confusion among Catholics concerning the distinctions between tradition, history, and custom. For well over a millennium, Catholic rulers wedded their imperial conquests, inquisitions, and religious wars to their faith. They fought for God and the cross; evangelism was a political as well as religious act. From this we learn that Christian nationalism seizes on historical moments in which the church actively supported nationalist goals that included the establishment of religious unity as a means of unifying the citizens of a nation. Thus, Catholic history can be seen as a critical aspect of tradition, the unfolding of God's plan for a universal Catholic Church, a valued tradition to be followed.

Further, those who endorse illiberal political values also make use of the ambiguity of the term "nation." How different nationalist groups understand a "nation" manifests itself in a spectrum. At one end are those who understand the term "nation" as referring to a race of people or a narrowly defined tribe, which is how the term was understood in the Middle Ages. The ethnic understanding of the term was also important in a variety of liberation movements in the modern period, including, for example, the Solidarity movement's resistance to communist rule in Poland. Nations are, in this sense, peoples who have a shared history, language, and ethnicity. A nation may or may not have its own state. This ethnic or racial way of understanding the term "nation" is manifested in Poland and Hungary, but also in Austria and Spain. Other Catholics understand a nation primarily in terms of the sovereign state, which can be seen in France and the United States. As we have noted, nationalism itself remains one way people establish an identity and join together to build society. Nationalism framed in terms of sovereignty runs the danger of privileging some groups and discriminating against others, but the arguments and rationales for discrimination are overtly framed in terms of national interests such as preserving unity, promoting national security, or protecting the country's cultural heritage. This form of nationalism, for a Catholic, also affects international relations insofar as it prioritizes one's own sovereign nation above all other nations.

"Nationalism from a Catholic perspective," therefore, is a contradiction in terms. "Catholic" literally means universal. As the *Catechism of the Catholic Church* explains, universality is one of the fundamental marks or identifying features of the Catholic Church.[2] An exclusive nationalism that transcends all other identities is completely contrary to fundamental dogmas of Catholicism as found in scripture, tradition, and the teachings of the magisterium of the church. One of the clearest statements on the incompatibility of Catholicism and nationalism comes from Pope John Paul II. In a message for World Migration Day in 1999, he cited Leviticus 25:23, "This land is mine; for you are strangers and sojourners with me,"[3] to show that Christians should see themselves as having a heavenly rather than earthly homeland. He continued:

These biblical categories have become significant again in the present historical context, which is strongly marked by substantial migratory flows and a growing ethnic and cultural pluralism. They also underscore that the Church, present in every clime, is not identified with any particular race or culture since, as the Epistle to Diognetus recalls, Christians "live in their homeland, but as guests; as citizens they participate in all things, but are detached from all things as strangers. Every foreign country is a homeland to them and every homeland a foreign country. . . . They dwell on earth but are citizens of heaven."[4]

John Paul II explained that this vision "helps Christians to reject all nationalistic thinking and to avoid narrow ideological categories." Christians must adopt this perspective, he argued, in order to free the gospel from "cultural encrustations that inhibit its inner dynamism."[5]

John Paul II taught that Catholicity cannot be restricted to Roman Catholics. Drawing on the command to love one's neighbor from Leviticus 19:18 and Paul's description of Christ as breaking down divisions between people in Ephesians 2:14, he declared: "Catholicity is not only expressed in the fraternal communion of the baptized, but also in the hospitality extended to the stranger, whatever his religious belief, in the rejection of all racial exclusion or discrimination, in the recognition of the personal dignity of every man and woman and, consequently, in the commitment to furthering their inalienable rights."[6]

John Paul said that the question Christians should ask is not, "Who is my neighbor?," but, "To whom should I become a neighbor?" The pope's answer was that the Christian must become the neighbor to anyone who is in need.[7]

As we shall see, John Paul stood firmly within the Catholic tradition and in accord with the teachings of Vatican II when he made these statements, which raises the question of why some Catholics declare that exclusivist and "othering" nationalism either is in accord with their faith or is grounded in it. In order to answer this question, we must consider the characteristics of Catholic nationalism, its roots in history, and the Catholic understanding of tradition. Because Catholic nationalists claim that they are aligned with tradition and use this claim to dismiss the authority of sources that would contradict their efforts to exclude refugees, marginalize minority groups, and ignore the common good of all, we concentrate more on how the apostolic tradition interpreted scripture than on the scriptures themselves. Once we understand tradition in doctrinal terms, we see that one must choose between Catholicism and the narrow reading of Catholicism adopted by those endorsing illiberal democratic principles.

Catholic Illiberal Nationalism

Over the last decade, Catholic nationalism in its illiberal form as an identity marker has grown tremendously in Europe and in the

United States. In Poland, Catholic nationalists portray themselves as fighting a culture war against the European Union's efforts to "Islamicize" Eastern Europe and to erase their homeland.[8] Poles have taken to the streets chanting, "Pure Poland, white Poland," and carrying banners declaring "Pure Blood, Clear Mind!"[9] Polish Catholic nationalists target teenagers and young adults, teaching them that Catholicism is the only true religion and that the Polish commitment to its Catholic identity is the reason for its superiority to other nations.[10] Similar Catholic nationalist movements based in an ethnic understanding of nationalism have arisen across Europe, from Italy to Hungary, Croatia to Slovenia.

These movements represent a significant challenge to the democracies in Eastern Europe. A 2017 report from the Pew Research Center reveals that slightly more than a quarter of the population in Poland and Hungary felt that, in some circumstances, nondemocratic governments are preferable; people who do not care what type of government they have make up 18 percent of Poland and 21 percent of Hungary.[11] Such nationalists do not need majorities to seize governments when the commitment to democracy is so anemic. In Croatia, ethnic nationalists with a xenophobic agenda were able to hold a slim majority in the government in 2017—even though 54 percent of the population affirmed democracy as preferable to any other form of government and 65 percent reported that they believe society is better when it consists of people from different nationalities, religions, and cultures.[12]

Catholic illiberal nationalism has also been growing in influence in older democracies. In France, Austria, and Spain, Catholic leaders espousing illiberal politics have gained significant power. In these contexts, their nationalism is based on the notion of the sovereign state rather than on ethnic identity, though there are ethnic aspects in the Western European countries as well. In the United States, many Catholics have been drawn to opposition to political correctness, immigration, and LGBTQ rights. While these movements are often not explicitly or even nominally religious, prominent Catholics are involved in the movement, such as Steve Bannon, who served as President Trump's central campaign advisor.

Because the United States has never been a Catholic country, Catholic nationalism there is quite distinct from its European counterparts; however, there has been a long tradition in American political discourse of referring to the United States as a Christian nation or as holding Judeo-Christian values. Even so, it is not clear how many U.S. Catholics support a nationalist perspective. The American National Election Study showed that Trump, who ran on a nationalist platform, won 56 percent of the white Catholic vote but only 19 percent of the Latino Catholic vote. Some of that support was due to opposition to abortion, regulations, taxes, or Hillary Clinton.[13] Though much of Trump's support from Catholics may not have been motivated by his populist nationalist agenda, a significant number of Catholics did not recognize his form of nationalism as a moral disqualification. Of course, Pat Buchanan long espoused a nationalist agenda, and he had numerous predecessors including Father Coughlin and Senator Joseph McCarthy. The question for U.S. Catholics is not so much whether to support Catholic illiberal nationalism, but whether a Catholic should support nationalist politicians, groups, policies, and laws.[14]

In the United States, the interaction between religious leaders and nationalist groups is complex. The Catholic bishops have long supported immigration and the expansion of a more generous social safety net for the poor, but their activism against gay marriage was framed in a way that allowed nationalists to co-opt their message. Representatives of the United States Conference of Catholic Bishops (USCCB) signed a letter, along with some other Christian and Jewish leaders, in 2012, "Marriage and Religious Freedom: Fundamental Goods That Stand or Fall Together," which succeeded in galvanizing opposition to LGBTQ rights. The executive summary of the letter concluded: "The law [legalizing same-sex marriage in certain states] not only will coerce and impose disincentives, but will also teach that religious objectors must be marked as if they were bigots. We encourage all people of good will to protect marriage as the union between one man and one woman, and to consider carefully the far-reaching consequences for the religious freedom of all Americans if marriage is redefined. May all of us work together to strengthen and preserve the unique meaning of marriage and the precious gift of religious liberty."[15]

Illiberal political forums promoted this message of fear as a means to motivate conservatives to vote. Since the release of the letter, more than a dozen states have passed some form of religious liberty law that allows for discrimination against LGBTQ people.[16] While we doubt the USCCB intended to provide rhetorical ammunition for groups that also oppose immigration, support the death penalty, and advocate an "America First" approach to economics and international relations, this is precisely what they did.

Whether we are considering this form of Catholic nationalism in Europe or in the United States today, it shares four common features. First, it opposes accepting Muslim refugees and immigrants. Second, it opposes the extension of civil rights and protections to LGBTQ people. Third, it presents the narrower good of the nation without considering the common good of humanity. Finally, it either proposes or justifies oppressive and exclusionary laws on the basis of Catholicism. This does not mean that opposing homosexual marriage or wishing to limit how many Muslims can immigrate into a country makes a Catholic illiberal. For example, a Catholic could support civil protections for LGBTQ people and still oppose homosexual marriage, or a Catholic could be concerned about how many refugees a country admits while promoting policies to provide aid to those refugees. However, in our read of how religious communities should respond to the critical issues of our day, a Catholic should never lose sight of the universality of the church and the common good or try to justify oppression by means of his or her faith.

Unfortunately, Catholics have done many things inconsistent with Catholic teaching over the long course of their history. It is the confusion of what faith demands of Catholics and the actual history of what Catholics have done to promote the faith that feeds those Catholics who advocate for illiberal nationalism. It is an easy mistake to make because faith is deeply connected to history in Catholicism. Catholicism teaches that God reveals Godself through history, particularly in the incarnation of Jesus Christ. The transmission of this revelation comes through scripture, and a particular read of the Catholic past, traditions, and memory is itself embedded in various historical contexts.[17] As we shall see, the confusion over what constitutes tradition and what is simply historical is nothing new. Both Martin Luther and John Calvin were able to use inconsistencies and contradictions in conciliar statements, papal decretals, and the writings of the saints to undermine the idea that Catholic doctrine is infallible. The Catholic Church's response to the questions raised by the Protestant reformers is critically important for revealing the nationalists as what they are: "false teachers among you, who will secretly bring in destructive opinions" (2 Peter 2:1 NRSV).

A Brief History of the Catholic Church's Political Role

The Catholic Church's relationship to the state has developed as political paradigms have changed, but throughout its history, the Catholic Church has strongly resisted attempts to identify the faith with any particular group of people or any particular state. In fact, a failure to resist was defined as the heresy of Donatism in the fifth century. At the same time, as a visible, organic society on earth, the Catholic Church reflected the historical and cultural contexts of its members. The Catholic Church emerged in an imperial context, then adapted to feudalism, and then to the rise of the nation-states in the early modern period. More recently, the Catholic Church has come to embrace democracy. Catholicism can adapt in these ways because the apostolic tradition does not speak to political or economic theories. The New Testament presents what is, at best, an ambivalent attitude toward the state. Satan is presented as the prince of the world in Luke 4:5–7, and the Apocalypse is suffused with references that identify the antichrist with the emperor. At the same time, Saint Paul warned the Christian community in Rome to be obedient to civil authority, since all authority is established by God, which was practical advice for a persecuted religious minority.

The Catholic Church's ambivalence toward the state runs throughout European history. Emperor Constantine's conversion to Christianity marks the true beginning of the Catholic Church's political entanglement with the state, which promptly led to the development of monasticism as a reform movement. The relationship with the Roman Empire almost immediately became problematic, as Constantine and his successors involved themselves in theological disputes over the Trinity, Christology, and icons. The emperors had inherited a belief that religious unity was necessary for political unity, but the more they tried to resolve divisive doctrinal disputes, the more they engendered resistance.

Christian bishops and apologists supported imperial initiatives as well as opposed them, but the Roman popes began to strongly and consistently assert independence from and even authority over secular rulers beginning in the fifth century. When it became clear that the Roman Empire could no longer defend Rome, Pope Leo declared that though emperors might abandon their capitals and empires themselves disappear, "there abides that which truth itself has ordained, and so blessed Peter, in retaining the rock-like strength he has received, does not abandon the government of the Church committed to him."[18] As the Roman Empire disintegrated in the West and finally collapsed in 476, the popes and the clergy increasingly took over governmental functions.

The clergy's involvement in governance was not based on doctrinal considerations. The exodus of the Roman elite left a political void that the popes and the clergy filled. In addition to their spiritual primacy, Leo the Great and the popes that followed began to speak of their office in terms of "principatus," which was a political title reserved for the emperor. Pope Gelasius set an important precedent in his letters to Emperors Zeno and Anastasius, stating that emperors cannot define Christian principles. He wrote that there are two powers governing the world, the sacred authority of pontiffs and the power of kings; moreover, he claimed that Christian emperors had to submit their actions to the bishops.[19]

Over the course of the sixth through the eighth centuries, instability in Italy led to the emergence of an actual papal state, which lasted until 1870. This was not the only example of the church mix-ing the spiritual and religious with raw political power. In order to convert Europe, medieval missionaries concentrated on converting kings, queens, and other nobles to the faith. Like Constantine, these rulers saw religious unity as necessary for political unity and per-suaded people to adopt the new faith. Their efforts to persuade people included a great deal of propaganda and even violence, which served to form national myths of origin. A trip to the cathedral in Aachen or in Rheims provides ample evidence of the ways the em-perors and kings associated their rule with divine providence.

In addition to legitimating imperial and royal power, religious propaganda was put in the service of warfare. The Crusades are a notorious example of the church's involvement in warfare, particu-larly against Muslims, though there were Crusades against the Al-bigensians and against other Christians as well. The Reconquista of Spain and the various wars with the Ottoman Turks in the sixteenth century served to reinforce Christian national identity as well as the heathen characterization of Islam. As the Christian rulers sought to enforce religious unity, they persecuted religious minorities. The Jews were always targets in these campaigns, and Catholic theolo-gians provided justifications for European rulers to seize Jewish property or to expel Jews from their borders. The church even pro-vided specialists, inquisitors, who could identify and root out reli-gious minorities and dissidents in order to aid the state in maintain-ing religious unity.

This history provides Catholic nationalists with a wealth of historical sources from the Catholic Church that were meant to stoke religious hatred and intolerance. It is not surprising that Polish nationalists used the Feast of Our Lady of the Rosary, which commemorated the victory of Christian forces over the Turkish navy in 1571, to call people to come together at the country's bor-ders to pray for "other European nations to make them understand it is necessary to return to Christian roots so that Europe will re-main Europe."[20] Marcin Dybowski, a Polish Catholic political leader, used the opportunity to explain that "a religious war be-tween Christianity and Islam is once again underway in Europe, just like in the past."[21] However, European Catholics are not facing a military invasion by the Turks in a religious war; instead, they are being asked to admit refugees who have been persecuted and displaced by conflicts in their home countries. Because Dybowski conflates faith with Poland's historical Catholic identity, followers are encouraged to identify opposition to immigration as Catholic faithfulness.

After the Protestant Reformation began, Europe was engulfed in a cataclysm of violence. There were the wars of religion between Catholic nations and Protestant nations, civil wars, and atrocities from the Knights' Revolt (1522–23) and the Peasant's Revolt (1524–26) to the Eighty Years' War (1568–1648) and the Thirty Years' War (1618–48). The vestiges of these conflicts remain visible all over Europe. You can still see the cages hanging from St. Lambert Church that held Anabaptists who had been flayed alive and put on display. The violence and horror caused by these conflicts led to a revolution in how church and state should relate to each other that began with the Peace of Westphalia in 1648. The treaty instituted a new political order in the Holy Roman Empire based on sovereign states.

Westphalia recognized that states would reflect the faith of their rulers, but it granted equal protection to Catholics, Lutherans, and Calvinists before the law in all of the states that signed the treaty. Gradually, these ideas influenced other European countries, such as France and Great Britain, and incorporated more religious faiths. After the religiously targeted genocides against the Armenian Christians (1915–22), the Assyrian Christians (1915–23), the Greek Orthodox in Anatolia (1914–22), the Jews and Serbian Orthodox Christians in Croatia (1941–45), and the Jews throughout Europe by the Nazis (1939–45), the liberal democracies committed to extending equal protection to people of all faiths. This process culminated in the United Nations Universal Declaration of Human Rights, article 2, which states: "Everyone is entitled to all the rights and freedoms set forth in this Declaration, without distinction of any kind, such as race, colour, sex, language, religion, political or other opinion, national or social origin, property, birth or other status. Furthermore, no distinction shall be made on the basis of the political, jurisdictional or international status of the country or territory to which a person belongs, whether it be independent, trust, non-self-governing or under any other limitation of sovereignty."[22] Although many countries have not lived up to this declaration, it remains a foundational document for modern democracies.

Following World War II, the Catholic Church began to adapt its political thinking to the new democratic realities, just as it had adapted to working in an imperial, feudal, and monarchical context. The Catholic Church came to recognize that the idea of a Catholic nation as a principle of political organization was no longer viable. That isn't to say the idea hasn't lingered in places like Northern Ireland, where the church has continued to run the school system, but it has been recognized that faith thrives in the context of a free and pluralistic society because faith must be freely embraced. Nonetheless, Catholicism still has a complicated history when it comes to democracy, a problem of how to incorporate or reject traditions, sacred texts, and historical experience when engaging and participating in democratic states.

Because Catholics have lived in and worked under diverse forms of government in their history, it is easy to find sources justifying imperial, feudal, and monarchical systems of government in church documents. It is also easy to find antidemocratic texts from the late eighteenth century well into the first half of the twentieth century. Though the church initially took an open if somewhat guarded stance toward the idea of democracy in the late eighteenth century, the anticlerical policies of the French Revolution led Pope Pius VI to condemn the principles of the revolution and the new French constitution in March 1791.[23] Tensions grew between the clergy and the revolutionaries, and in August 1792 revolutionaries massacred over two hundred priests in Paris. The French revolutionaries closed monasteries, shuttered seminaries, and seized church property in the name of liberty. Napoleon exported these policies across Europe, decimating the Catholic Church. So it is not surprising that, forty years after the massacre of the Parisian priests, Pope Gregory XVI, who was an actual monarch in the Papal States, portrayed democracy and religious liberty as flowing from a poisonous stream of antireligious fervor.

Gregory XVI also suppressed Italian revolutionaries who were seeking political liberty. Even after the popes lost their monarchical status, they continued to oppose fundamental tenets of modern democracy well into the twentieth century. Pope Pius X expressed his opposition to religious liberty and the separation of church and state in his 1907 encyclical *Pascendi Dominici Gregis*. This encyclical was then referenced in Pius X's Oath against Modernism, which all clergy, religious superiors, and professors of theology and philosophy were required to take from 1910 until 1967.[24] Nationalists now use these very sources and this very historical experience to justify their illiberal policies against liberal democracies and their commitment to protect religious minorities, Muslim refugees, and members of the LGBTQ community. Nationalists can do so because they grant the pre–Vatican II papal encyclicals the same authority as, or more authority than, they grant to the documents of Vatican II, in part because they see the church's antidemocratic history as tradition. Their position is grounded in the idea that the church cannot and does not change.

As history makes clear, however, the Catholic Church has changed and continues to change on many matters. Cardinal John Henry Newman argued that Christianity's strength and perfection was revealed in its ability to adapt to new contexts without losing its identity. He described the nature of a perfect idea this way: "In time it enters upon strange territory; points of controversy alter their bearing; parties rise and fall around it; dangers and hopes appear in new relations; and old principles reappear under new forms. It changes with them in order to remain the same. In a higher world it is otherwise, but here below to live is to change, and to be perfect is to have changed often."[25] All of this change implies, as Newman admitted, that some developments might be unfaithful to the original idea. Indeed, this possibility is central to the concept of reform in the Catholic Church. As we shall see, what cannot change is the gospel as presented in the scriptures and the apostolic tradition. The gospel or the revelation provides the test for determining whether or not a change is legitimate. The Catholic Church's official stance toward religious liberty, separation of church and state, and democracy changed decisively at Vatican II. This change did not appear ex nihilo; instead, it largely emerged out of the Catholic experience of democracy in the United States, where Catholic bishops were strong supporters of the separation of church and state and of religious liberty. As the leaders of a religious minority, they recognized how these principles afforded their communities protection and allowed them to grow in a pluralistic society. Drawing on traditions that go back to John England, who was the first bishop of Charleston, South Carolina (1820–42), John Courtney Murray, S.J., demonstrated how Catholicism and democracy were compatible. After having been silenced from 1954 until 1963, he was invited to help draft a document on religious liberty during Vatican II. In December 1965, the council released *Dignitatis Humanae*:

> The Vatican council declares that the human person has a right to religious freedom. Freedom of this kind means that everyone should be immune from coercion by individuals, social groups and every human power so that, within due limits, no men or women are forced to act against their convictions in religious matters in private or in public, alone or in association with others. The council further declares that the right to religious freedom is based on the very dignity of the human person as known through the revealed word of God and by reason itself. This right of the human person to religious freedom must be given such recognition in the constitutional order of society as will make it a civil right.[26]

The right to religious freedom is grounded in human dignity and is revealed by faith and reason, but the council also grounded religious freedom in the philosophy of personalism—the claim that the person is the key in the search for self-knowledge, for correct insight into reality, and for the place of persons in it—as well as in the concept of the common good.

The common good of a society is to promote the conditions of social life which allow a person to achieve a "fuller measure of perfection with greater ease."[27] Here "a person" denotes an individual in relation to a community, which means that a person's physical, social, psychological, and spiritual dimensions must be considered in order to achieve a just society.[28] The Second Vatican Council taught that it is the common responsibility of individual citizens, social groups, civil authorities, the church, and other religious communities to protect the right to religious freedom. Further, it stated that civil authorities must see to it that there is no religious discrimination before the law.[29]

Given the Catholic Church's history, the council members were careful to show how religious freedom is in harmony with the apostolic tradition. *Dignitatis Humanae* declared: "One of the key truths in catholic teaching, a truth that is contained in the word of God and is constantly preached by the Fathers, is that human beings should respond to the word of God freely, and that therefore nobody is forced to embrace the faith against their will."[30] In other words, Vatican II recognized that medieval theology that denied the role of free will in salvation and that justified forced conversions was a corruption of apostolic tradition. Vatican II taught that God's regard for the freedom and the dignity of the human person is clearly revealed in the life of Jesus Christ, who acted humbly and patiently in attracting and inviting disciples. Christ did not come as a political Messiah (Matthew 4:8–10), but he came to serve and to "give his life as a ransom for many" (Mark 10:45).[31] As the council explained: "His kingdom does not establish its claims by force (Matthew 26:51–53), but is established by bearing witness to and hearing the truth and it grows by the love with which Christ, lifted up on the cross, draws people to himself (John 12:32)."[32]

The Second Vatican Council's reference to the word of God and the constant preaching of the Fathers indicates how the council members evaluated the authority of the documents that had condemned religious liberty and other democratic tenets. They were indicating that they had evaluated the matter in light of the apostolic tradition and found support for the principle of religious liberty both in the New Testament and in the teaching of the Church Fathers. Certainly, there are ambiguities that remain in the Catholic understanding of normative, binding, or infallible tradition, but the Council of Trent provided some clarity on what is and what is not tradition. This is important because it provides a test for determining whether something can change, as well as whether a change is legitimate. Vatican II used this dogmatic principle from the Council of Trent to reevaluate some of the teachings of the magisterium that had taken place after the apostolic era. It is also the principle people need to understand in order to expose the error of nationalism. The Catholic nationalists do not just stand in opposition to the recent teachings of the popes and the teachings of Vatican II. As now understood, their position entails rejecting the Council of Trent as well.

Defining Tradition

In the sixteenth century, Luther's and Calvin's critiques forced the Catholic Church to clarify what it meant by binding tradition, which, in any communitarian sense, is the lived experience of the faithful. There was no consensus on what constituted tradition, and since the end of the thirteenth century, a debate had been ongoing as to the relative authority of scripture, history, canon law, and prophetic revelations. Leaving prophecy aside for our purposes, the debate over scripture and tradition at Trent clearly illustrates that the credibility of the Catholic Church rests on a clear distinction between history, custom, and what are considered traditions so embedded in the lived experience of Christians as to be considered infallible.

In the polemics and apologetics between Catholic theologians and Protestants, Catholic apologists took varying positions in their responses to Luther's principle of *sola scriptura* (scripture alone) as the only infallible authority. Catholics claimed that scripture must be seen through the lens of its Christian interpreters. Cardinal Cajetan argued that the infallible revelation included scripture and its interpretations in the apostolic tradition, the holy doctors, and the councils of the church.[33] By way of contrast, Sylvester Prierias responded to Luther by arguing, "In its irrefragable and divine judgment, the church's authority is greater than the authority of scripture." From this he concluded, "Whoever does not rest on the doctrine of the Roman Church and of the Roman pontiff as on the infallible rule of faith from which even sacred scripture draws its strength and authority, is a heretic."[34] Jacques Almain also placed the authority of the church over the scriptures. Almain claimed the church may define points of doctrine not in scripture, for she has received these points "orally from the Apostles"; however, he placed the ultimate authority in the councils of the church rather than in the papacy.[35]

The problem for the Council of Trent was that Protestant objections to the authority of the church and of her traditions were fairly consistent, but Catholic answers were not. Tradition or traditions potentially included unwritten oral traditions, liturgical matters, practices, the teachings of the Church Fathers, the writings of the saints, conciliar decrees, and papal decretals. Since some of these sources contradict others, it was impossible to discern what was and was not Catholic tradition. It is similar to the confusion of those who point to long-abandoned papal encyclicals or the Feast of Our Lady of the Rosary to justify their antidemocratic and exclusionary policies. The bishops at the Council of Trent realized that it was urgent to develop a coherent understanding of tradition. On February 18, 1546, the word was limited to apostolic traditions, which the bishops identified as the hallmark of revelation. However, this led Bishop Bertano of Fano to object: "As soon as they [Lutherans] see that the apostles' traditions are received by us, they will say: how many traditions do they receive, which they themselves violate? For it is certain that to receive communion under both kinds, to stand from Easter to Pentecost, to pray toward the East, are apostolic traditions. . . . It is not enough to say we receive only what has reached down to us. For adversaries will say . . . that we receive what we like, those we dislike, we exclude."[36] Since this was going to be a dogmatic teaching of an ecumenical council, the bishops had to state clearly what is and is not binding and infallible tradition or call the very concept of the church's infallibility into question.

After more than a week of debate, the Council of Trent clarified the authority of scripture and tradition for the Catholic Church. On April 8, 1546, Trent identified three characteristics of binding or infallible tradition. The first condition for an infallible or irreformable tradition is that the doctrine must come from the apostolic period. However, the Council of Trent restricted the idea of tradition further by limiting it to matters of faith or morals. There is some debate as to exactly how to understand each of these characteristics of tradition. For example, it is not entirely clear when the apostolic period ends, but, generally speaking, it extends to the death of those who knew the apostles, who themselves knew Jesus. Given that the apostle John supposedly died in 100 CE, it is hard to imagine this period lasting beyond 175 CE. There have also been times, for example, when it was not clear whether something was a matter of faith or science, as in the notorious case of Galileo. Though Trent did not clearly distinguish between matters of science and matters of faith and morals, the council deliberately excluded customs, liturgical practices, and canon law.

Trent's position on tradition was explicitly reaffirmed at the Second Vatican Council in the dogmatic constitution *Dei Verbum*. *Dei Verbum* describes tradition this way: "God graciously arranged that what he had once revealed for the salvation of all peoples should last forever in its entirety and be transmitted to all generations. Therefore, Christ the Lord, in whom the entire revelation of the most high God is summed up (see 2 Corinthians 1:20, 3:16–4:6), having fulfilled in his own person and promulgated with his own lips the gospel promised beforehand by the prophets, commanded the apostles to preach it to everyone as the source of all saving truth and moral law, communicating God's gifts to them."[37] Ironically, most of what are considered in the Catholic Church as inherited traditions are not apostolic. These nonapostolic traditions, practices, policies, and laws can be good, bad, or morally neutral. Catholic nationalists around the world often rely on these "inherited" traditions to justify racist, homophobic, and xenophobic behavior. Yet because the traditions they claim as justification arise from particular historical and cultural circumstances, such traditions can be revised, suppressed, or abandoned. Although local customs may have value, they must yield to scripture and the apostolic tradition.

Catholicism also claims that tradition makes progress in the church over time, with the help of the Holy Spirit. How can tradition develop if it is restricted to apostolic matters of faith and morals? Here it is helpful to understand that the term "tradition" comes from a verb that means "to hand down." This process of handing down the gospel in different times and places leads to deeper insight into its meaning.[38] These deeper insights have led to changes in how the Catholic Church understands issues like slavery, torture, social justice, and the death penalty. Nonetheless, these deeper insights must be grounded in and consistent with scripture and the apostolic tradition. With scientific progress, including the social sciences, the meaning of the revelation becomes clearer. For us, it is painful as we look back to imagine how the Catholic Church ever supported torturing and executing people for their religious convictions, conducting witch hunts, or holding trials by ordeal. Of course, we do understand historical context, the reality of what was deemed acceptable not only by the church but by the societies in which Christians lived. That said, our growing awareness of what is just and right in human development constantly clarifies and enhances what it means to love our neighbors and to recognize human rights.

A Renewed Commitment to Human Rights

Catholic teachings on human rights are rooted in the belief that every person, as a living image of God, deserves respect; they also hold that Christians are called beyond respect or tolerance, to the active solicitude of love. As the Second Vatican Council stated:

Today, there is an inescapable duty to make ourselves the neighbor of every individual, without exception, and to take positive steps to help a neighbor whom we encounter, whether that neighbor be an elderly person abandoned by everyone, a foreign worker who suffers the injustice of being despised, a refugee, an illegitimate child wrongly suffering for a sin of which the child is innocent, or a starving human being who awakens our conscience by calling to mind the words of Christ: "As you did it to one of the least of these my brothers and sisters, you did it to me" (Matthew 25:40).[39]

Holding true to these claims, it seems increasingly obvious that Catholics should not refuse to help refugees, discriminate against LGBTQ people, or exclude people based on religion or ethnicity. Moreover, Catholics are called upon to love their enemies and do good to those that hate them, as Jesus commanded in Matthew 5:43–44 and Luke 6:27.[40] In other words, Catholics should not support discriminatory policies and laws—even when they are framed in terms of national security and claim to follow the teachings of Christ. Vatican II declared that any kind of "social or cultural discrimination in basic personal rights on the grounds of sex, race, color, social conditions, language or religion must be curbed and eradicated as incompatible with God's design." Moreover, the council urged both governments and private organizations "to safeguard basic human rights under every political system."[41]

Although Catholics have failed, sometimes spectacularly, at treating everyone with respect and love in its long history, the apostolic tradition affirms that Catholics may not legitimately discriminate against or hate anyone. This tradition is well attested in the writings of the saints as well. For example, Saint Maximus the Confessor taught that the person who has even a trace of hatred toward anyone at all becomes completely foreign to the love of God, because the love for God in no way admits of hatred for humanity. He explained: "'The one who loves me,' says the Lord, 'will keep my commandments' and 'this is my commandment, that you love one another.' Therefore, the one who does not love his or her neighbor is not keeping the commandment, and the one who does not keep the commandment is not able to love the Lord."[42] Maximus taught that Christians must meet the basic needs of everyone, whether they are just or unjust, good or evil. Imitating God requires loving all equally, the virtuous and the wicked. He said that it is not enough to believe. Christians have to do the work of love. "The work of love," he explained, "is the deliberate doing good to one's neighbor as well as long-suffering and patience and the use of all things in a proper way."[43]

The through-line from scripture and tradition as expressed by the magisterium is clear that everyone has inherent dignity and rights; but more importantly, all three sources of authority mandate that everyone, including the most wicked people, must be treated with respect, with love, with mercy, and with patience. Catholics cannot claim that their faith justifies the racist exclusion of immigrants and refugees, because the Catholic faith demands that every Christian has a duty to meet the needs of anyone in need. Catholics cannot claim their faith justifies discriminatory laws and inflammatory language about LGBTQ people because all are beloved images of God. The Catholic faith teaches that every Catholic must work to eradicate discrimination so that everyone in a society is accorded access to the same resources and cultural benefits. It is by learning how to extend yourself in love to the person you fear or see as sinful that Christians learn how to love as Christ commanded. This extension to those that seem impure can be seen in the way that Saint Francis of Assisi embraced and kissed a leper at the outset of his ministry.

Catholicism cannot support efforts to exclude people out of a concern to preserve a Catholic or Christian culture because the church is a sacrament or an instrument of the unity of the human race in communion with God. Poland may have a majority of Catholics, but Poland—or Italy or Croatia or France—cannot ever be "Catholic." Vatican II declared: "By its nature and mission the church is universal in that it is not committed to any one culture or to any political, economic or social system."[44] Moreover, the church is not tied exclusively or indissolubly to any race or nation, way of life, or set of customs.[45] The church calls on all Catholics and all people to put aside conflicts and to build just human associations. Though the Catholic Church did not commit itself to democracy as the only political system, it did call all regimes to recognize the basic rights of the person, the family, and the common good.[46] Those who use Catholic identity to nourish and sustain illiberal democratic movements act in rebellion against the clarity of this position.

Cultures contain gifts to humanity as well as imperfections and errors that need to be purified, which is why "culture must be subordinated to the integral development of the human person, to the good of the community and of the whole of humanity."[47] Though culture demands respect, such respect is conditional upon whether or not the culture safeguards the rights of the individual and of the community within the limits of the common good.[48] "It is not for the public authority to determine how human culture should develop," according to Vatican II, "but to build up the environment and to provide assistance favorable to such development, without overlooking minorities."[49] From this, we derive that it is a duty for all Christians to work diligently for political decisions that will ensure the recognition and implementation everywhere of everyone's right to human and civil culture in harmony with personal dignity, without distinction of race, sex, nation, religion, or social circumstances.[50] Although Vatican II predated the more contemporary perspective on gender, the intent was to rule out discrimination against all those who are marginalized or oppressed. Catholicism teaches that the aim of governments "should always be the formation of human persons who are cultured, peace-loving, and well disposed towards all, to the benefit of the whole human race."[51]

The commitment to the good of the entire human race does not allow for any political agenda that absolutizes the idea that a nation can place its good above the good of the community of nations. This claim has been used to foster populist and antidemocratic movements in Europe and the United States; however, Catholicism endorses international cooperation and the establishment of international organizations to work for the common good, and "especially to respond to intolerance around the world."[52] This cooperation includes economic matters in terms of both trade and international aid to developing countries.[53] Christians have an obligation to advocate for generous international cooperation and are encouraged to establish nongovernmental organizations with this purpose.[54]

Given Catholic doctrine on international cooperation, the rights of minorities, and the dignity of the human person, the rise of an illiberal nationalism that uses Catholic identity to gain support reveals the failure of the Catholic bishops and of the Roman Curia to make people conscious of these teachings. Vatican II affirmed that special attention should be given to incorporating these themes into both religious and civil education programs. Unfortunately, this did not happen consistently, and Rome did not reinforce the importance of these doctrines. Many Catholic schools continue to reinforce a narrow patriotism without balancing it against the idea of the common good and the demands of Christian love. While catechetical programs usually discuss social justice and human dignity, they generally fail to connect these teachings to political issues related to international affairs or civil rights. Except for the Catholics who have the means to attend a Catholic college or university, most will never encounter these teachings. That is a tragedy, and Catholic nationalists who fight against Vatican II in the name of national sovereignty have taken advantage of the void, but there are ways that Catholics can begin to roll back the forces of intolerance and hatred or, at the very least, to show that the Catholic faith condemns the agendas, policies, and behaviors of those forces.

What Should Be Done

To respond to the errors of Catholic nationalism, the Catholic Church needs to change how it educates Catholics, disciplines clergy who advocate for nationalism, and observes the liturgical matters. The first step is to show how Vatican II's support for human rights and international cooperation was grounded in a return to scripture and apostolic tradition. There must be an effort to distinguish between the apostolic tradition and the various historical accretions, customs, and liturgical retrojections used by politicians and political movements in the name of the Catholic Church to persuade people to join their cause. Catechetical materials, Catholic school curricula, and seminary syllabi—particularly in the fields of church history and moral theology—need a thorough self-reflective review with the aim of removing elements at variance with the apostolic tradition. Formation programs for both ordained and lay ministers need to incorporate requirements for field education working with minority, immigrant, and LGBTQ people and communities. These programs should encourage and, if possible, provide experiences working with Catholic NGOs in developing countries. Dioceses and parishes should facilitate discussion groups for Catholics to compare the teachings of the Catholic Church with the positions of politicians and parties as well as with existing laws and policies.

There is a need to educate Catholic clergy, theologians, and religious educators on the integral relationship between Catholic teachings on human rights and the institutions that protect and promote them. The freedom of religion entails freedom of association and of speech as well. Such freedoms mean little without an ability to communicate through independent media, whether in print or online. Equal treatment under the law requires strong constitutional rights and an independent judiciary. Christians must be taught to recognize the importance of cultivating civility in political discourse, which is difficult to accomplish without the existence of political parties able to give voice to the opposition. Vatican II states: "They [Christians] should recognize the legitimacy of differing points of view on the organization of worldly affairs and should show respect for the individual citizens and groups who defend their opinions by legitimate means."[55] Catholics need to understand how doctrines advocating for international cooperation and the common good of humanity require strong institutions, such as the World Trade Organization, as well as multilateral efforts, such as the Paris Climate Accords. Making these connections such in a way that Catholics can see them clearly will require collaboration between Catholic educators, public policy experts, economists, and communications professionals.

At the same time, there is a desperate need to discipline members of the religious orders, priests, and bishops who ignore the central doctrines of the common good and the inherent rights of the human person. While remaining true to present claims about what constitutes acceptable Catholic behavior, the Catholic Church still can sanction priests who wish to deny civil rights to LGBTQ people, to ban immigration by Muslims, or to foster hatred of Jews. If the bishops fail to discipline these people, then Catholics should publicly protest their failure to adhere to the teachings of the church and should petition Rome to act.

The Vatican needs to reevaluate how the liturgical calendar and religious art in Catholic churches reinforce ethnic and religious discrimination as well as nationalist propaganda. Religious art that presents Jews and Muslims as subhuman ought to be removed from all places of worship or covered during all liturgical celebrations and public events. The same is true of the art that reinforces nationalist ideologies. If there is a desire to display these artworks for historical purposes, then perhaps the buildings should not be used for liturgical purposes. Feast days such as Our Lady of the Rosary and The Most Holy Name of the Blessed Virgin Mary should be suppressed immediately because they are contrary to the universal church. New feast days promoting human dignity and solidarity should be established in the liturgical calendar. Local customs should also be reviewed in light of the Catholic commitment to human dignity and promoting the common good in every diocese. The Curia should work to draw up guidelines to assist dioceses in evaluating liturgical practices, the celebration of feast days, and the use of religious art. One of those guidelines ought to mandate that representatives of minority groups and marginalized people should be invited to participate in these reviews.

These concrete steps would provoke a great deal of resistance from Catholic nationalists, who believe that church and state are one, but they would demonstrate that the Catholic Church is committed to its own teachings. Although we doubt that there is much that would convince committed Catholic nationalists to abandon their errors, it is possible to hamper their ability to recruit more Catholics to their cause. Doing so will require an effort to raise awareness among the bishops of the ways that Catholic nationalists threaten the unity of the church by their rejection of the authority of the magisterium and of the apostolic tradition itself. Bishops must be reminded that they "have the obligation to foster and safeguard the unity of the faith and to uphold the discipline which is common to the whole Church."[56] At the same time, Catholic educators and ministers must work to empower all Catholics to carry out their religious duty to combat injustice, oppression, arbitrary domination, and intolerance.[57] With some coordination between Catholic organizations—such as Jesuit Refugee Services or Partnership for Global Justice, and the Roman Catholic Curia—and local bishops, these steps could quickly be implemented, at least in Europe and the United States. Although fighting for human dignity and the institutions that promote human rights will require fortitude in the face of intense opposition, Catholics should remember that fortitude is a gift of the Holy Spirit for those who "hunger and thirst for justice" (Matthew 5:6, my translation).

Catholics must keep the vision of the heavenly Jerusalem in mind as they take up the task of responding to those who use the faith to promote hatred and intolerance. The Apocalypse presents us with a model that makes it clear that Christians cannot accept exclusionary and discriminatory policies or laws as legitimate because they have no place in God's kingdom. After identifying the multitude of Jews that will be given a place of honor before the throne of God, John continued:

> After this I looked, and there was a great multitude that no one could count, from every nation, from all tribes and peoples and languages, standing before the throne and before the Lamb, robed in white, with palm branches in their hands. They cried out in a loud voice, saying, "Salvation

belongs to our God who is seated on the throne, and to the Lamb!" And all the angels stood around the throne and around the elders and the four living creatures, and they fell on their faces before the throne and worshiped God, singing, "Amen! Blessing and glory and wisdom and thanksgiving and honor and power and might be to our God forever and ever! Amen." (Revelation 7:9–12 NRSV)

CHAPTER FIVE

The Post-Holocaust Protestant Church as the Defender of Pluralistic Democracy

The Reformation was a rebellion against what Luther and others claimed was an encrusted, corrupt church that had strayed from the biblical roots of Christianity and the unmediated experience of God's presence. The freedom to read the Bible directly without dependence on a priest or through the lens of the apostolic traditions of the Church Fathers became foundational to Protestant tradition. If the Catholic Church emanating from Rome was the universal mother church, the Protestant Reformation opened the door to more local jurisdictions. That led, over the centuries, to churches that were intimately linked to the rising nation-states of Europe. There was now a Church of England with the monarch as titular head, and there were state-aligned national churches in much of northern Europe. Even where the church was not an official state church, as a result of religious wars often tied to rising nationalism in Europe, church affiliation helped to ground allegiance to the nation or the nationalist political movement. For Protestants in Europe, there was no significant church-state separation. As J. C. D. Clark explains, "The individual was tied to the polity by allegiance, and Christianity was the ideology that interpreted that tie. . . . It is possible to see how large a part religion played in the matrix of ideas."[1] Faith was linked to national identity, much as Protestant churches in the United States, mainly but not exclusively in the South, were aligned with segregationist state governments.

In the United States, as we have noted, no one church dominated. The colonies, all products of emigration from Europe, reflected Christian diversity. That said, what they shared was the Reformation and the establishment of Protestantism as the dominant Christianity. As historian Steven Green explains, four pillars define the ways Christian Protestants associated faith with American destiny. The first was the experience of the Pilgrims as forebears of nationhood. The second was the hagiographic accounts of the founders of the republic as Christian leaders. The third was the belief, much as we described, that civil law emerged from Christian principles. And, of course, the fourth pillar rested on the belief that the fate of America is guided by divine providence. It is these four pillars that form the backbone of today's American Protestant nationalism.[2]

While not united as one church, Protestants did share an evangelical belief that the world should know the gospel of Christ. This led to missionary work around the globe, which, when accompanied by the colonial successes of European empires, often meant the subjugation of indigenous populations, especially in Africa. When one considers the maps of imperial conquest, the picture drawn of Protestant evangelism indeed has a colonial tint. And Protestant denominations, from the German Evangelical Church in Namibia and Nauru, to the Presbyterians in Malawi and Zambia, to Anglicans in Uganda and South Africa, became powerful arms of the imperial states. Preaching the gospel and conversion were, as is now so clear, acts of colonization and oppression. As Kenton Clymer notes in writing about the lands conquered in the Spanish American War, "The Protestant churches [in the United States] helped prepare a national temper receptive to the acquisitions and doubtlessly also helped influence [President] McKinley, the country's most prominent Methodist."[3] It would be easy to dismiss Protestant churches as irrelevant to defending liberal democracy at best and complicit in great evil at worst.

Even within Europe and America, Protestants played a significant role in territorial expansion as well as empire building. Those
who promoted the doctrine of Manifest Destiny in America, for example, grounded that doctrine in the "white man's burden," advocating a strong Christian American nation as "an extension of the
history of salvation" and convinced that "God must have provi-
dentially intervened in that conflict on the side of 'his people,' the
Americans." America is an "anointed land, set apart by a divine
plan for an extraordinary existence as a nation and an extraordinary
mission to the world."[4]

Well into the twentieth century, Protestant churches were compromised by their acceptance of nationalist impulses, certainly
manifest most directly in the formal German Protestant alignment
with Nazism and the silence of fellow Protestant churches around
the world. These impulses still exist among some Protestants—impulses to endorse, in the name of the nation, policies and politicians
who seek to undermine core democratic values of equality and
human and civil rights. And the response by church bodies to their
past has been slow. The Presbyterian Church in the United States,
for example, acknowledged late in the game Protestant complicity
in segregation. It was only in 2014 that they stated, "Those churches
segregated worshipers by race, barred blacks from membership and
black churches from joining presbyteries, participated in and defended white supremacist organizations, and taught that the Bible
sanctioned segregation and opposed inter-racial marriage."[5]

As Katharine Henderson laments, in a passage we earlier
quoted in chapter 3:

Division is nothing new in the church. But the theological
divisions over doctrine, theology, governance and "brand"
that have historically plagued the followers of Jesus, even
before they were called Christian, have been exploited to
win votes, garner political power and divide people from
one another. The theological rifts over public issues, especially slavery and enduring racism—never adequately exca-
vated or exorcized—live on and are now joined by other

ones such as abortion, same sex marriage and the role of women in the home, the church and public life. These classic debates over public issues are now exacerbated by the demographic changes that will make America no longer a white majority nation over the next decades. Already for the first time, white Protestants are no longer a religious majority. Whether consciously or unconsciously these changes create a sense of displacement for some who identify as white and Christian, providing an opportunity to evoke fear by the current administration, rendering people who are poor, for example, enemies when they should be natural allies.[6]

She goes on to explain the challenge facing Protestants; she focuses on the United States, but her words here are well applied to Europe as well:

Many Christians have forgotten that their first allegiance belongs to God and not the nation-state. At its worst, this toxic brew of political and reactionary Christianity creates a hospitable ecosystem for extremism, the kind that provoked Dylan Roof to murder members of Mother Emanuel Church in Charleston during Bible study, or a crowd of young white men in white shirts carrying torches reminiscent of burning crosses in Charlottesville, while spewing hate filled anti-Semitic speech: "Jews will not replace us." This mixture of faith and politics leads courts to use religious freedom as the rationale for legislation that upholds a businessman's right based on private religious belief to refuse to bake a wedding cake for a gay couple.[7]

How, then, do Protestants engage faithfully in the struggle to sustain liberal democracy and to confront the appeal to Christian identity by political leaders who want to fuel and sustain racist and homophobic attacks? What is the role of the church in defending pluralistic values today, especially in the context of anti-immigrant sentiment and efforts to undermine not only the right of asylum but democracy itself? The divisions within the Protestant community demand an examination and correction in the ways Protestant Christians properly apply their past in contemporary political debates to avoid aligning themselves with antidemocratic forces. Given the historic failures of so many Protestant churches in Europe and the United States to protect "the Other" as the world was engulfed in Fascism, and given that they looked aside in the face of slavery and segregation, and given that they supported the conquering imperialism of their own governments, Protestants have much work to do. Today, once again, the threat to liberal democracies is real, and Christians must act in their defense.

As Jim Winkler, the president of the National Council of Churches of Christ, to which many Protestant and Orthodox denominations belong, explains:

> There are those who try to use Christian identity toenflame hatred. It is a mistake, however, to conflate all Christianity or even conservative Christianity with these movements. The relationship of the alt-right, white supremacists, and white nationalists with Christianity is strange and complex. It is not their faith that joins them. These three groupings generally share a common theme of racism, anti-Semitism, and prejudice. For me and for the National Council of Churches, we reject the notion perpetrated by adherents of Christian nationalism that the United States is a Christian nation in which the Christian faith and American identity are inseparable. This is not a political claim, but a deeply theological one. Christians should be patriots. But a faithful Christian cannot be a nationalist; the nation cannot replace God. That is a form of idolatry.[8]

A Christian Theology of Civic Engagement

Finding theological responses to endorse the institutions and values of democracy beyond denominational resolutions is then critical both for the future of Protestant Christianity as a moral agent and for the democracies in which Protestants are a major force. For these reasons, we turn to a German theologian whose voice still resonates even after his brutal murder in the Flossenbrück concentration camp. Dietrich Bonhoeffer's ethics of the churches' responsibilities to God and to the nation offers a rich response to the current political debate over illiberal nationalism. It allows us to focus in particular on the embattled right of asylum and immigration, as this issue, perhaps more than any other, roils Europe and the United States. In focusing on immigration, on who constitutes a real European or American (not to speak of so many other nationalities such as Israeli, Indian, or Brazilian), we enter the dark world of populist nationalism with its challenge to the leadership of Protestant churches in the fight for human and civil rights for all within a pluralist, democratic state.

Victoria Barnett explains that nationalism, anti-Semitism, ethnocentrism, and populism have played a role in different historical periods and national contexts and that the ways that citizens and their institutions respond are crucial. Political culture is an expression of what we are willing to tolerate, what compromises we make and the reasons why we make them—and those are the factors that can undermine and even destroy a political culture. As we well know, the veneer of ethics and moral behavior in the public square can be surprisingly thin. Human beings are easily swayed and enraptured. Peer pressure and crowd behavior are powerful forces. In her introduction to a new edition of a crucial text from the German Protestant theologian Dietrich Bonhoeffer from 1942, Barnett writes:

We are used to living by a particular set of rules, values, and expectations of behavior, individually and socially, and it is often easier for institutions like the civil service, universities, businesses, and religious bodies to conform than to resist. When the rules change, it can be difficult to find our bearings, let alone chart a new course that can address and if necessary challenge what is happening around us. These are the themes that Dietrich Bonhoeffer addressed. . . . His context was Nazi Germany, but his observations about what happens to human decency and courage when a political culture disintegrates continue to resonate around the world today.[9]

The heated debate around migration, raging since 2015 throughout Europe and in the United States since the 2016 presidential campaign, is a critical test case for the disintegration of a political culture whose highest ideal is liberal democracy. It also calls for a religious response.

In the time of the Holocaust, Christians in Germany overwhelmingly were either perpetrators or bystanders. There were theologians, such as Helmut Gollwitzer and Dietrich Bonhoeffer, who argued that Christian faith ultimately calls its followers to defend "the other" and to resist state injustice and persecution. But the long history of Protestant anti-Jewish rhetoric and theology and a militaristic nationalism made it easier for Protestant Christian leaders to turn their heads. Prophetic voices of confession and resistance were the exception. Few rejected the nationalist use of the Protestant tradition; opposition was rare. Throughout the Christian world, one does not find many leaders who condemned even the most striking and ominous element of Nazi ideology. Indeed, many Christian leaders before and throughout the Nazi era cited Christian teachings as a justification for anti-Jewish rhetoric and policies. The same could be said of Protestants in America, who, as we have shown, used biblical texts and Christian history to endorse and sustain slavery and, later, Jim Crow laws.

The contemporary challenges to the Protestant community to learn from its past failures to address the evils of colonialism, racism, and anti-immigrant rhetoric and policies are apparent. In 2016, Donald Trump was elected president of the United States with an illiberal democratic campaign, gaining over 80 percent of the Protestant evangelical Christian vote, which also included a majority of all white Protestants. The Social Democrats in Protestant Sweden and Fidesz in Hungary energetically campaign in the name of Christian nationalism. And in Germany, the outcome of coalition negotiations in Germany in 2018 was a "Grand Coalition," which meant the AfD became the main opposition party in the Bundestag, a major disruption to long-held perceptions of the Federal Republic as a stable and centripetal polity.[10]

The coleader of the AfD has described the Nazi era as a brief stain in Germany's otherwise grand history, paraphrasing Jean-Marie Le Pen's similar claims in mobilizing French populist voters when he ran for president of the republic. Addressing the youth division of the AfD at a conference in June 2018 in Seebach, Thuringia, Alexander Gauland said: "Only those who acknowledge history have the strength to shape the future. . . . Hitler and the Nazis are just bird shit in more than 1,000 years of successful German history." He added that, while accepting responsibility for twelve years of Nazi rule, Germans "have a glorious history—and that, dear friends, lasted longer than the damn 12 years."[11] The rise of the AfD in Europe's largest democracy, igniting anti-Islamic and antimigrant sentiments, and openly sympathizing with neo-Fascists and their worldview, arguably poses a critical historical challenge to Protestants who are committed to defend liberal democracy and its human rights values.

In searching for a Christian prophetic voice that is relevant to our times, we can turn to those Protestant theologians and leaders who challenged the antidemocratic nationalist impulses of the 1930s, especially in Germany. Pastor Helmut Gollwitzer, having witnessed the "Pogromnacht" on November 9, 1938, in his Berlin parish, shook up his congregation in a sermon delivered on the annual Christian "Day of Prayer and Penance," a few days later. The churches' failure to protect the Jews, Gollwitzer argued, not only was a moral disaster but was destroying the very basis for Christian worship and prayer. He challenged the right of any pastor to preach repentance on such a day, claiming that they had allowed their mouths to be muzzled. He chastised his followers, asking how it was possible that faithful Christians, following all the years and centuries of preaching, had arrived at this moment of violence and hatred. He continued:

What do we expect God to do, if we come to him now singing, reading our Bibles, praying, preaching, and confessing our sins as if we can really count on his being here and on all this being more than empty religious activity? Our impertinence and presumption must make him sick. Why don't we at least just keep our mouths shut? Yes, that might be the right thing to do. What if we just sat here for an entire hour without saying a word, no singing, no speaking, just preparing ourselves silently for God's punishment, which we have already earned?[12]

In light of the catastrophic failure of the church to protect its Jewish neighbors, Gollwitzer, toward the end of his sermon, called for social and political action: "Now just outside this church our neighbor is waiting for us—waiting for us in his need and lack of protection, disgraced, hungry, haunted, and driven by fear for his very existence. That is the one who is waiting to see if today this Christian congregation has really observed this national day of penance. Jesus Christ himself is waiting to see."[13]

Dietrich Bonhoeffer, Refugees, and the Obligation of the Church to Fight Injustice

As John Green notes, for Dietrich Bonhoeffer, Christian faith entailed a new perception and understanding of human existence: "A Christian is one for whom interaction with others is engagement with the real person of Christ. Christ's presence is ubiquitous, but is revealed in the *sanctorum communio*. The *sanctorum communio* exists only in the actual social, historical, bodily reality of the human world."[14] Bonhoeffer's theological paradigm, which is social, public, and political, marks a shift from the intrasubjective orientation of the medieval-Reformation paradigm. According to Bonhoeffer, the church as the *sanctorum communio* is that community which represents all humanity not only as a partner in sin but above all as the promise of new humanity when the spirit of Jesus in socially embodied word and sacrament unites people in mutual freedom for each other. He adds that, as a corporate community, "Christ existing as a Church community [Christus als Gemeinde existierend] aims the church-community into the communities of nations and peoples as a sign of peace and justice, of hope and love, of faith and freedom."[15]

Already in his 1933 essay "The Church and the Jewish Question," Bonhoeffer acknowledges three different dimensions in which the church has the obligation to resist political injustice. Christians must question state injustice and call the state to responsibility. They must help the victims of injustice, whether they are church members or not. Bonhoeffer believed, according to Barnett, that ultimately Protestant churches must be willing not only to resist oppression but to "fall into the spokes of the wheel itself" in order to halt the machinery of injustice.[16] He uses the metaphor of "falling into the spokes of the wheel" in order to assert an activist resistance to the tyrannical policies of the Nazi government by disrupting the wheels of antidemocratic revolution.[17]

Once again, in our day, Christians are called to active resistance with the hope that, this time, they will heed Bonhoeffer's call to action. The compelling issue at this moment is refugees and the right of asylum, a challenge to liberal democracies to hold true to the values of human rights, that each human being is an image of God. For those seeking to undermine these principles, refugees are the perfect target, the ultimate "Other" who threaten the nation by polluting its Christian identity, threatening with their alien cultures, taking from true citizens their livelihoods. No issue seems to galvanize partisan populist nationalists, from Poland to France, from Texas to Italy, more effectively than refugees pounding at the gates of the nation.

Following World War II, there seemed to be a universal consensus that persons persecuted on political grounds shall have the right of asylum.[18] Included in the Universal Declaration of Human Rights, the right of asylum was accepted throughout Western Europe and the United States. In 1993, after the reunification of Germany and the collapse of the Eastern Bloc, Germany received an unprecedented number of asylum applications. Sadly, the German government responded with an amendment to its constitution that imposed massive restrictions on asylum. The new article, 16a, while formally upholding the right of asylum in article 16, goes on to significantly circumscribe that right. It argues that, since Germany is surrounded by states deemed "safe," at least in theory, no person entering Germany by land has an automatic right to asylum. The safe-country-of-origin policy instructs German authorities to reject asylum seekers from a country listed as safe or where the German government does not find a risk of persecution. Due to this amendment, the constitutional entitlement to asylum has become almost meaningless.[19] Similar limitations were replicated in other nations, such as Austria, Slovenia, and Denmark, and especially in the United States, as immigration, refugees, and asylum became politically explosive.

In 2015, the dramatic number of refugees from the Syrian civil war trapped at the EU border temporarily changed the approach of the German government. In August 2015, Germany decided to suspend the Dublin Procedure for Syrians, which meant that refugees from that country no longer had to be sent back to the first EU country they had entered. German chancellor Angela Merkel declared, "Wir schaffen das" (We can do this), as Europe was confronted with the largest refugee crisis it had seen since the end of World War II. The wars in the Middle East, particularly in Syria, resulted in the German government granting protection to hundreds of thousands of refugees. Merkel called it a "national duty" to do so.[20]

For more than thirty years, the principle of church asylum in Western nations has offered, at least in theory, temporary protection for refugees without a legal residence status who would face unacceptable social hardship, torture, or even death if forced to return to their country of origin.[21] Now refugees in Europe were facing assault, arrest, and deportation, often back to the very dangers that caused them to flee. In the United States, government policies that undermine the economies of many Latin American countries have led to the rise of gang violence in Central America and Mexico as terrified families flee north. In light of the deterioration of conditions in so many countries, parishes are expected to feel bound by their Christian faith to protect people from expulsion. Parishes offering church asylum are asked to place themselves between refugees and the civil authorities carrying out deportations in order to delay the process and seek legal recourse allowing the asylum seekers to remain. Christians once again are being asked to "throw themselves into the spokes of the wheel," so that the doors of churches and parsonages will stand in the way of state power. Church grounds are considered sacred spaces not to be entered by state authorities with their mandates to deport asylum seekers, and volunteers—church members and pastors—are called upon to become the voices of the refugees, speaking to police officers and authorities.[22]

In quantitative terms, church asylum in Europe may be insignificant, just as Bonhoeffer's defense of Nazi victims could not end the slaughter. Though hugely significant for individual refugees, church protection is just a drop in the ocean compared with the number of those deported from Europe and the United States; even more so for the many thousands who have died at the borders or in the water. Yet the symbolic value of Protestant churches demanding asylum for refugees—protesting, petitioning, and protecting—stands in stark contrast to the Nazi era, a visible form of Christian repentance.[23] The church thus becomes the moral force, and church asylum its act of resistance, calling on citizens to rise up in protest and voice their commitment to protect asylum seekers, as was seen in Holland when hundreds arrived day and night to sing and pray to protect a refugee family from deportation.[24]

When a church grants asylum while also preaching the gospel from the pulpit, it does not rely on any legal norms other than those of Christian faith and international law. It is, however, basing its actions on the assumption that the pressures on liberal democracies, especially pressures exerted by those who do so in the name of Christianity, cause state actors to break those fundamental legal norms and core gospel commands. Certainly this has been the case in the United States, where an attorney general of the United States could cite the apostle Paul's Letter to the Romans, chapter 13, to defend the administration's cruel policy—a form of torture—separating immigrant children from their parents at the border, leaving them in filthy conditions where children have died.[25]

It is possible that applications for refugee status, for protection from deportation, or for a residence permit on humanitarian grounds have been refused even when the situation does in fact call for protection from forcible deportation. Thus, the churches in Germany argue: "Congregations which take a stand for the realization of these human and basic rights therefore do not question the State under the rule of law but make a contribution to the preservation of legal peace and the basic values of our society."[26] The Charter of the New Sanctuary Movement in Europe, drafted in 2010, highlights the biblical command urging Christian parishes to provide church asylum: "All of Europe must become a safe haven, a 'sanctuary' for migrant men and women. To this we commit ourselves—in the conviction that God loves the strangers and that in them we encounter God (Matt. 25, 31ff.)."[27] Similar statements can be found in Protestant denominations as well as the National Council of Churches of Christ in the United States.[28]

Nevertheless, church asylum can be a breach of law, attacked by opponents as a lack of patriotic passion for the nation. In a number of cases, German clergy and members of church boards responsible for providing church asylum have been charged with supporting the illegal stay of foreigners.[29] Christians are threatened with arrest on the U.S.-Mexico border for aiding weary migrants by providing food and water.[30] Ultimately, the conscience of Christians can be in conflict with state rulings or actions, a disruption that jolts and jams the spokes of the wheel.

The cruelty of national anti-immigrant policies is tinged with a xenophobic racism as fewer and fewer refugees find safe haven. The dramatic situation of refugees being forcibly held in detention centers around the Mediterranean Sea and on the U.S. southern border and the tragic fate of thousands of refugees drowned en route to sanctuary pose a humanitarian crisis that challenges liberal democracies at their core. This is contrary to what has been an international consensus concerning refugees, and certainly it is a challenge to the gospel of Christ, which calls for compassion and love toward the stranger. That is why this issue, perhaps more than any other at this moment, has become a focal point of church action. As a result, the Churches' Commission for Migrants in Europe accordingly declared in October 2018: "In light of ever more restrictive asylum policies and practices we reiterate the right for all to access a full and high-quality asylum procedure inside the EU irrespective of the path a person took into the EU. . . . In a situation where border-states of the EU are currently left alone we reemphasize the vision of 'solidarity first.' Solidarity and sharing are understood as something where stronger shoulders carry more than the weaker ones, and where everyone contributes what they can."[31]

The Church as Protector of Liberal Democratic Values

The discourse on migration is a focal point in any effort to safeguard progressive Christian democratic values today. To be sure, it is the responsibility of Protestant churches, both their pastors and their congregants, to speak with a prophetic voice and take direct political action against anti-Semitism and anti-Muslim assaults, racism, homophobia, hate speech, threats to a free press, and other forms of illiberal assaults on democracy. However, fighting for the right of asylum today is arguably the most important demonstration of the churches' commitment to democratic values, because it often encompasses the other threats.

All of Bonhoeffer's three dimensions of church resistance to political injustice are relevant to the right of asylum, and, seventy-five years after the defeat of Nazism, Protestant churches are challenged to defend the principles of liberal democracies against those who use the name of Christ to promote inhumane policies that undermine each person as an image of God.

First, Christians must give voice to opposing injustice. The churches have to question state policies and call the state to responsibility. Rev. Manfred Rekowski stated in July 2018, when visiting sea rescuers in Malta who had been banned from operating: "This practice of closing borders has been spreading for years and is undermining international and European refugee law. From history we know: the first to die is the law and then the human being."[32] And on the occasion of World Refugee Day, when Protestants are asked to stand in solidarity with asylum seekers and endangered refugees, Rekowski further challenged governments to reject policies that cause human beings to be turned away at borders, to be sent from one country to another, or to die at sea, and he declared that "this policy of outsourced responsibility is unacceptable." Perceiving the potential for devastating impact on the future of Europe and the principles of liberal democracies, he added: "If we accept what is happening beyond our borders in Libyan camps and thousands of people drowning in the Mediterranean year after year, there are consequences for us in Europe. Our own dignity, our own humanity, are in danger of decay. The importance of our own rights and freedoms is reflected by our willingness to share them with those seeking protection. From a Christian understanding, human dignity and human rights are indivisible."[33]

Similarly, in the United States, the National Council of Churches of Christ stated:

We feel that the thrust of our basic immigration law neither reflects Christian concern adequately nor furthers our national interest sufficiently. In particular, we are critical and ashamed of the racial and cultural discrimination in the present basis of our immigration quota system, resting as it does largely upon the national origins of our white population according to the census of 1920. We welcome the efforts of leaders in Government to codify, clarify, and improve legislation on this vast, complex, and in many ways, technical subject.

We believe that through increased Christian concern in immigration, the churches and their members can make a fuller witness to our faith that, under God, men and nations are responsible to each other and for the welfare of all mankind.[34]

Second, the churches have an obligation to help victims of injustice. Providing temporary shelter in cases of church asylum serves this purpose, as it enables legal procedures to determine whether the authorities' decisions need to be revised. Christians must provide financial support for the refugee work of churches and church institutions, aiding immigrants around the globe to bolster local humanitarian assistance and support victims of injustice.[35]

Third, resistance to political injustice may require "falling into the spokes of the wheel." Even though church asylum is frequently considered in violation of the law, Christians must make the opposite claim by fearlessly declaring that church asylum helps to protect the rule of law and the constitutional right of asylum. Still, even this may not be enough. Where nationalist illiberal movements assume state authority, as they already have in many countries, more dramatic activism and protest will be required of Christians if they are to comply with Christian demands to challenge injustice. Protestant churches, through prayer and righteous action, have to commit themselves to keeping the liberal democratic values of human rights and constitutional structures in the European Union and the United States alive.

John de Gruchy, in his essay on Bonhoeffer's political witness then and now, calls Christians to action, reminding them that the reason Germans and other Christians around the world failed to show civil courage in the time of the Nazis was that those Christians refused to accept their duty to God and their prophetic calling to defend liberty and human dignity. He concludes with a manifesto of religious obligation:

> Christians should be engaged in the struggle for democracy, understood as an open-ended, developing project in which the rule of law, the protection of human rights, and the freedom from any form of tyranny is affirmed, and in

which the economic market is transformed in the interests of overcoming grinding poverty and the destruction of the environment. This is as much a challenge for Christians in the established liberal democracies of the West as it is for Christians across the world. It is both a global and an ecumenical imperative, which should engage people of all faiths together with their secular compatriots.[36]

Each Human Being as an Image of God

A Jewish Response to Religious Nationalism

Posing the Questions

Judaism does not speak with one voice on any issue, lacking, as it does, a singular decisor or an authoritative catechism, so no one can authoritatively make claims about how Judaism should approach civic and political affairs. Jewish tradition is multivoiced, reflecting radically varied contexts, ages, and geographic communities, a potentially rich dialogue that spans millennia. This chapter will provide recognition of the variety of historic Jewish responses to engaging the "other," particularly in political and civic affairs, yet will follow a path to a principled pluralist Judaism, emerging both from within the tradition and from modern Jewish involvement in civil society. It is from this vantage point that we will address the essential principles and processes of discernment that a Jew committed to democracy, civil liberties, and human rights, as well as a relationship with other communities, might bring to a conversation about these subjects. Given a political climate that challenges pluralist democracies, it is still possible from within a hoary tradition to highlight behaviors and beliefs that will endorse and encourage support for democratic principles. A Jewish response to these political conditions rests on three claims grounded in Jewish texts and traditions.

God Is Everywhere, So Make Room for Diversity

The first claim affirms that access to the experience of God is available to all human beings, as expressed in the midrashic claim that "entrances to holiness are everywhere (*eyn makom panu'i miney*). The possibility of ascent is all the time, even at unlikely times and through unlikely places."[1] Any engagement with the state, as patriots engaged in civil society, is grounded in an understanding that God's presence is far-reaching and well beyond the boundaries of Judaism. This naturally leads to a conception of Jewish pluralism not as concession, but as part of a divine plan, the most effective mechanism to upgrade the presence of God in the world. This is not relegated to the synagogue or theological arcana, but must be expressed and lived in the real social and political worlds Jews inhabit. This core pluralism is best expressed within Judaism in the words of Rav Abraham Kook, chief rabbi of Palestine and one of the most powerful and respected voices of twentieth-century Judaism: "For the building is constructed from various parts, and the truth of the light of the world will be built from various dimensions, from various approaches, for 'these and those are the living words of God. . . .' It is precisely the multiplicity of opinions, which derive from variegated souls and backgrounds, that enriches wisdom and brings about its enlargement. In the end, all matters will be properly understood and it will be recognized as impossible for the structures of peace to be built without all those views which appear (to us) to be in conflict."[2]

This fundamental principle offers absolute support to the discourse of democracy, respectful debate, willingness to listen, honoring of the integrity of all those within the community, because a diverse polity, not one that ostracizes or expels those who are different or have alternative views, is mandatory in civic affairs. Even radically opposite views can still be the word of God.

God Has Many Faces, No One Knows Them All

This in turn will lead us to a second Jewish understanding that informs the ways a Jew meets a non-Jew. At the Jewish core is a deep challenge to absolutist religious claims, a challenge which derives from a Jewish understanding of God's revelation as a multifaceted approximation of God's word, but certainly not the same as God. As the founding rabbis of the first centuries of the Common Era understood the oral tradition, revelation continues to unfold as humans better apprehend God's will. Therefore, no one can ever claim absolute knowledge of God. No one, therefore, and no religious, political, or social tradition can own all of God's truth. To make that claim would be to submit to idolatry. Jews will resist those who claim they alone know God or what God demands. This is particularly important, as Jews live in most of the world as a minority and must constantly challenge those forces—from religious majorities to illiberal nationalist movements—that make absolutist claims about who belongs to the nation or the nature of the nation itself. Jewish patriotism thus values the nation as a political and social system that fosters open dialogue; it eschews violent rhetoric that degrades and humiliates. Jewish patriotism honors critique and constant challenge to upgrade and solidify pluralist democratic values that include rather than exclude. From intimate engagement with history, Jews know that they can only flourish in a society that honors the rights of the individual.

Even if Jews are a minority, Judaism must be examined in terms of its perception of other religious and ethnic communities and its treatment, in theory if not in practice, of those who are not part of the Jewish community. The Jewish tradition calls for continuous critique of what is inherited, sometimes through challenges to the canon or traditional readings and sometimes even resulting in the elimination of those elements of the tradition which undermine the fundamental pluralism and openness at the core of the lived Judaism we seek to promote. It becomes evident that the Jewish test of a religion's power and value is whether it can thrive in a democratic political system, even one that has Jewish identity at its core and that creates partnerships with other religious communities to seek God's truths, provides meaning to those who follow it, and advances God's goodness and healing in the world. The logic for excising the "othering" texts and traditions of Judaism results from an exploration that will challenge the monotheist and Enlightenment positions that the veracity and authenticity of any religion is based on whether that religion is true or false. Actions take precedence over belief.

Human Obligation to Repair a Broken World

The demand for sacred engagement in civil affairs, from combatting racism to embracing refugees, from defending the rights of marginalized fellow citizens to making strides to protect the environment, is a religious act. This derives from the Jewish understanding that human beings, created in God's image, are partners with God in repairing the brokenness of the world (*shutafim laKadosh Baruch Hu*). Jewish tradition calls us to always ask how far we've progressed in this endeavor and how much Judaism—or any other faith—has shown the way. The degree to which a religion is capable of succeeding in providing meaning, motivation, and behaviors that upgrade all life reflects the truths it has to offer. It is this world, not a focus on the spiritual realm alone, that is in need of repair; as a religion grounded in deed rather than catechism, Judaism must engage the politics, the distribution of power, and the treatment of all human beings within society.

Entrances to Holiness Are Everywhere

Judaism continues to struggle over how the Other is seen, whether there is a place in God's plan for those of other faiths and truths other than as a danger or as idolatry. Biblical Israel seemed to fear the religious Other (if not all "others") as a seductive force that would tear the faithful from obedience to God.[3] Indeed, a section of

Psalm 115 is recited on Jewish festivals, as a reminder of the false-ness of other faiths:

They have mouths, but cannot speak;
Eyes, but cannot see;
They have ears, but cannot hear,
Noses, but cannot smell. . . .
Those who fashion them,
All who trust in them,
Shall become like them.[4]

Aleynu, the liturgical culmination of each service recited three times a day, is meant to attest to the unique and singular truth of Judaism:[5]

It is incumbent upon us to praise the God of all. . . .
Who did not make us as all other nations and peoples
Who did not give us their portion or destiny. . . .
We therefore hope in You, God,
And may we soon behold the glory of Your might:
Sweeping away the false gods of the earth,
Utterly destroying idolatry. . . .
So that all humanity will invoke Your name.

The placement in the liturgy of the *Aleynu*, although it was written in the early centuries of the Common Era, dates to the thir-teenth century, long after classical idolatry had ended. Verses ex-cised under Christian pressure, "for they bow down to nothingness and emptiness, and pray to a god that will not save," have in recent years been reintroduced in certain circles in Israel and abroad. The notion that other religions are dangerous and impure, as old as bib-lical Israel in the Psalm cited above, runs through Rabbinic Juda-ism[6] and into medieval times.[7] As Seth Farber explains:

Many Jewish commentators viewed this discussion as an opportunity to reflect on the "chosenness" of the Jewish people and, as a result of their being chosen by God, their superiority. Some, like Rabbi Judah HaLevi in the Medieval period and Rabbi Abraham Isaac HaKohen Kook [cited so positively above] in the modern period, took it as a sine qua non that the Jewish community was endowed with an essence that differentiated its collective soul from the souls of others. Though for Rabbi Kook, this did not lead him to separate from the world around him—particularly when it came to the non-religious Jewish world—the notion of the Jew being superior in some meta-physical way still permeates his thought.[8]

With respect to Christianity, though his point would apply to other faiths as well, Jacob Katz notes: "Avoidance of contact with the visible expressions of the Christian faith became almost an instinct with the Jew, who felt himself endangered spiritually, and perhaps even physically, whenever he encountered a Christian gathering performing its religious rites."[9] It is fair to say that, since Jewish theology is inextricably rooted in the Jewish historical experience, memory will shape any encounter with other Abrahamic faiths—the Crusades, the Spanish Inquisition, anti-Jewish riots and pogroms, anti-Israel behaviors, and, of course, the Holocaust.[10] For Jews, recalling carnal memory and not philosophy or classical theological discourse is an essential aspect of discernment that informs encounters with other communities. History is the language of Jewish theology. What "you" did to "us" begins (and often ends) dialogue between Jews and the rest of the world. Ironically, for some, this disposition plays into a nationalist demand to threaten, defame, and expel the "Other"—as we noted in Israeli politics— whereas, for progressive Jews, Jewish history demands compassion and welcoming the "Other." Even when we recognize the minority status of Jews in most parts of the world, the use of Jewish identity to create a tight-knit community that sees itself responsible only for its members while excluding "*goyim*" (the perjorative word for anyone not Jewish) is a trap into which even liberal-minded Jews often fall. This anachronistic memory of ghettoes and exile must not metastasize into contemporary government or communal practice.

That said, this instinctual tendency of "othering" does reflect a lachrymose read of the many ways Jews learn history—in every generation "we" are threatened by nefarious external forces. Just as the biblical redactors and the rabbis of Judaism's early centuries sought to divide the world between "us" and "them," medieval Jews—often segregated and unable to imagine political, let alone social, intercourse with their Christian or Muslim counterparts—felt endangered by contact. The cathedral, with its icons and dark chambers and the faithful crossing themselves, was naturally threatening. The Muslim rulers, however noble, enforced policies that not only separated Jew from Muslim but confirmed the domination of Islam by forbidding Jewish equal standing with Muslims while enacting humiliating laws. One need not list the rules and regulations or even the pogroms and riots that occurred in Europe and North Africa to recognize that Jews formed their personal and communal identity not only from within but also in the ways their lives reflected against the Other. Civil leaders were no better, excluding Jews as aliens, drawing ugly stereotypes and giving citizenship only grudgingly if at all. Some prayer traditions expect Jews, upon awakening, will recite, "Blessed are you God, who has not made me a Gentile [as in Other]."[11]

This "othering" can extend as well to those whose Jewish identity is not accepted by those who claim greater piety, an issue made more contentious by the oppressive role of the Israeli Chief Rabbinate and its control over personal status issues in the State of Israel. In one extreme form, for example, Chief Rabbi Lau refused to say that Jews murdered in Pittsburgh in 2019 were in fact praying in a synagogue because the synagogue where the massacre took place did not conform to his version of Jewish ritual. Such views affect who can marry and to whom, who will be buried in a Jewish cemetery (Israeli soldiers killed in combat whose religious status is questioned would not be allowed to be buried in a Jewish cemetery), or who is registered as a Jew or as a rabbi in Israel. In present-day Israel, the ultra-Orthodox make up only 12 percent of the population but exert control over the country's religious life with absolutist claims that deny the authenticity of any other way of being Jewish. Their belief that they alone are authentic Jews and that only God's word as they interpret it has true legitimacy and not the policy decisions of the duly elected leaders and appointed civil authorities represents a threat to Israeli democracy.

Language that denigrates and incites violence is used repeatedly to attack fellow Jews. The Sephardic chief rabbi's attacks on non-Orthodox Jews are illustrative: "They brought terrible destruction on the Jewish people in the Diaspora"; they have "uprooted every foundation of the Torah"; "their entire intention is to harm the holiness and purity of Torah"; they "corrupt and sabotage" the land of Israel (literally, the vineyard of the Lord of Hosts).[12] Such language, spoken in the name of Orthodoxy, undermines democratic pluralism and assaults diversity even within the Jewish world. This use of a narrow definition of Jewish identity gives credibility to the attacks by secular Jewish leaders such as Benyamin Netanyahu on those defending a pluralist Israel.

A more dangerous "othering" within the Jewish people occurs when Jewish tradition is used to incite violence or even murder in the name of God. The Talmud tells of assassins during the Roman period who murdered any Jew who disagreed with the revolt and even threatened the life of the central rabbi of that time, Yohanan Ben Zakkai.[13] Prime Minister Yitzhak Rabin, assassinated in 1995, was called a *rodef*, one who pursues Jews and must be killed in self-defense; the murder of a young woman participating in a Gay Pride parade by an Orthodox extremist who saw her as polluting the Holy Land is a painful example of religious violence in God's name.[14] Since right-wing settlers saw Rabin as endangering Jewish lives by returning Palestinian lands and saw Gay Pride as a pollution, these assassins claimed that rabbis endorsed the murders they committed. Although one does not find this level of violence in Europe or the United States, the justifications offered for it flow into the ways Judaism is viewed wherever Jews reside, whatever the religious practice. Such arguments are made in the name of sustaining nationalist Jewish power and territorial hegemony, not in terms of observance.[15]

The rise to power of the illiberal democratic parties signaled also a harsh attitude toward non-Jewish minorities within Israel. In this call to protect Jewish identity, the movement moved from veneration of the State of Israel as a fulfillment of Jewish destiny to the "Land" or the Temple Mount in Jerusalem as the flowering messianic dream, thus replacing the rule of civil law with religious-fueled fervor in which Palestinians can only be an enemy.[16] This is the origin of Israel's illiberal tendency, which continues to be influential until this very day.[17]

Whatever role such discrimination against fellow Jews or other faith communities may have served in earlier ages, its damage to Judaism has become more apparent now. As Laurence Silberstein and Robert Cohn explain, the Jewish experience of the Other confirms in so many ways that "the relationship of culture and power is clearly evident in the practices of exclusion and othering that characterize ethnographic practices."[18] And such "othering" is never exactly benign because, as Jacques Derrida notes, the Other compels a community to question itself, being shadowed and haunted by those it claims are Other.[19] "Insofar as identity presupposes alterity, any effort by a group to establish the parameters of its own identity entails the exclusion and/or silencing of the voices of Others. Consequently, the process of identity formation entails acts of violence against the other."[20]

Identity formation becomes dangerous when the absolutist values that some assert in the realm of theology and religious command spill over into the political sphere as well. Judaism can be used to justify assassination, violence such as burning down Arab orchards, or defacing Christian or Muslim religious sites. A Jew such as Stephen Miller can become the architect of xenophobic antirefugee policies while a Jewish leader, such as the Jewish U.S. ambassador to Israel, David Friedman, could call other Jews who oppose Israeli hegemony over the whole land of Israel *kapos*, Nazi lackeys. The rabid nationalist rhetoric used by Donald Trump to describe fellow citizens and potential immigrants should shake the Jewish minority in America to its core. But some endorse dehumanizing Muslims and applauding Israeli expansionist policies and attacking Muslim members of Congress, declaring such actions "good for the Jews" and thus ignoring what is good for all those residing in the United States. That helps explain why most Orthodox (Haredi) and even Modern Orthodox Jews in the United States supported Donald Trump at a comparable rate to that of white evangelical Protestants.[21]

For many, a Judaism based on praising a God "who did not make us as all other nations and peoples," whose gods and, therefore, whose lives are nothingness and emptiness, says little constructive about who and what Jews are. And a Judaism that denigrates even those within its own community as a source of contamination and sin rejects the pluralist core of Judaism, which eschews any singular practice, belief, or authority. In fact, Judaism has learned and even incorporated a great deal from those it has marked as the Other, even if the source of such appropriation was denied.

There are certainly some texts declaring that non-Jews could be good people, that they could earn their place in the world to come, and even that gentile religions and civilizations could do good. Although experiencing themselves as under attack by a hostile world, the rabbis who founded Rabbinic Judaism in the early centuries of the Common Era could not deny the obvious—that there were righteous gentiles and that other cultures produced just and constructive societies.[22] Within most Jewish circles, there is now little debate on the matter. The great majority of twenty-first-century Jews engage in a wide range of relationships with members of other faiths, including serious and deep dialogue. This should and often does lead to encounters that transcend acceptance and, instead, seek partnerships in which, as Irving Greenberg notes, "each partner affirms that its truth/faith/system alone cannot fulfill God's dreams. The world needs the contribution that the other religion can make for the sake of achieving wholeness and perfection for all. A partner affirms (today, I would say: celebrates) that God assigns different roles and different contributions to different groups."[23]

While certainly understandable, fear and anger and the "other-ing" of religious and ethnic groups cannot frame the way Jews en-counter others in the world. So how can a community grounded in ancient texts and generations of exegetical commentaries and legal codes further support democratic institutions and processes and defend them against assault?

An understanding of the monotheistic bond between Judaism, Christianity, and Islam underpins instances of cooperation among the three faith communities. A recent example is the Jewish, Chris-tian, and Muslim organizations that have joined together in the United States to support immigration reform and challenge police profiling and attacks on Muslims under the Trump administration.

The Noahide covenant (Genesis 9) narrates God's renewal of covenant with humankind. It mandates a basic rule for human behavior, from which the rabbis derived laws that provide both a biblical and rabbinic acceptance of the potential righteousness of all humanity and its inclusion in God's covenantal promise. Mai-monides makes this point, but with the limitation that gentiles must acknowledge the authority of Torah, and he affirmed that those who observe these core humanist commandments are counted among the righteous and have a place in the world to come.[24] This returns us to the core belief that, since God is not knowable and there are many pathways to sacredness, the Noahide covenant does mean that every human being can work to repair the world as a valid expression of this divine pact with humanity.

Again, the midrash is so helpful in its recognition that access to the sacred and awareness of God is not limited to any one space, language, or set of behaviors or beliefs. Otherwise, it seems to us, there would be no need to claim that "there is no place on earth without the Presence [of God]."[25]

The Battle against Idolatry

Judaism stakes its historical legitimacy on the revealed awareness that God is beyond human consciousness, infinitely impossible to comprehend. Idolatry, then, must imply much more than bowing to graven images onto which the worshiper has projected super-natural powers. The pagan world knew that their gods did not actually reside in the sculpted form. The Torah's attack on idolatry had less to do with the pagan forms than with the pagan belief that gods are themselves subservient to a natural order. Nothing can impede Judaism's contention that the world can be improved exactly because God and we enter history as partners to challenge the accepted absolutist claims of those who accept the world as it is. It is here that we can see how contemporary Judaism, with an eye toward human improvement, should be comfortably at home in pluralist liberal democracies.

The pagan world to which the Bible responds revels in pre-determination. Change is impossible, the natural world and the universe itself are complete, and we are forced to acknowledge our particular condition as unchanging. The fate of the pagan gods is regulated by natural cycles over which they have no control. Human life was thought to be similarly bound by irresistible forces.

It was possible for the pagan world to contain many gods because, no matter how many there were, they still were not free. Ultimately, the gods had to bow to the absolute control of the natural world. The hierarchies of the gods were mirrored in the human societies that worshiped them. Birth determined a person's status and fate. But Judaism declared that Pharaoh and Caesar, along with all of the natural world, were subservient to a force beyond human apprehension—the only absolute.

The protection of individual freedom in a liberal democracy—religious and otherwise—is at odds with any absolutist claim, no matter its source. Whether religiously or politically inspired, the idea of a nation to which some people can belong and others cannot is an absolutist claim that amounts to idolatry, as does the idea that one person or one group of people possesses full knowledge of God, that it has access to the divine truth. That goes for Judaism as well, so that the Torah, halakhah, or rabbinic rulings cannot claim absolute knowledge of God's will. Contemporary theologian Gordon Tucker amplifies this point: "It is ultimately futile to try to capture all that can (or perhaps must) be known in the systems we devise, no matter how cleverly and piously. There are inevitably truths greater than those that humanly conceived and designed formalizations can capture for us—be they number theory, or physics, or ethics, or religion. As given in a quote of unknown attribution brought by [the dean of Modern Orthodoxy, Rabbi] Soloveichik, there is 'music that is better than it can be played.'"[26]

Not even a Torah that was given to Moses on Mount Sinai should be understood as absolute truth—and it is in this embrace of pluralism that Judaism offers a response to attacks on liberal democracy. The Zohar refers to the idolatrous nature of those who seek a literal reading of the Torah:

> So this story of Torah (the Five Books of Moses) is but the garment of Torah.
> The body is clothed in garments, the stories of this world.
> Fools of the world look only at the garment, the story of Torah; they know nothing more.
> Those who know more do not look at the garment but rather at the body under that garment. . . .
> In the time to come they are destined to look at the soul of the soul of Torah.[27]

Although the thirteenth-century Spanish Kabbalist authors of the Zohar were most certainly elitist mystics, their claim resonates with an earlier *midrashic* text that touches a primal understanding of revelation at Sinai itself and expresses the democratic nature of Judaism, the belief that everyone stood at the foot of the mountain and each person's uniqueness was crucial to revelation itself: "All the people saw the voices"—How many voices were there? The Torah was meant to be heard in voices according to the strength of each human listener, as it says in Psalms, "The voice of God is in the power"—the power of each human being.[28]

That is why the rabbis insisted, as a cardinal axiom of faith, that the oral law is as divinely given as the written law. The making of the law is an ongoing human enterprise that belongs to mortal and fallible human beings, who cannot deign God's truth, but can modestly grasp only an approximate version that is, at the moment, accessible to them. The rabbis go so far as to forbid God to intervene when the Great Assembly of Rabbis is trying to make a decision on some thorny issue. They tell a story about Rabbi Eliezer, who offers a legal argument that is validated by God's intervention with divine miracles. But even the voice of God is ignored, and God's will overruled, by the majority of rabbis. "Rabbi Yehoshua stood up and protested: 'The Torah is not in heaven!' (Deut. 30:12). We pay no attention to a divine voice because long ago at Mount Sinai You wrote in your Torah at Mount Sinai, 'After the majority must one incline.' (Ex. 23:2)."[29]

Noam Zion elaborates:

> Rabbi Yehoshua rejects the interpretative move of Eliezer who "consults the author" regarding the authoritative reading of the Torah. Yehoshua claims **authorial intention is irrelevant to interpretation** even if the words of God are called *mitzvot*, that is, expressions of God's will. . . . Thus Rabbi Yehoshua's viewpoint is a radical one. He uses it to challenge a God who in the story is unsure that giving up control of the interpretation of Torah is good. "It is not in Heaven" is then a **radical** defense of human interpretation by rejecting the prophetic voice from heaven that would have stopped controversy by authenticating one view.[30]

This is not relativism, that all views are equally valid, but undermines Divine sanction as a justification for action and endorses a pluralism that harmonizes well with liberal democratic values and norms. Within respectful civic discourse, absolute standards can live and function together even when they conflict only if the

Other's humanity is honored. "The deepest insight of pluralism is that dignity, truth, and power function best when they are pluralized, e.g., divided and distributed, rather than centralized and absolutized."[31] No illiberal democracy, with its absolutist nationalism, can offer a political system that would uphold these values.

This is the democratic Jewish response to the absolute truth claims of other religious and political cultures as well as an internal critique against those who have fetishized Torah and halakhah into idolatrous forms, especially where those who hold this attitude have power, as in Israel and sections of New York City. Principled pluralism that functions within a liberal democratic political environment is an effective way to partner with God, to humbly seek justice and practice mercy as fellow citizens and all human beings who seek to approach God by doing good.

Judaism, with all its traditions and history and rich texts, cannot achieve its messianic dream alone. Although its contributions may be rich, it offers only a partial response to the modern condition and the demands of society building. As Mark Johnson notes: "It takes no great insights to recognize that our moral understanding is complex, multidimensional, messy, anything but transparent and utterly resistant to absolutes and reductive strategies. . . . We negotiate our way through this tangled maze of moral deliberation, one step at a time, never sure where we will end, guided only by our ideals of what we, and others, and our shared world might become."[32]

Judaism revels in the messiness of moral deliberation, be it the context of theology or politics or the establishment of economic or social standards of justice. This messiness, and not God's truth, is both principle and process. There should be no surprise when Jews challenge hoary faith assumptions and bridle when truth claims are too coherent, too compelling, too absolute, leaving no space for alternative views. Those political leaders who speak in absolutist terms will find engagement with Jews particularly prickly. Judaism recognizes and respects the different paths we all have taken to reach this moment.

Excising "Othering" from Contemporary Judaism

Judaism, or, better yet, Jews—especially in Israel, where Jewish law plays a heightened and special role—are still struggling with their own diversity as well as other faiths and peoples. If Judaism sees potential entrances to holiness everywhere and hears in contradictory voices the living word of God, what do we do with those elements of the Jewish past that have, for the very understandable reasons of oppression, anger, and fear, deviated from the core Jewish pluralist message?

This is a real issue, now that there is a state where Jews hold a majority and there are significant populations of Jewish voters in the United States who could affect the outcome of elections. In the case of Israel, Elan Ezrachi voices concern for where the Jewish-identified state is heading:

Imagining a State of Israel that could be democratic, with majority rule in a unicameral Parliament, liberal, protecting individual civil and human rights, and Jewish, has become increasingly difficult. As a result, the threats to pluralist, democratic values as embodied in Israel's Declaration of Independence, are real. Settlers who use their Jewish identity to make claims for land have founded unauthorized settlements in contravention of the rule of law and, to deepen the issue, some government agencies secretly fund the projects. And settlers who claim they act out of Jewish tradition, often exonerated, have been responsible for acts of violence against Palestinians and against Israeli Jews who support peace efforts.[33] The acceptance of violence in the name of God among some Israeli Jews includes veneration at the tombs of the Jewish supremacist Meir Kahane and Baruch Goldstein, the man who murdered twenty-nine Muslims in prayer. Some secular Government ministers cheered the release of Elor Azaria, a soldier who received a hero's welcome, after being convicted of murdering a Palestinian terrorist who had already been neutralized.[34] Support for and use of violence against opponents, all in the name of God and Torah, is one sign that the core values of democracy are under assault.[35]

This read of Jewish tradition is not limited to extremists in Israel. David Friedman was appointed under President Trump as U.S. ambassador to Israel and also is Jewish. He, along with other American and European Jews, helped to fund an organization cited as terrorist that promotes violence against Palestinians.[36] After millennia without power, Jews are struggling to determine the nature of their support for the principles of liberal democracy.

From our standpoint, the inherited traditions that these Jewish supremacists maintain to justify their actions no longer can reside alongside a liberal and pluralist democratic world. Included in the categories of traditions that must be rejected as a desecration of God are all biblical genocidal claims, even if never actualized, as well as the acceptance of slavery, capital punishment, homophobia, and, of course, the overall inequality of men and women that is found in the Bible and rabbinic tradition. And the notion that a Jew can decide that another Jew is a *rodef*, a pursuer, or dismiss other Jews as heretics or "worse than Hitler" must also be eradicated from Jewish vocabulary. One can certainly explain the sociological context of key texts, find the literary and legal elements taken from other traditions, or make a positive comparison to more brutal cultures. But that is no longer adequate. Because we are to be faithful to the Torah's vision that each human being is created as an image of God, imbued with infinite value, cherished uniqueness, and the right to divine equality, Jews are therefore commanded to reject degrading and "othering" texts and traditions because they diminish God in the universe.[37]

And Judaism must not limit its rejection to the Bible, but is obligated to examine those elements of Rabbinic Judaism which further exacerbate many of these issues, whatever their original intentions. Among the sacred texts received but now to be rejected are the words of Shimon Bar Yohai, one of the great rabbis of the Mishnah, which was compiled during the early centuries of the Common

Era. "The best of the Gentiles should be killed," he wrote,[38] which laid the groundwork for passages such as this one: "Cattle may not be left in inns of idolaters because they are suspected of bestial sodomy; a Jewish woman may not remain alone with them since they are suspected of lewd lechery; and a Jewish man may not remain alone with them for they are suspected of murder."[39]

Beyond such "othering" projections in the legal midrashic tradition, popular liturgical texts are permeated with the belief that the goyim—what became a pejorative term from the Hebrew word for "nations"—are trying to destroy us, and we must therefore call on God to destroy them first. So, after reciting the verse that in every generation, "they" have arisen to destroy us, the Passover Haggadah adds: "Pour out Your wrath on the nations that know You not. . . . Pour out Your rage upon them and let Your fury overtake them. Pursue them in anger and destroy them from under the heavens of the Eternal."

Today, such words desecrate God's name even if we understand the pained context in which they were authored and included in the tradition. They cannot be taught without the critique and rejection built in, for Jewish tradition eschews reading the Bible without commentary. Contemporary commentary infused with a principled Jewish pluralism would need to place caution symbols next to the unacceptable words, just as Jews demand that Christians excise or reframe anti-Jewish liturgical and Gospel texts and that Muslims rid themselves of anti-Jewish diatribes.

There are counter texts and admonitions that better reflect the contemporary pluralism that Jews can value in the many countries in which they live. To care for the widow and the orphan because "we" were slaves in Egypt is repeated in one fashion or another over thirty-six times in the Bible, more than any other commandment. And rabbinic commentary adds depth to the commandment. A Jew is commanded to care for the stranger, to feed him, to clothe her, to offer work, to try to heal, and to bury gentiles who have no one else to care for them.[40] And the Mishnah declares that Jews must seek out the welfare of the gentiles—even idolaters—because Jews must value the paths that lead to peace.[41] It is an easy task to apply these ancient principles to asylum seekers, undocumented migrants, the marginalized and oppressed in society.

Sensitized to the capacity of religion today to wreak damage in the name of God, we are pushed to explore more effective ways to teach the faithful to engage each other and those of other faiths, politics, and cultures. This includes engaging as a community in a deep and thorough investigation of all Jewish sacred texts. It means making informed and conscious decisions about which texts will continue to be taught and how to teach them. Religions must take responsibility for the violence, divisiveness, bigotry, and prejudice in their sacred narratives. As religious human beings, Jews are commanded to eradicate idolatry from the world. Before asking this of other faiths, Jews must apply this commandment to Judaism.[42]

Seeking Truths

In excising or overriding dangerous "othering" scriptural and traditional voices from the past, we have a problem if we claim that "all these (contradictory) words are the living word of God." How do we deal with true evil, with views that undermine and deny the godliness of each individual? This is no different than the problem democracies face when those who seek to destroy democratic institutions and undermine liberal democratic values use the very instruments of democracy to do so. It is hard to balance the belief that every human being is created in God's image when one is facing those who deny that truth, who denigrate and dehumanize those who do not conform to their absolutist standards. Civil discourse does have a minimal threshold, a respect for the diversity and humanity of the "Other." If that threshold is undermined and threats of violence or expulsion or genocide enter the religious or civic space, then it is possible to deny legitimacy to those who would so act. Pluralism does not mean abandoning the very principles by which a liberal democracy successfully functions.

That said, to see the image of God in the Other opens pathways to a shared language of discourse that allows a wide range of diversity participation in conversation, creating partnership and disagreement with fervor and conviction. To do so, we reject true-false dichotomies or reframe them to instead respect each other's narratives. Emmanuel Levinas, the twentieth-century French thinker, claims that this is adult faith, accepting the loss of a consolatory heaven, recognizing that God has withdrawn from the world and we are left to do the work of healing "through the intermediary teaching, the Torah. It is precisely a discourse, not embodied in God, that assures us a living God among us."[43] And when the Torah is wrenched from its dialogic character, its multivoiced potential, and seeks objective and scientific truths, it can become a destructive agent. Torah functions best in a diverse, multivoiced society whose followers share a commitment to protect each other's civil and human rights.

Yes, we all are dependent on the stories we tell, and, therefore, the framework or ground rules of our lives and our faith depend on the story. What must be asserted is that our sacred narratives and the truth statements and meaning we derive from our sacred narratives are significant only when they are contextual and helpful in the human enterprise of repairing the world. And they are always limited and must never be absolutized. This is not only a critique of archaic medieval religious wars. The sadness is that, rather than accept that there are multiple narratives, each with the potential to illumine an aspect of the infinite God, too many believers have attempted for the past few hundred years to prove that there is but one single true metanarrative. That said, building a nation that would dehumanize and marginalize others in the name of the majority's religious identity, that attacks those who do not follow the majority's sways as heretics, that diminishes the humanity of those who dissent in the name of God, is a desecration of God.

On an absolutist scale that eschews democratic values, the destruction of a "false" religion by murdering its adherents, bombing its holy sites, denigrating its symbols, and denying the veracity of its story and its history makes perfect sense. In so doing, religion becomes both unnecessarily polarizing and dangerous. The antidote: if your understanding of God's truth commands you to destroy and dehumanize in God's name, don't give up on God. Give up on that truth. The same can be said of many nationalist political ideologies. Here, perhaps, in a simple question one finds the essential principle by which Jews today must seek to explain themselves and challenge others: What have you done because you are a believer?

This does not diminish dialogue, but expands its obligation to be more than conversation among erudite thinkers. As Abraham Joshua Heschel, a twentieth-century theologian, writes: "Philosophy, to be relevant, must offer us a wisdom to live by—relevant not only in the isolation of our study rooms, but also in moments of facing staggering cruelty and the threat of disaster."[44] We certainly should encourage theological discourse, plumbing our beliefs and exploring our religious concepts. Leora Batnitzky's analysis of the Jewish thinker Franz Rosenzweig[45] reminds us that we must not give up on this kind of controversial theological discourse, in which the aim is not to come to an agreement, but to deepen our judgment of one argument over and against the other for the sake of deepening our self-judgment. Otherwise, don't we lose the appreciation of the richness and the diversity of theological insights that the religious traditions provide? The same must be said in support of political discourse.

Rich dialogue, whether political or religious—or both together—among diverse participants can open each participant to another voice, to be challenged on the most profound level, to provoke radical reassessments, enriching the narratives and allowing all who partake a generative exploration of alternative ways to see the world. Where such dialogue feels most valuable is when participants are impelled to return to their own religious beliefs and behaviors ever more capable and motivated to pursue goodness, more generous toward those we once would have called Other, more willing to roll up our sleeves and reengage in acts of healing. Silencing, defaming, ostracizing, and dehumanizing those with whom we disagree is, in our reading, not only a political abomination but a venal sin.

Epilogue

Religious Leadership, Civil Discourse,
and Democracy

Tribalism is alive and well, perhaps as prescribed by our DNA. We have enough information about the evolution of human beings and communities to understand that identifying who is friend or foe is deep in our genetic makeup. Facial recognition and the ability to experience fear of a strange or hostile face emerge in infants by the age of six months.[1] Yuval Harari provides perhaps the most nihilistic statement of this biological fact: "Evolution has made Homo sapiens, like other social mammals, a xenophobic creature. Sapiens instinctively divide humanity into two parts, 'we' and 'they.'"[2] Kinship determines whom to trust, and xenophobia is an effective form of self-defense. That alone could explain the rise of illiberal democracy that seeks to include the pure and marginalize and expel everyone else. But Jonathan Haidt argues that kinship networks can expand to create larger units. Societies that were most successful, the ones that "beat out" others in an evolutionary battle to survive, are those that could move beyond kinship fidelity to band together and work as a team against less organized enemies.[3]

As we surveyed the present state of affairs, it was easy to wonder if we have in fact evolved beyond the infantile reflex that divides the world between friend and foe, safety and dire threat. There is ample evidence for the most hopeful as well as the most pessimistic assessment of how teams, tribes, ethnic groups, and nations create a sense of obligation and devotion to those who share their salient identity. On one hand, soccer fans during the World Cup respond as if their nation's fate depends on whether their team makes a goal, while on the other, scientific collaborators from so many different countries could, in the face of a global pandemic, join in the search for a vaccine and protocols that will save and cure millions they will never meet.

Certainly, tribal pride and commitment has had a role to play in the advancement of humanity. Nations have nurtured a global community that strives to create a better society. And there is a strong psychological argument that the ability to expansively love and respect others is first nurtured within smaller units, starting with the family. One does not love all humanity without loving individual people first. We have shown the deep need for a shared sense of community, the failure of globalized liberal democracies to provide such shelter, and the power of populist nationalism to galvanize and unite community. That said, in its extreme forms, tribal collective identity has wrought untold killing and destruction. What we see now, in contrast to the lofty claims of the Enlightenment and its progeny, is that the belief that humanity has arrived at a new evolutionary stage of global connection may be highly overstated. The use of religious identity to fuel populist revolt and stoke fear and anger, the subject of this book, remains as potent today as it has been for millennia.

As more and more politicians proudly and piously declare themselves nationalists with God on their side, the need to protect the independence and vitality of democratic institutions becomes ever more crucial. Timothy Snyder writes in *On Tyranny*: "It is institutions that help us to preserve democracy. They need our help as well. Do not speak of 'our institutions' unless you make them yours by acting on their behalf. Institutions do not protect themselves. They fall one after the other unless each is defended from the beginning. So choose an institution you care about—a court, a newspaper, a law, a labor union—and take its side."[4]

For faith communities, nothing protects their rights to believe and practice as effectively and completely as democracies that enshrine freedom of religion at their core. On pragmatic grounds alone, defending the autonomy of the courts and civil servants, the integrity of the voting process and an independent press, all building blocks of a free and open society, should be a religious as well as a civic duty. As authors, we hope to have impact through what we write. As activists, we join in the struggle to protect and strengthen the democratic institutions that are vulnerable to attack. As religious folk, we seek to mobilize faith communities to rise up to support the institutions that ensure our liberty and protect our rights.

All the nationalist cases we have examined share certain features which authors across the political spectrum continue to cite as dangerous pathways that undermine liberal democracies committed to human and civil rights. That is why we write and engage in the civic affairs of our nations and reach out to support democratic governments across the globe. Religion that endorses constructive civic engagement and that eschews hatred, xenophobia, and denigrating the "other" must be marshaled as a vital force for freedom; the types of faith presented in this book mean to inspire us to move off the sidelines into the center of these efforts to combat those who try to weaponize religion to fuel populist nationalist movements.

There is nothing conservative about defending the existing democratic political systems, calling on religious leaders to support and sustain their political institutions and the norms and values of democracy. We well recognize that governments are not perfect and that aspirations for equality and equity remain unfulfilled even as we acknowledge the experience of so many who feel that their governments are abandoning them. Disparities are widening, dividing globalized elites from the majority who feel left behind. Liberal democracies will need to find a way to provide a sense of shared destiny even as they protect and enhance laws and social norms that expand human and civil rights. There is much work to be done, and religious leaders can be in the forefront of constructive and critical change. It is the role of religious leaders and faith-based institutions to work hard to bridge the polarization that feeds the sicknesses of hatred and xenophobia in society and equip their followers to reach out to heal the schisms and soothe the anger. Reactionary reflex responses to such challenges are never healthy, and certainly the prophetic voice of religious leaders should demand that democracies address their own weaknesses and failures. That said, attempts to disenfranchise citizens or cow them into submission are not courageous efforts to expand freedom and equality, but attempts to undermine existing civil rights protections. Challenging existing inequalities, civil disagreement among political opponents, and debates over differing policy choices are all signs of democratic health. As one participating voice among many in the public square, religious leaders and their communities of faith, whether politically on the right or left, should be part of these conversations. That too is a sign of democratic health. And religious vitality.

Yet we have clearly demarcated where populist, xenophobic, and religiously weaponized nationalism threatens and weakens key democratic norms and institutions. Demonizing opponents by "othering" them because of their race, religion, ethnicity, national status, and all the other ways demagogues manipulate to gain or maintain their power threatens not just human rights, but human lives. Denigrating opponents as traitors and criminals becomes a catchall that is meant to "other" them and invariably becomes a dangerous attack on the opponent's humanity, targeting them for verbal abuse or even violence. Using deceit as a political weapon, undermining the independent news media as fake and enemies of the people, and closing down dissent or using a range of legal actions to suppress it while attempting to legitimize distortions and lies are all now actions of choice from the Philippines to Brazil, from Washington to Warsaw. And the overt call to violence and use of violence to threaten and intimidate, whether in language or in behavior, is a reminder of how democratic processes can morph into threats of tyranny. We are witness at this very dangerous moment in history to a collapse of a shared consensus as to what is true and right and just.

In each of these assaults on democracy, religion can play a destructive or protective role. Religious identity can be used to buttress the good of the whole society or as a battering ram to fuel hatred. We seek to distinguish between a democratic patriotism that supports human and civil rights and respects the pluralist realities of society—for us, a religious individual's love for, and willingness to work on behalf of, their nation—and populist nationalism, which narrows the religion by turning fealty to the nation into a form of idolatry.

For many decades, treaties and alliances steadied and limited the hegemonic tendencies that in the past century led to world-wide conflagration. As more and more societies experimented with democratic forms of governance, feeble and tentative as they may have been, many faith communities also reached out to embrace democratic norms and a more pluralist engagement in the public square. As some societies, disappointed and angry, abandon liberal democratic norms and institutions, faith communities can force-fully respond by strengthening those norms and institutions from the pulpit, in collective declarations of support, and through active political advocacy. And they can help nurture personal meaning and a commitment to shared values that could well assuage the pains so many experience in their daily lives.

We have written this book with confidence that religious leaders will communicate that the use of their religion to fuel nationalism is, in fact, a dangerous religious malfunction. We have written to faith communities in the hope that they will be more deeply en-gaged in the civic affairs of their countries as vocal and activist ad-vocates for democratic norms and institutions. We have written so that political analysts and pundits will immerse themselves more deeply in how faith communities translate belief into action and sa-cred scripture into policy prescriptions. And we write in the hope that political leaders will eschew the demagogic path of weaponiz-ing the religious identity of their citizens to fuel illiberal populist nationalism.

The book of Ecclesiastes in the Bible poetically describes the reality that some moments are more fraught than others:

> There is a time for everything and a season for every activity
> under the heavens:
> a time to be born and a time to die,
> a time to plant and a time to uproot,
> a time to kill and a time to heal,
> a time to tear down and a time to build,
> a time to weep and a time to laugh,
> a time to mourn and a time to dance,
> a time to scatter stones and a time to gather them,
> a time to embrace and a time to refrain from embracing,
> a time to search and a time to give up,
> a time to keep and a time to throw away,
> a time to tear and a time to mend,
> a time to be silent and a time to speak,
> a time to love and a time to hate,
> a time for war and a time for peace.
> (Ecclesiastes 3:1–8; my translation)

We do not choose the time to be born, and seldom the time to die, nor can we choose whether we are born in an age of peace and prosperity or one of hatred and terrible devastation. We cannot control these aspects of our lives. And it is also hubris to believe that any one of us alone can change the course of history. But we still can act, as individuals and as communities, to stem the hemorrhaging of the post–World War II consensus under which nations committed themselves to a new era of civility, endorsing democracy and interconnected global responsibility—consensus that, while not perfect, seemed to work for seventy years. The reasons for such commitment might not have been noble—fear of nuclear retaliation, the desire to be included in the United Nations or to receive aid, leaders wanting the stature of international recognition. And it certainly was not a perfect time of love and peace, laughter and dance. Yet the adage is more acutely true than ever that liberal democratic governments, while far from perfect, are still a better choice than any other political system.

We offered the teaching of Dietrich Bonhoeffer, murdered by the Nazi regime, who told us that what matters "is not the beyond but this world, how it is created and preserved, is given laws, reconciled and renewed," and that God's presence is revealed in the *sanctorum communio*, the sacred community that exists only in the actual social, historical, bodily reality of the human world. This places a powerful claim on people of faith and on their leaders, demanding that they ensure that their religion and religious identity will be a source for good, for healing, and for reconciliation, promoting a more just and compassionate world. And it is to you, the reader, to whom we present this challenge: bring the ideas and ideals of this book into being. Those in faith communities, whether as leaders or participants, can collectively change the current trajectory through their actions and attitudes. It is toward this goal that we joined to author this book.

NOTES

Introduction

1. Anderson is quoted in Nathan Heller, "Structure of Equality," 48.
2. See Carse, *Finite and Infinite Games*.
3. Hawley, *Making Sense of the Alt-Right*, introduction.
4. Cremer, "Defenders of the Faith."
5. Lepore, "In Every Dark Hour," 20–21.
6. Tufecki, *Twitter and Tear Gas*, 6.
7. Eatwell and Goodwin, *National Populism*, xiii.
8. Taguieff, *Sur la Nouvelle Droit*, 32–35.
9. Brubaker, "Between Nationalism and Civilizationism," 1192.
10. Eatwell and Goodwin, *National Populism*, 39.
11. Plattner, "Illiberal Democracy and the Struggle on the Right," 10.
12. Eatwell and Goodwin, *National Populism*, xxii.
13. Williamson, "Chaos in the Family, Chaos in the State."
14. Hochschild, *Strangers in Their Own Land*, 157 (emphasis original).
15. Case and Deaton, "Mortality and Morbidity in the 21st Century."
16. Tamir, *Why Nationalism*, 10–11.
17. Ibid., 155.
18. Alissa Wahid, "My Islam, Your Islam, Our Islam."
19. Walzer, *Paradox of Liberation*, 7.
20. Krastev, *After Europe*, 40.
21. Avineri, "Ignored by Liberal Elites."
22. Eatwell and Goodwin, *National Populism*, 11.

23. Lepore, "In Every Dark Hour," 21.

24. Rambachan, "Hindu Theological Critique of Hindutva."

25. Lepore, *These Truths*, 568.

26. Ibid., 662.

27. See Miles, *Religion as We Know It.*

28. Weigel, "Pope John Paul II and the Dynamics of History."

29. Appleby, *Ambivalence of the Sacred*, 27.

30. Brown-Dean, *Identity Politics in the United States*, 162.

31. Henderson, "Christianity as the Antidote to Christian Nationalism."

32. Saperstein, "Use and Abuse of Jewish Tradition," 33.

33. For example, Yuli Tamir's *Why Nationalism* has but a single reference in her index to religion, as Michael Walzer observed to her with concern in conversation at Columbia University, April 26, 2019, as reported to the authors.

34. Shulman, "Challenging the Civic/Ethnic and West/East Dichotomies."

35. Asad, "Construction of Religion as an Anthropological Category."

36. Plecita, "Importance of Christianity and Customs/Traditions."

37. Over 70 percent of Jews in Europe do not attend synagogue, even on the High Holidays. See Zieve, "70% of European Jews Won't Go to Shul."

38. Brubaker, "Between Nationalism and Civilizationism," 1196.

Chapter One

1. Elman, "Does Democracy Tame the Radicals?"

2. Pew Research Center, "Religious Belief and National Belonging in Central and Eastern Europe."

3. Levitsky and Ziblatt, *How Democracies Die.*

4. Appiah, *Lies That Bind*, 36.

5. Bakshi, "Continent Divided."

6. Sumiala, "Introduction: Mediatization in Post-Secular Society."

7. "Religious Symbols Take Center Stage."

8. Erlanger, "Sweden Was Long Seen as a 'Moral Superpower.'"

9. Ibid.

10. See "Religion in Charleston, West Virginia," BestPlaces, https://www .bestplaces.net/religion/city/west_virginia/charleston.

11. Searcey, "72-Hour War over Christmas."

12. Hjelm, *Is God Back?*, 15.

13. Appiah, *Lies That Bind*, 20.

14. Feldman, "Megyn Kelly Assures Everyone That Santa Is White."
15. Appiah, *Lies That Bind*, 25.
16. Gelman, "Psychological Essentialism in Children."
17. See Casad and Bryant, "Addressing Stereotype Threat Is Critical."
18. Berger, "Secularism in Retreat," quoted in Hjelm, *Is God Back?*, 4.
19. Corbett and Corbett, *Politics and Religion.*
20. In fact, a majority of young Germans do define themselves as religious, a reality ignored by many German social scientists. Sixty-two percent of Germans claim church affiliation even if they do not attend services very often. Lam, "Religion in the EU."
21. Day, *Believing in Belonging*, 22.
22. Koch, "Introduction: Revisiting Civil Religion."
23. Day, *Believing in Belonging*, 194.
24. Stanley, *How Fascism Works.*
25. Casanova, "Politics of Nativism."
26. Cremer, "Defenders of the Faith."
27. Elcott and Sinclair, "Flexibility in American Religious Life."
28. Richie, "Neither Naïve nor Narrow."
29. Elcott and Sinclair, "Flexibility in American Religious Life."
30. Douglas, *Purity and Danger.*
31. Levitsky and Ziblatt, *How Democracies Die*, 23–24.
32. Bakshi, "Continent Divided." Hindutva is the movement to claim the unique and singular Hindu nature of the Indian nation.
33. See Chaudhury, "OHCHR Has Filed Petitions."
34. Braunstein and Taylor, "Is the Tea Party a 'Religious' Movement?," 55.
35. Fukuyama, "End of History?," 1.
36. See Levitsky and Ziblatt, *How Democracies Die*; Day, *Believing in Belonging.*
37. Pew Research Center, "Religious Belief and National Belonging in Central and Eastern Europe."
38. Day, *Believing in Belonging*, 55–58.
39. Eatwell and Goodwin, *National Populism*, 38.
40. Porter-Szűcs, "PiS in Their Own Words."
41. Alternative für Deutschland, "Manifesto" (2017).
42. Rambachan, "Hindu Theological Critique of Hindutva."
43. Levitsky and Ziblatt, *How Democracies Die*, chapter 1.
44. Grynbaum, "After Another Year of Trump Attacks, 'Ominous Signs.'"
45. Madison, Federalist Papers, no. 10.

46. "Die Kirchen in Deutschland schrumpfen."

47. See Greenwald, "Glenn Greenwald: I Was Assaulted Live on Air."

48. See the article on the rise of violence in Germany: Halasz, Schmidt, and Kottasová, "Two More Suspects Arrested after Far-Right Supporter Confesses."

49. Farber, "Finding the Godliness in All Humanity."

50. Weiqian, "Christian Religiosity and Support for Populist Radical Right Parties in Europe," 6.

51. Tversky and Kahneman, "Judgment under Uncertainty."

52. Regarding surveys attesting to a drop in trust, see, e.g., Quinnipiac University Poll, Surveys on President Trump's approval ratings.

53. Trust in journalists is dropping. For example, in the U.S., it dropped from 68% in 1972 to 41% in 2019. See Ritter, "How Much Does the World Trust Journalists?"

54. See Henderson, "Attorney General Sessions Task Force Is a Tool for Division."

55. Elcott and Sinclair, "Flexibility in American Religious Life."

56. Winkler, "Christian Call to Engage the World."

57. See the account of Pope Francis's statement in Glatz, "'Joy of the Gospel.'"

Chapter Two

1. Becher, *Der Aufstand des Abendlandes*; Bock, "Negotiating Cultural Difference"; Coury, "A Clash of Civilizations?"; Eatwell and Goodwin, *National Populism*; Kaufmann, *Whiteshift*.

2. Betz and Meret, "Revisiting Lepanto"; Brubaker, "Between Nationalism and Civilizationism"; Marzouki, McDonnell, and Roy, *Saving the People*; Minkenberg, "Religion and the Radical Right"; Roy, *L'Europe est-elle chrétienne?*

3. Bednarz, *Die Angstprediger*; Morieson, "Religion and Identity at the 2017 Dutch Elections"; Norris and Inglehart, *Cultural Backlash*.

4. "Deutschen werden christliche Wurzeln wichtiger"; Pollack and Rosta, *Religion and Modernity*.

5. Arzheimer and Carter, "Christian Religiosity and Voting for West European Radical Right Parties"; Daenekindt, de Koster, and van der Waal, "How People Organise Cultural Attitudes"; Immerzeel, Jaspers, and Lubbers, "Religion as Catalyst or Restraint of Radical Right Voting?"; Lubbers and Scheepers,

"Explaining the Trend in Extreme Right-Wing Voting"; Montgomery and Winter, "Explaining the Religion Gap in Support for Radical Right Parties in Europe"; Orth and Resing, *AfD, Pegida & Co.*

6. Krause, "Christliche Symbole bei Pegida-Demo 'pervers.'"

7. Bednarz, *Die Angstprediger*; Montgomery and Winter, "Explaining the Religion Gap in Support for Radical Right Parties in Europe"; Orth and Resing, *AfD, Pegida & Co.*; Thielmann, *Alternative für Christen?*

8. "Die Kirchen in Deutschland schrumpfen."

9. Thieme and Liedhegener, "'Linksaußen,' politische Mitte oder doch ganz anders?"; in fact, churches are even criticized for being too far on the left and too hostile toward new right-wing movements.

10. Lindner, "Eine unheilige Allianz"; "'Rolle wie im Dritten Reich'"; "AfD attackiert Kirchen für Einsatz in der Flüchtlingskrise."

11. Strohm, *Die Kirchen im Dritten Reich*; Troeltsch, *Die Soziallehren der christlichen Kirchen und Gruppen.*

12. Cremer, "Resistance of the Protestant Church in Nazi Germany"; van Norden, *Der Deutsche Protestantismus im Jahr der nationalsozialistischen Machtergreifung.*

13. NSDAP was the initialism that stood for the party better known among English speakers as the Nazi Party. The letters stand for Nationalsozialistische Deutsche Arbeiterpartei (National Socialist German Workers' Party).

14. Cremer, "Resistance of the Protestant Church in Nazi Germany"; Gruber, *Katholische Kirche und Nationalsozialismus,1930–1945.*

15. Portier, "L'État et les religions en France"; Willaime, *Lumières, Religions, Laïcité.*

16. Strohm, *Die Kirchen im Dritten Reich*, 7 (translation by Elcott). In December 1941 Hitler claimed, "The war will end, and I will make it my ultimate life's work to bring the church question to its final solution. Only then will the German nation be fully secure." Ibid.

17. Cremer, "Resistance of the Protestant Church in Nazi Germany."

18. Kalyvas and van Kersbergen, "Christian Democracy."

19. Müller, "Towards a New History of Christian Democracy," 245.

20. Kaiser and Wohnout, *Political Catholicism in Europe, 1918–45*; Linden, *Global Catholicism.*

21. Ringshausen, "Widerstand und die Krichen."

22. Schlaich, Heckel, and Heun, *Gesammelte Aufsätze.*

23. Müller, "Towards a New History of Christian Democracy," 251.

24. Böckenförde, *Staat, Verfassung, Demokratie*; Krings, "Von strikter Trennung zu wohlwollender Neutralität."

25. Kaiser and Wohnout, *Political Catholicism in Europe, 1918–45*.

26. Graf, *Der Protestantismus*.

27. Zander, *Die Christen und die Friedensbewegungen*.

28. Püttmann, *Ziviler Ungehorsam und christliche Bürgerloyalität*.

29. Alternative für Deutschland (AfD), "Programm für Deutschland (Manifesto)."

30. "AfD-Stellvertreter Gauland: 'Wir sind keine christliche Partei.'"

31. Amann, *Angst für Deutschland*, 59; Arzheimer, "AfD."

32. Gebhardt, "Eine 'Partei neuen Typs'?," 87.

33. "AfD erstmals zweitstärkste Partei nach der Union."

34. Amann, *Angst für Deutschland*.

35. "AfD wandelt sich von Professoren- zur Prekariats-Partei."

36. Eatwell and Goodwin, *National Populism*; *Bundestagswahl*; Fukuyama, *Identity*; Kaufmann, *Whiteshift*; Pew Research Center, "As Election Nears, Voters Divided."

37. Bornschier, *Cleavage Politics and the Populist Right*; Goodhart, *Road to Somewhere*; Harari, "Nationalism vs. Globalism."

38. De Wilde et al., *The Struggle over Borders*; Dostal, "The German Federal Election of 2017: How the Wedge Issue of Refugees and Migration Took the Shine off Chancellor Merkel and Transformed the Party System."

39. Frank, *What's the Matter with Kansas?*; Fukuyama, *Identity*; Lilla, *Once and Future Liberal*.

40. Frank, *What's the Matter with Kansas?*, 5.

41. Betz, "Exclusionary Populism in Western Europe in the 1990s and Beyond."

42. Eatwell and Goodwin, *National Populism*; Mudde and Kaltwasser, *Populism*.

43. Crowley, "Man Who Wants to Unmake the West."

44. An analysis of AfD's positions through the manifesto project of Wissenschaftszentrum Berlin (WZB) shows the decline in positive references to the market economy and a simultaneous rise of positive mentions of national identity and negative references towards multiculturalism over the years. See Wissenschaftszentrum Berlin, "Manifesto Project."

45. "Alexander Gauland bezeichnet Übergriffe in Chemnitz als normal."

46. "AfD: Besetzer der Reichstagstreppe keine Demokratiegefahr," Berlin.de, September 3, 2020, https://www.berlin.de/aktuelles/berlin/6281967-958 092-afd-besetzer-der-reichstagstreppe-keine-.html.

47. Kaufmann, *Whiteshift*; McCulloch, "Nouvelle Droite in the 1980s and 1990s"; Rydgren, *Movements of Exclusion*.

48. Prange, "How the Catholic Church Ties in to Poland's Judicial Reform"; "Hungarian PM Sees Shift to Illiberal Christian Democracy in 2019 European Vote."

49. Müller, "What Happens When an Autocrat's Conservative Enablers Finally Turn on Him?"

50. Cremer, "Defenders of the Faith."

51. Marzouki, McDonnell, and Roy, *Saving the People*, 2.

52. Casanova, "Politics of Nativism," 489.

53. Menzel, "Schwarz-Rot-Dumpf."

54. Vorländer, Herold, and Schäller, *Wer geht zu PEGIDA und warum?*

55. Roos, "Katholische Soziallehre und Kultur der Entwicklung." Roos's concept of the cultural-ethical triangle analyzes organizations' Christian orientation through (1) the analysis of their policies, (2) the personal virtues of their leading personnel, and (3) their attitude toward the institutional churches.

56. Alternative für Deutschland, *Programm für Deutschland (Alternative für Deutschland Manifesto)*.

57. "Rolle wie im Dritten Reich."

58. Heimbach-Steins and Filipović, *Grundpositionen der Partei "Alternative Für Deutschland,"* 71.

59. Deutscher Bundestag, *Datenhandbuch Deutscher Bundestag*.

60. Alternative für Deutschland Hessen 2018, *Hessen. Aber Sicher!*; Alternative für Deutschland Bayern, *Bayern. Aber Sicher! Wahlprogramm Landtagswahl Bayern 2018*.

61. "Rolle wie im Dritten Reich"; Höhne and Wensierski, "Neue rechte Allianz."

62. "Kein religiöses Symbol?"

63. Steppat and Giesel, "Spätentscheider verhindern das Schlimmste für CSU."

64. Arzheimer and Carter, "Christian Religiosity and Voting for West European Radical Right Parties"; Daenekindt, de Koster, and van der Waal, "How People Organise Cultural Attitudes"; Dargent, "Les catholiques français et le Front national"; de Koster et al., "Progressiveness and the New Right"; Fourquet, *À la droite de Dieu*; Immerzeel, Jaspers, and Lubbers, "Religion as Catalyst or Restraint of Radical Right Voting?"; Lubbers and Scheepers, "Explaining the Trend in Extreme Right-Wing Voting"; Montgomery and Winter, "Explaining the Religion Gap in Support for Radical Right Parties in Europe"; Perrineau, *La France au Front*.

65. Betz and Meret, "Revisiting Lepanto."

66. "Election Analysis, 2005."

67. Daenekindt, de Koster, and van der Waal, "How People Organise Cultural Attitudes"; de Koster et al., "Progressiveness and the New Right"; Cleuziou, "Sens commun."

68. Pew Research Center, "Being Christian in Western Europe."

69. Arzheimer and Carter, "Christian Religiosity and Voting for West European Radical Right Parties," 985.

70. Roy, "French National Front."

71. Bornschier, "Why a Right-Wing Populist Party Emerged in France but Not in Germany," 138.

72. Püttmann, "AfD und Kirche."

73. "Katholiken-Präsident stuft AfD als rechtsradikal ein"; "Dresdner Frauenkirche macht wegen Pegida das Licht aus"; Kraetzer, "AfD legt sich mit der evangelischen Kirche"; Orth and Resing, *AfD, Pegida & Co.*; Deutsche Bischofskonferenz, "Bischöfe: AfD nicht mit christlichem Glauben vereinbar."

74. Pollack and Rosta, *Religion and Modernity.*

75. Dargent, "Les catholiques français et le Front national"; Fourquet, *L'archipel français.*

76. "AfD-Stellvertreter Gauland: 'Wir sind keine christliche Partei.'"

77. "Wenn die Gottlosen für das christliche Abendland demonstrieren."

Chapter Three

1. Levitsky and Ziblatt, *How Democracies Die*, 23–24.

2. Whitehead, Perry, and Baker, "Make America Christian Again." See also Bellah, "Civil Religion in America"; Gorski, "Conservative Protestantism in the United States?"

3. Whitehead, Perry, and Baker, "Make America Christian Again," 147.

4. Justice and Berglund, "Trump, Palin Challenge ORU Students."

5. Corbett and Corbett, *Politics and Religion in the United States*, 23.

6. Whitehead, Perry, and Baker, "Make America Christian Again," 151.

7. Fox, *Introduction to Religion and Politics*, 13.

8. Dickinson, *Pennsylvania Journal.*

9. See Green, *Separation of Church and State.*

10. "God in the White House."

11. Everson v. Board of Education.

12. Abington School District v. Schempp.

13. Lemon v. Kurtzman.

14. Wallace v. Jaffree.

15. Porterfield, "Religion's Role in Contestations over American Civility," 43.

16. Ibid., 41.

17. Story, *Commentaries on the Constitution*.

18. Abington School District v. Schempp, cited in Carper and Hunt, *Praeger Handbook*, 354.

19. De Vogue, "Supreme Court Keeps Mojave Cross Case Alive."

20. Town of Greece v. Galloway.

21. Burwell v. Hobby Lobby Stores, Inc.

22. Zeskind, "Christian Coalition and Republican Party."

23. Mudler, "Moral World of John Foster Dulles."

24. Young, Review of *Family Values and the Rise of the Christian Right*.

25. Reagan, "Remarks at the Annual Convention of the National Religious Broadcasters." Reagan quoted from John 3:16 and 2 Chronicles 7:14 in the King James Version of the Bible.

26. Clayton and Elgar, *Civility and Democracy in America*, 45.

27. Friedman, "2016 Republican Platform on Religious Liberty."

28. UVA Center for Politics, "New Poll: Some Americans Express Troubling Racial Attitudes."

29. See Whitehead, Perry, and Baker, "Make America Christian Again"; Braunstein and Taylor, "Is the Tea Party a 'Religious' Movement?"

30. Winthrop, *Model of Christian Charity*. The passage alludes to Deuteronomy 30:19–20: "I have set before you life and death, blessing and cursing: therefore choose life, that both thou and thy seed may live: That thou mayest love the LORD thy God, and that thou mayest obey his voice, and that thou mayest cleave unto him: for he is thy life, and the length of thy days." The image of a city on a hill alludes to Matthew 5:14: "Ye are the light of the world. A city that is set on an hill cannot be hid" (both passages are quoted from the King James Version).

31. For an example of the kind of biblical prophecy that seventeenth-century English settlers referenced as a basis for their orientation toward the land and peoples they encountered in America, see Deuteronomy 7:1–16.

32. Lease, "History Is a Weapon."

33. See "Be Strong," a quotation attributed to Dr. David Jeremiah.

34. Bushman, preface to *From Puritan to Yankee*.

35. Religion and the Founding of the American Republic.

36. Gerbner, epilogue of *Christian Slavery*.

37. Ibid.

38. Milgrom, *Leviticus 1–16*, 43.

39. Douglas, *Purity and Danger*, 133.

40. Milgrom, *Leviticus: A Book of Ritual and Ethics*, 15.

41. See Elcott and Sinclair, "Flexibility in American Religious Life"; Elcott, "Why Evangelicals Are Okay with Voting for Roy Moore."

42. See Elcott and Sinclair, "Flexibility in American Religious Life."

43. Whitehead, Perry, and Baker, "Make America Christian Again."

44. Pence, "Remarks by the Vice President on Healthcare and Tax Reform," 2017.

45. See Christerson and Flory, "Rick Perry's Belief That Trump Was Chosen by God Is Shared by Many."

46. See "Hurricane Gus Update," blog post commenting on how Rev. Gus Booth challenged the IRS rules on endorsing candidates from the pulpit.

47. Dias and Peters, "Evangelical Leaders Close Ranks with Trump."

48. Jerry Falwell, quoted in Rapp, *God's Country*, 43. See also Newman, "From John F. Kennedy's 1960 Campaign Speech to Christian Supremacy," 693.

49. Park, "Revolutionary Roots of America's Religious Nationalism."

50. Wallace, "Segregation Now, Segregation Forever" (Wallace's inauguration speech).

51. Ladd, "Pastors, Not Politicians."

52. See Nelson and Swanson, "Full Transcript," providing the full transcript of President Trump's remarks in a press conference he held after the march.

53. Henderson, "Christianity as the Antidote to Christian Nationalism."

54. Braunstein and Taylor, "Is the Tea Party a 'Religious' Movement?," 56.

55. Fox, *Introduction to Religion and Politics*, 7.

56. Porterfield, "Religion's Role in Contestations over American Civility," 46.

57. Whitehead, Perry, and Baker, "Make America Christian Again," 19.

Chapter Four

1. The source can be found in Alan of Lille, *Art of Preaching*, 1. The original was written in the late twelfth century in Paris and became the standard preaching manual in the thirteenth century. Many of its principles were incorporated into the subsequent textbooks.

2. See *Catechism of the Catholic Church*, #830–31. Number 831 cites *Lumen Gentium* 13: "All men and women are called to belong to the new people of God. This people therefore, whilst remaining one and unique is to be spread throughout the whole world and to all ages in order that the design of God be fulfilled: he made human nature one in the beginning and decreed that all his children who were scattered should be finally gathered together as one." All English citations of Vatican II are from Flannery and Northport, *Basic Sixteen Documents*.

3. My translation.

4. John Paul II, "Message for the 85th World Immigration Day."

5. Ibid.

6. Ibid., 6.

7. Ibid., 5.

8. Ojewska, "Catholic Nationalism."

9. Paul Hockenos, "Poland and the Uncontrollable Fury of Europe's Far Right."

10. Ojewska, "Catholic Nationalism."

11. Pew Research Center, "Religious Belief and National Belonging in Central and Eastern Europe." The material cited is from subsection 8, which concentrated on democracy, nationalism, and pluralism.

12. Ibid.

13. Statistics cited from Reese, "Pollsters Confused about Catholic Voters."

14. Southern Poverty Law Center's website lists eleven organizations as hate groups under the rubric "Radical Traditional Catholicism"; but having reviewed their materials, I find that they are better described as either anti-Semitic, homophobic, or both rather than as nationalists. The Southern Poverty Law Center notes that these groups reject the authority and even the legitimacy of the popes and the Second Vatican Council. Insofar as they formally deny the legitimacy of papal and conciliar teachings, not to mention the tradition behind them, these groups have been required to remove the term "Catholic" from their names and publications by local bishops. Though there appears to be cross-fertilization between some of these groups and other nationalists, I will not be addressing them directly.

15. "Marriage and Religious Freedom."

16. Mississippi passed the Religious Liberty Accommodations Act, which makes it legal to discriminate against people if the discrimination is based on the belief that marriage is only between one man and one woman, that sexual relations can only take place within the confines of marriage, and that gender is

immutably determined at birth. On May 4, 2017, President Trump signed an executive order that directed the attorney general to support and defend religious freedom laws allowing for discrimination against LGBTQ people. See Gessen, "How Trump Uses 'Religious Liberty' to Attack L.G.B.T. Rights."

17. *Dei Verbum* 7–10, *Catechism of the Catholic Church.*

18. Leo the Great, *Sermon 3*, 3, quoted in Meyendorff, *Imperial Unity and Christian Divisions*, 150.

19. Leo the Great, *Sermon 3*, 16.1, citing Pope Gelasius.

20. See, for example, Agence France-Presse, "Polish Catholics Come Together at the Country's Borders."

21. Ibid.

22. United Nations, Universal Declaration of Human Rights.

23. For a full discussion see Bokenkotter, *Church and Revolution*, 7–38.

24. Pius X, *Pascendi Dominici Gregis.*

25. Newman, *Essay on the Development of Christian Doctrine*, 40.

26. See *Dignitatis Humanae* 2, quoted in *Catechism of the Catholic Church.*

27. Ibid., 6.

28. See *Gaudium et Spes* 25, quoted in *Catechism of the Catholic Church.*

29. *Dignitatis Humanae* 6, quoted in *Catechism of the Catholic Church.*

30. *Dignitatis Humanae* 10, quoted in *Catechism of the Catholic Church.*

31. Ibid., 11.

32. Ibid.

33. Tavard, *Holy Writ or Holy Church*, 115.

34. Ibid., 116–17.

35. Ibid., 114.

36. Ibid., 203–4.

37. *Dei Verbum* 7, quoted in *Catechism of the Catholic Church.*

38. Ibid., 8.

39. *Gaudium et Spes* 27, quoted in *Catechism of the Catholic Church.*

40. Ibid., 28.

41. Ibid., 29.

42. Maximus the Confessor, *Four Hundred Chapters on Love*, 37.

43. Ibid., 1.40 (p. 39).

44. *Gaudium et Spes* 42, quoted in *Catechism of the Catholic Church.*

45. Ibid., 58.

46. Ibid., 42.

47. Ibid., 59.

48. Ibid.
49. Ibid.
50. Ibid., 60.
51. Ibid., 74.
52. Ibid., 84.
53. Ibid., 85.
54. Ibid., 89.
55. Ibid.
56. See *Lumen Gentium* 23, quoted in *Catechism of the Catholic Church.*
57. *Gaudium et Spes* 76, quoted in *Catechism of the Catholic Church.*

Chapter Five

1. Clark, "Protestantism, Nationalism, and National Identity," 272.
2. Green, *Inventing a Christian America*, 201, cited in Goodnight, "William Apess, Pequot Pastor," 1.
3. Clymer, "Religion and American Imperialism," 29.
4. Wilsey, "Our Country Is Destined to Be the Great Nation of Futurity," 50.
5. Zylstra, "Presbyterian Church in America Apologizes."
6. Henderson, "Christianity as the Antidote to Christian Nationalism."
7. Ibid.
8. Winkler, "The Christian Call to Engage the World."
9. Barnett, *After Ten Years.*
10. Lees, "The 'Alternative for Germany' (AfD)," 296.
11. "AfD's Gauland Plays Down Nazi Era as 'Bird Shit.'"
12. Gollwitzer, "Sermon about *Kristallnacht*," 118.
13. Ibid., 124.
14. Green, "Exploring the Traditionalist Alliance," 23.
15. Ibid., 35.
16. Barnett, *After Ten Years.*
17. Pangritz, "'To Fall within the Spokes of the Wheel,'" 106.
18. "Asylum and the Rights of Refugees."
19. Just, "Rise and Features of Church Asylum," 136.
20. Prange, "How the Catholic Church Ties in to Poland's Judicial Reform."
21. German Ecumenical Committee on Church Asylum, "Welcome: German Ecumenical Committee on Church Asylum."

22. Neufert, "Church Asylum," 36.

23. Just, "Rise and Features of Church Asylum," 44.

24. Gregory, "Family Shielded from Deportation in Dutch Church for Three Months Finally Granted Asylum."

25. Zauzmer and McMillan, "Sessions Cites Bible Passage."

26. Church Office of the Evangelical Church in Germany and the Secretariat of the German Bishops' Conference in co-operation with the Council of Christian Churches in Germany, 1997, in-house statement, 75.

27. German Ecumenical Committee on Church Asylum, "Welcome: German Ecumenical Committee on Church Asylum."

28. National Council of the Churches of Christ, "Immigrants, Refugees and Migrants."

29. Ibid.

30. Livni, "Does Freedom of Religion Protect Americans?"

31. "Declaration of the Participants of the 15th European Asylum Conference," 2.

32. "Visit to the Idomeni Refugee Camp." Rekowski is the highest representative of the Protestant Church in the Rhineland (EKiR) and chair of the Advisory Commission on Migration and Integration of the Evangelical Church in Germany (EKD).

33. "Flight Ban for Sea Rescuers Is an Amputation of Humanitarian Assistance."

34. National Council of the Churches of Christ, "The Churches and Immigrationl [sic]."

35. "Visit to the Idomeni Refugee Camp."

36. De Gruchy, "Dem Rad in die Speichen Fallen," 443.

Chapter Six

Adapted from a presentation and publication at Boston College, 2009.

1. Bamidar Rabbah 12:4, with added commentary by Lawrence Kushner. See Kushner, *Honey From the Rock*, 48.

2. Kook, *Essential Writings of Abraham Isaac Kook*, 1:330.

3. See, for example, Deuteronomy 12.

4. Elcott translation, here and in other biblical quotations in this chapter.

5. See "Liturgy: Daily Prayers."

6. See, for example, Mishnah Avodah Zarah 4:7 or Babylonian Talmud, Megillah 25b.

7. See Katz, *Tradition and Crisis*, chapter 4.

8. Farber, "Finding the Godliness in All Humanity."

9. Katz, *Tradition and Crisis*, 43.

10. Note that in a "first"-ever event, an address given by a rabbi—in this case, the chief rabbi of Haifa, Shear-Yashuv Cohen—to a synod of bishops could not avoid the history of Roman Catholic–Jewish relations: the church's efforts on behalf of Jews during World War II. See "Haifa Chief Rabbi at Vatican: Wartime Pope Let Jews Down."

11. For all but the Orthodox Jewish community, this blessing has either been reframed—"Blessed are you God who have made me Israel"—or removed entirely.

12. Hasit, "How Dare Rabbi Amar Call Conservative and Reform Jews Corrupt?"

13. Babylonian Talmud, Gittin 56a–b.

14. See Kifner, "Zeal of Rabin's Assassin Linked to Rabbis of the Religious Right."

15. See, for example, Tibon, "'Racist and Reprehensible.'"

16. Persico, "End Point of Zionism," 104. He argues that veneration of the Temple Mount has supplanted Kookist emphasis on the holiness of the state, which he regards as "not a *religious* revival but an ethnonational project, grasping the Temple as a symbol for Jewish sovereignty" (emphasis added).

17. Scham, "Nation That Dwells Alone," 207–15.

18. Silberstein and Cohn, *Other in Jewish Thought*, 5.

19. Ibid., 7.

20. Ibid.

21. See Deutsch, "'Borough Park Was a Red State.'"

22. Mishnah Avodah Zara 4a; Bereshit Rabbah, Bereshit 9:13.

23. Greenberg, *For the Sake of Heaven and Earth*, 43.

24. Maimonides, *Yad, Hilkhot Melakhim* 9.1.

25. These words are another way of translating Bamidar Rabbah 12:4, which was quoted near the beginning of this chapter (see note 1 above).

26. Tucker, "Can a People of the Book Also Be a People of God?," 17.

27. Zohar, 44–45. All translations in this chapter are my own.

28. Mekhilta d'Rabbi Yishmael (see also Shemot Rabbah 29:1; Pesikta Drabbati on Exodus 19).

29. Babylonian Talmud, Baba Metzia 59b.

30. Zion, *Elu v'Elu*, 19.

31. Greenberg, *For the Sake of Heaven and Earth*, 201.

32. Johnson, *Moral Imagination*, 260.

33. See Berger, "In First, Settler Who Carried Out 'Price Tag' Attacks Convicted of Membership in Terror Group"; Magid et al., "Left-Wing Activists Injured in Reported Assault by Settlers."

34. Kubovich and Landau, "Elor Azaria."

35. Ezrachi, "When Jewish Identity Meets a Modern Nation-State."

36. Kampeas, "Israeli 'Terror' Group Funded by David Friedman Blames Listing on 'Ignorance.'"

37. Elcott, *Sacred Journey*, 10–12.

38. Palestinian Talmud, Kiddushin 4:11.

39. Mishnah Avodah Zarah 2:1.

40. Babylonian Talmud, Gittin 61a.

41. Mishnah Gittin 5:9.

42. Landres and Berenbaum, *After the Passion Is Gone*, xiii, 348.

43. Levinas, *To Love the Torah More Than God*, 219, cited in Handelman, *Slayers of Moses*, 172.

44. Heschel, *Who Is Man?*, 13.

45. Batnitzky, "Dialogue as Judgment, Not Mutual Affirmation," 523–44.

Epilogue

1. Field, "Problems in Infancy."

2. Harari, introduction to *Sapiens*.

3. Haidt, "Profiles in Evolutionary Moral Psychology."

4. Snyder, *On Tyranny*, 22.

BIBLIOGRAPHY

Abington School District v. Schempp, 374 U.S. 203 (1963).

"AfD attackiert Kirchen für Einsatz in der Flüchtlingskrise." *Frankfurter Allgemeine Zeitung*, May 26, 2016. https://www.faz.net/aktuell/politik/inland/kirchentag-afd-attackiert-kirchen-fuer-einsatz-in-der-fluechtlingskrise-14253596.html.

"AfD erstmals zweitstärkste Partei nach der Union" [AfD for the first time is the second strongest party in the union]. *Die Zeit*, September 21, 2018. https://www.zeit.de/politik/deutschland/2018-09/deutschlandtrend-wahl-afd-spd-union-grosse-koalition-umfrage-horst-seehofer.

"AfD Politicians Unwanted on Catholic Day." Statement by Thomas Sternberg, president of the German Catholic Central Committee. FOCUS Online, May 25, 2016. https://www.focus.de/regional/leipzig/kirche-veranstalter-afd-politiker-auf-katholikentag-unerwuenscht_id_5566721.html.

"AfD's Gauland Plays Down Nazi Era as 'Bird Shit' in German History." Deutsche Welle, June 2, 2018. https://www.dw.com/en/afds-gauland-plays-down-nazi-era-as-a-bird-shit-in-german-history/a-44055213.

"AfD-Stellvertreter Gauland: 'Wir sind keine christliche Partei'" [We are not a Christian party]. *Frankfurter Allgemeine Zeitung*, May 24, 2016. http://www.faz.net/aktuell/politik/fluechtlingskrise/alexander-gauland-betrachtet-afd-nicht-als-christlich-14250064.html.

"AfD wandelt sich von Professoren- zur Prekariats-Partei" [AfD Is Changing from a Party of Professors to a Precariat Party]. *Die Welt*, March 21, 2016. https://www.welt.de/politik/deutschland/article153514296/AfD-wandelt-sich-von-Professoren-zur-Prekariats-Partei.html.

Agence France-Presse. "Polish Catholics Come Together at the Country's Borders, Praying to Save Poland." Public Radio International, October 7, 2017. https://www.pri.org/stories/2017-10-07/polish-catholics-come-to gether-countrys-borders-praying-save-poland.

Ahrens, P., and H. Rebenstorf. "Rechtspopulismus Unter Evangelischen Christen—Empirische Befunde der Kirchen und Religionssoziologie" [Rightwing populism under the Evangelical Church: Empirical findings from the churches and sociology of religion]. *Zeitschrift Für Evangelische Ethik* 62, no. 3 (2018): 183–99.

Alan of Lille. *The Art of Preaching*. Translated by G. R. Evans. Kalamazoo, MI: Cistercian Publications, 1981.

Albright, Madeleine. *The Mighty and the Almighty: Reflections on America, God, and World Affairs*. New York: Harper Perennial, 2007.

"Alexander Gauland bezeichnet Übergriffe in Chemnitz als normal" [Alexander Gauland Describes Violence in Chemnitz (Death Camp) as Normal]. *Die Zeit*, August 29, 2018. https://www.zeit.de/gesellschaft/zeitgeschehen /2018-08/chemnitz-alexander-gauland-ausschreitungen.

Alternative für Deutschland. *Programm für Deutschland (Alternative für Deutschland Manifesto)*. Berlin: Alternative für Deutschland, 2015.

Alternative für Deutschland. "Programm für Deutschland (Manifesto)." Berlin: Alternative für Deutschland, 2015.

Alternative für Deutschland. *Manifesto for Germany: The Political Programme of the Alternative for Germany*. Approved at the Federal Party Congress, Stuttgart, 2016. Berlin: Alternative für Deutschland, 2017. https://www .afd.de/wp-content/uploads/sites/111/2017/04/2017-04-12_afd-grundsatz programm-englisch_web.pdf.

Alternative für Deutschland Bayern. *Bayern. Aber Sicher! Wahlprogramm Landtagswahl Bayern 2018* [Bayern. Why surely! Election program for the State Election 2018]. (Bayern: Alternative für Deutschland Bayern, 2018). https://www.afdbayern.de/wahlen-2018/wahlprogramm-landtagswahl -2018/.

Alternative für Deutschland Hessen 2018. *Hessen. Aber Sicher! Wahlprogramm Landtagswahl Bayern 2018* [Hessen. Why surely! Election Program for the State Election 2018]. (Hessen: Alternative für Deutschland Hessen, 2018). https://www.afd-hessen.de/landtagswahl-2018/.

Alternative für Deutschland. *Manifesto for Germany: The Political Programme of the Alternative for Germany*. Approved at the Federal Party Congress. Berlin: Alternative für Deutschland, 2018. https://www.afd.de/grund satzprogramm-englisch/.

Alternative für Deutschland. *Bayern. Aber Sicher! Wahlprogramm Landtags wahl Bayern 2018* [Bayern. Why surely! Election program for the State Election 2018]. https://www.afdbayern.de/wahlen-2018/wahlprogramm-landtagswahl-2018/.

Amann, Melanie. *Angst für Deutschland: Die Wahrheit über die AfD* [Anxiety for Germany: The truth about the AfD]. Munich: Droemer, 2017.

Amital, Yehuda. "The Ethical Foundations of Rav Kook's Nationalist Views." Gush.net, http://gush.net/alei/2-1kook.htm.

Ammerman, N. T. "American Evangelicals in American Culture: Continuity and Change." In *Evangelicals and Democracy in America*, edited by Steven Brint and Jean R. Schroedel, vol. 1, *Religion and Society*, 44–73. New York: Russell Sage Foundation Press, 2009.

Anderson, Christopher. "Ritual Purity and Pastoral Care Reform." In *A Companion to Pastoral Care in the Late Middle Ages (1200–1500)*, edited by Ronald J. Stansbury, 23–39. Brill's Companions to the Christian Tradition 22. Leiden: Brill, 2010.

Anderson, Margaret Lavinia. *Practicing Democracy: Elections and Political Culture in Imperial Germany*. Princeton: Princeton University Press, 2000.

Appiah, Kwame A. *The Lies That Bind: Rethinking Identity, Creed, Country, Color, Class, Culture*. New York City: Liveright Publishing, 2018.

Appleby, R. Scott. *The Ambivalence of the Sacred: Religion, Violence and Reconciliation*. Lanham, MD: Rowman & Littlefield, 2000.

Arzheimer, Kai. "The AfD: Finally a Successful Right-Wing Populist Eurosceptic Party for Germany?" *West European Politics* 38, no. 3 (2015): 535–56. https://doi.org/10.1080/01402382.2015.1004230.

Arzheimer, Kai, and Elizabeth Carter. "Christian Religiosity and Voting for West European Radical Right Parties." *West European Politics* 32, no. 5 (2009): 985–1011.

Asad, Talal. "The Construction of Religion as an Anthropological Category." In *Genealogies of Religion: Discipline and Reasons of Power in Christianity and Islam*. Baltimore: Johns Hopkins University Press, 1993.

Association of Religion Data Archives. *Faith Matters Survey*. University Park: Association of Religion Data Archives, Pennsylvania State University, 2006. www.thearda.com.

"Asylum and the Rights of Refugees." International Justice Resource Center, n.d. https://ijrcenter.org/refugee-law/.

Avineri, Shlomo. "Ignored by Liberal Elites." *Haaretz*, August 1, 2019. https://www.haaretz.com/life/books/.premium-the-left-wing-case-for-nationalism-1.7603631.

Bakshi, Rajni. "A Continent Divided: Hindu Nationalism and the Challenges before Liberal Democracy in Multireligious India." Unpublished manuscript provided to authors.

Barnett, Victoria. *After Ten Years: Dietrich Bonhoeffer and Our Times*. Minneapolis: Fortress, 2016.

———. Articles for Dietrich Bonhoeffer exhibition. Washington, DC: United States Holocaust Memorial Museum, 2018. https://www.ushmm.org/information/exhibitions/online-exhibitions/special-focus/dietrich-bonhoeffer.

Batnitzky, Leora. "Dialogue as Judgment, Not Mutual Affirmation: A New Look at Franz Rosenzweig's Dialogical Philosophy." *Journal of Religion* 79, no. 4 (1999): 523–44.

Bean, Lydia. *The Politics of Evangelical Identity: Local Churches and Partisan Divides in the United States and Canada*. Princeton: Princeton University Press, 2014.

Becher, Phillip. *Der Aufstand des Abendlandes: AfD, Pegida & Co.* [The uprising of the West]. Köln: PapyRossa Verlag, 2016.

Bednarz, Liane. *Die Angstprediger: Wie rechte Christen Gesellschaft und Kirchen unterwandern* [The fear preacher: How right-wing Christians infiltrate society and churches]. Munich: Bundeszentrale für politische Bildung, 2018.

———. "Fromm und Rechts—Das Passt Zusammen" [Religious and right-wing—which fits together]. In *Alternative für Christen? Die AfD und Ihr Gespaltenes Verhältnis Zur Religion* [Alternative for Christians? The AfD and its split relationship to religion]. Index Theologicus. Neukirchen-Vluyn: Neukirchener Verlag, 2017.

Bellah, Robert. "Civil Religion in America." *Dædalus* 96, no. 1 (Winter 1967): 1–21.

Bender, Justus. "Das Dilemma der AfD" [The dilemma of the AfD]. *Frankfurter Allgemeine*, October 22, 2018. https://www.faz.net/aktuell/politik/inland/richtungsentscheidung-die-afd-politiker-im-dilemma-15851351.html.

Berger, Peter L. "Secularism in Retreat." *National Interest* 46 (Winter 1996): 3–12.

Berger, Yotam. "In First, Settler Who Carried Out 'Price Tag' Attacks Convicted of Membership in Terror Group." *Haaretz*, March 29, 2018. https://www.haaretz.com/israel-news/.premium-settler-who-carried-out-price-tag-attack-convicted-of-terror-group-1.5959079.

"Be Strong." Quotation on the website of If714.org. https://www.if714.org/alerts/be-strong/.

Bethge, Eberhard. *Dietrich Bonhoeffer: Man of Vision, Man of Courage*. New York: Harper and Row, 1970.

Betz, Hans-Georg. "Exclusionary Populism in Western Europe in the 1990s and Beyond." United Nations Research Institute for Social Development, 2004.

———. *La droite populiste en Europe: Extrême et démocrate?* [The popular right in Europe: Extremists or democratic?]. Paris: Autrement, 2004.

Betz, Hans-Georg, and Susi Meret. "Revisiting Lepanto: The Political Mobilization against Islam in Contemporary Western Europe." *Patterns of Prejudice* 43, no. 3–4 (2009): 313–34.

Blum, Lawrence. "Stereotypes and Stereotyping: A Moral Analysis." *Philosophical Papers* 33, no. 3 (2004): 251–89.

Bock, J. J. "Negotiating Cultural Difference in Dresden's Pegida Movement and Berlin's Refugee Church." Unpublished manuscript provided to the authors.

Böckenförde, Ernst-Wolfgang. "Die Entstehung des Staates als Vorgang der Säkularisation" [The emergence of the state as a process of secularization]. In *Recht, Staat, Freiheit: Studien zur Rechtsphilosophie, Staatstheorie und Verfassungsgeschichte* [Law, state, freedom: Studies on legal philosophy, state theory, and constitutional history], 92–114. Frankfurt am Main: Suhrkamp, 1991.

———. *Staat, Verfassung, Demokratie: Studien zur Verfassungstheorie und zum Verfassungsrecht* [State, constitution, democracy: Studies on constitutional theory and constitutional law]. Frankfurt am Main: Suhrkamp, 1991.

Bokenkotter, Thomas. *Church and Revolution: Catholics in the Struggle for Democracy and Social Justice*. New York: Doubleday, 1998.

Bonhoeffer, Dietrich. *The Cost of Discipleship*. New York: Macmillan, 1966.

Bornschier, Simon. *Cleavage Politics and the Populist Right: The New Cultural Conflict in Western Europe*. Philadelphia: Temple University Press, 2010.

———. "Why a Right-Wing Populist Party Emerged in France but Not in Germany: Cleavages and Actors in the Formation of a New Cultural Divide." *European Political Science Review* 4, no. 1 (2010): 121–45.

Braunstein, Ruth, and Malaena J. Taylor. "Is the Tea Party a 'Religious' Movement? Religiosity in the Tea Party versus the Religious Right." *Sociology of Religion* 78, no. 1 (2017): 33–59.

Brint, Steven, and Jean Schroedel, eds. *Evangelicals and Democracy in America*. Vol. 1. New York: Russell Sage Foundation Press, 2009.

Brown, D. L. *Donald Trump Is Not My Savior: An Evangelical Leader Speaks His Mind about the Man He Supports as President.* Shippensburg, PA: Destiny Image, 2018.

Brown-Dean, Khalilah L. *Identity Politics in the United States.* Cambridge: Polity Press, 2019.

Brubaker, Rogers. "Between Nationalism and Civilizationism: The European Populist Movement in Comparative Perspective." *Ethnic and Racial Studies* 40, no. 8 (2017): 1191–1226.

Buckley, Madeleine. "Notable Christians Who've Had a Change of Heart on LGBT Issues." Religion News, July 12, 2017. https://religionnews.com /2017/07/12/notable-christians-whove-had-a-change-of-heart-on-lgbt -issues/.

Bunderson, Carl, and Matthew A. Rarey. "Archbishop Chaput: Be Catholic before You Are Democrat or Republican." *Catholic News Agency*, October 25, 2012. https://www.catholicnewsagency.com/news/archbishop -chaput-be-catholic-before-you-are-democrat-or-republican.

Bundestagswahl. Forschungsgruppe Wahlen e.V., September 24, 2017. http:// www.forschungsgruppe.de/Wahlen/Wahlanalysen/Newsl_Bund_170928 .pdf.

Burwell v. Hobby Lobby Stores, Inc., 573 U.S. 682 (2014).

Bushman, Richard L. *From Puritan to Yankee: Character and the Social Order in Connecticut, 1690–1765.* Cambridge, MA: Harvard University Press, 1980.

Campbell, D. E. "Religious 'Threat' in Contemporary Presidential Elections." *Journal of Politics* 68, no. 1 (2006): 104–15.

Carper, James C., and Thomas C. Hunt, eds. *The Praeger Handbook of Religion and Education in the United States.* Westport, CT: Praeger, 2009.

Carse, James. *Finite and Infinite Games.* New York: Free Press, 1986.

Carson, D. A. *Christ and Culture Revisited.* Grand Rapids: Eerdmans, 2008.

Cary Noel. *The Path to Christian Democracy: German Catholics and the Party System from Windthorst to Adenauer.* Cambridge, MA: Harvard University Press, 1996.

Casad, Bettina J., and William J. Bryant. "Addressing Stereotype Threat Is Critical to Diversity and Inclusion in Organizational Psychology." *Frontiers in Psychology* 7, no. 8 (2016).

Casanova, José. "The Politics of Nativism." *Philosophy & Social Criticism* 38, no. 4–5 (2012): 485–95.

———. *Public Religions in the Modern World.* Chicago: University of Chicago Press, 1994.

Case, Anne, and Angus Deaton. "Mortality and Morbidity in the 21st Century." *Brookings Papers on Economic Activity*, Spring 2017. https://www.brookings.edu/bpea-articles/mortality-and-morbidity-in-the-21st-century/.

Catechism of the Catholic Church. 2nd ed. Vatican City: Libreria Editrice Vaticana, 1997.

Cavanaugh, William T. "Telling the Truth about Ourselves: Torture and Eucharist in the U.S. Popular Imagination." *The Other Journal*, no. 15, *Aesthetics* (2009). https://theotherjournal.com/2009/05/08/telling-the-truth-about-ourselves-torture-and-eucharist-in-the-u-s-popular-imaginat/.

Chandler, Adam. "Why American Jews Eat Chinese Food on Christmas." *Atlantic*, December 23, 2014. https://www.theatlantic.com/national/archive/2014/12/why-american-jews-eat-chinese-food-on-christmas/384011/.

Chaudhury, Dipanjan Roy. "OHCHR Has Filed Petitions to Become Amicus Curiae in Europe and America Too." *Economic Times*, last updated March 5, 2020. https://economictimes.indiatimes.com/news/politics-and-nation/ohchr-has-filed-petitions-in-europe-and-america-too/articleshow/74484783.cms.

Christerson, Brad, and Richard Flory. "Rick Perry's Belief That Trump Was Chosen by God Is Shared by Many in a Fast-Growing Christian Movement." YubaNet.com, December 2, 2019. https://yubanet.com/usa/rick-perrys-belief-that-trump-was-chosen-by-god-is-shared-by-many-in-a-fast-growing-christian-movement/.

Clark, J. C. D. "Protestantism, Nationalism, and National Identity, 1660–1832." *Historical Journal* 43, no. 1 (March 2000): 249–76.

Clarke, Harold D., Matthew Goodwin, and Paul Whiteley. "Why Britain Voted for Brexit: An Individual-Level Analysis of the 2016 Referendum Vote." *Parliamentary Affairs* 70, no. 3 (2017): 439–64.

Clayton, Cornell W., and Richard Elgar. *Civility and Democracy in America: A Reasonable Understanding*. Pullman: Washington State University Press, 2012.

Cleuziou, Yann Raison du. "Sens commun: Un combat conservateur entre deux fronts" [Common meaning: A conservative fight on two fronts]. *Le Débat* 2 (2018): 105–14.

Clymer, Kenton J. "Religion and American Imperialism: Methodist Missionaries in the Philippine Islands, 1899–1913." *Pacific Historical Review* 49, no. 1 (February 1980): 29–50.

Coles, Robert. *The Call of Stories*. Boston: Houghton Mifflin, 1989.

Corbett, Michael, and Julia Corbett. *Politics and Religion in the United States*. New York: Garland, 1999.

Coulter, Dale M. "Evangelical Identity and Its Crises." *First Things*, November 30, 2017. https://www.firstthings.com/web-exclusives/2017/11/evangeli cal-identity-and-its-crises.

———. "Evangelical Identity in an Age of Trump." *First Things*, January 2, 2018. https://www.firstthings.com/web-exclusives/2018/01/evangeli cal-identity-in-an-age-of-trump.

Coury, D. "A Clash of Civilizations? Pegida and the Rise of Cultural Nationalism." *German Politics and Society* 34, no. 4 (2016): 54–67.

Cremer, Tobias. "Defenders of the Faith: Why Right-Wing Populists Are Embracing Religion." *New Statesman*, May 20, 2018.

———. "The Resistance of the Protestant Church in Nazi Germany and Its Relevance for Contemporary Politics." *Review of Faith & International Affairs* 17, no. 4 (2019): 36–47. https://doi.org/10.1080/15570274.2019.168 1728.

Crowley, Michael. "The Man Who Wants to Unmake the West." *Politico*, March/April 2017. https://www.politico.com/magazine/story/2017/03 /trump-steve-bannon-destroy-eu-european-union-214889.

Crowley, Sharon. *Toward a Civil Discourse*. Pittsburgh: University of Pittsburgh Press, 2006.

"Culture War over German Identity: Religious Symbols Take Center Stage." *Der Spiegel*, March 5, 2018. http://www.spiegel.de/international/germany /religious-symbols-at-heart-of-german-search-for-identity-a-1205572 .html.

Daenekindt, Stign, Willem de Koster, and Jeroen van der Waal. "How People Organise Cultural Attitudes: Cultural Belief Systems and the Populist Radical Right." *West European Politics* 40, no. 4 (2017): 791–811.

D'Antonio, William. *Laity, American and Catholic: Transforming the Church*. Kansas City: Sheed & Ward, 1996.

Dargent, C. "Les catholiques français et le Front national." *Études* 12 (2016): 19–30.

Day, Abby. *Believing in Belonging*. Oxford: Oxford University Press, 2011.

"Declaration of the Participants of the 15th European Asylum Conference." Statement of participants of the 15th European Asylum Conference, October 15–20, 2018, Chios and Athens, Greece. Churches' Commission for Migrants in Europe. N.d. https://ccme.eu/wp-content/uploads/2018/11 /2018-10-22_15th_European_asylum_Conference_declaration_final.pdf.

de Gruchy, J. W. "Dem Rad in die Speichen Fallen: Das Politische in der Theologie Dietrich Bonhoeffers" [A Spoke in the Wheel: The Political in the Theology of Dietrich Bonhoeffer]. In *Christianity, Democracy and New*

Realities: Bonhoeffer's Political Witness Then and Now, edited by Kirsten Busch Nielsen, Ralf K. Wüstenberg, and Jens Zimmermann, 432–44. Gütersloh: Gütersloher Verlagshaus, 2017.

de Koster, Willem, Peter Achterberg, Jeroen van der Waal, Samira Van Bohemen and Roy Kemmers. "Progressiveness and the New Right: The Electoral Relevance of Culturally Progressive Values in the Netherlands," *West European Politics* 37, no. 3 (2014): 584–604.

Deutsch, Nathaniel. "'Borough Park Was a Red State': Trump and the Haredi Vote." *Jewish Social Studies* 22, no. 3 (Spring/Summer 2017): 158–73.

Deutsche Bischofskonferenz. "Bischöfe: AfD nicht mit christlichem Glauben vereinbar." *Frankfurter Allgemeine Zeitung*, March 3, 2017. https://www.faz.net/aktuell/politik/inland/katholische-bischoefe-distanzieren-sich-von-der-afd-14917396.html.

"Deutschen werden christliche Wurzeln wichtiger" [Christianity remains for Germans ever more important]. *Frankfurter Allgemeine Zeitung*, December 19, 2017. http://www.faz.net/aktuell/politik/inland/christentum-wird-den-deutschen-immer-wichtiger-15350350.html.

Deutscher Bundestag. *Datenhandbuch Deutscher Bundestag*, Stand 15.12.2017 (2017).

de Vogue, Araine. "Supreme Court Keeps Mojave Cross Case Alive." ABC News, April 28, 2010. https://abcnews.go.com/Politics/Supreme_Court/supreme-court-refuses-ban-mojave-cross/story?id=9536679.

de Wilde, Peter, Ruud Koopmans, Wolfgang Merkel, Oliver Strijbis, and Michael Zürn, eds. *The Struggle over Borders: A Political Sociology of Cosmopolitanism and Communitarianism*. Cambridge: Cambridge University Press, 2019.

Dias, Elizabeth, and Jeremy W. Peters. "Evangelical Leaders Close Ranks with Trump after Scathing Editorial." *New York Times*, December 20, 2019. https://www.nytimes.com/2019/12/20/us/politics/christianity-today-trump-evangelicals.html.

Dickinson, John. *Pennsylvania Journal*, May 12, 1768. Reprinted in *The Founders on Religion*, edited by James H. Huston, 60–61. Princeton: Princeton University Press, 2005.

"Die Kirchen in Deutschland schrumpfen" [The churches in Germany are shrinking]. *Frankfurter Allgemeine Zeitung*, July 20, 2018. http://www.faz.net/aktuell/politik/inland/austritte-aus-der-kirche-nimmt-in-deutschland-weiter-zu-15700450.html.

Dockery, Wesley. "Two Years Since Germany Opened Its Borders to Refugees: A Chronology." *Deutsche Welle*, September 4, 2017. https://www.dw.com

/en/two-years-since-germany-opened-its-borders-to-refugees-a-chro
nology/a-40327634.

"Does the AfD Belong to the Catholic Day?" *Die Zeit*, May 25, 2016.
https://www.zeit.de/2016/23/leipzig-afd-katholikentag-streitgespraech.

"Do Not Diminish Refugee Protection." Statement by church president
Rekowski, June 20, 2018. Evangilische Kirche im Rheinland. https://www
.ekd.de/en/do-not-diminish-refugee-protection-1260.htm.

Dostal, J. M. "The German Federal Election of 2017: How the Wedge Issue of
Refugees and Migration Took the Shine off Chancellor Merkel and Transformed the Party System." *The Political Quarterly* 88, no. 4 (2017): 589–
602.

Douglas, Mary. *Purity and Danger*. London: Routledge, 2010.

"Dresdner Frauenkirche macht wegen Pegida das Licht aus" [The Frauenkirche
turns the lights out on Pegida]. FOCUS Online, February 9, 2015. https://
www.focus.de/regional/dresden/demonstrationen-dresdner-frauenkirche
-macht-wegen-pegida-das-licht-aus_id_4463244.html.

Eatwell, Roger, and Matthew Goodwin. *National Populism: The Revolt against
Liberal Democracy*. London: Pelican Books, 2018.

Elcott, David. *A Sacred Journey*. Northvale, NJ: Jason Aronson, 1995.

———. "Why Evangelicals Are Okay with Voting for Roy Moore." *The Conversation*, December 11, 2017. http://theconversation.com/why-evangeli
cals-are-ok-with-voting-for-roy-moore-88920.

Elcott, David, and Andrew Sinclair. "Flexibility in American Religious Life:
An Exploration of Loyalty and Purity." *Society of Policy Sciences* 50, no. 4
(2017): 649–73.

"Election Analysis, 2005." *Election Analysis*. 2018 edition. Sankt Augus-
tin, Germany: Konrad Adenauer Stiftung, 2018. https://www.kas.de/web
/wahlen.kas.de/wahlanalysen.

Elman, Miriam F. "Does Democracy Tame the Radicals? Lessons from Israel's
Jewish Religious Political Parties." *Asian Security* 4, no. 1, *Faith and Security: The Effects of Democracy on Religious Political Parties* (2008): 79–99.

Emont, Jonathan. "Islamic Intolerance Poses a Growing Threat to Indonesia's
Minorities." *Time*, April 20, 2016. http://time.com/4298767/indonesia
-intolerance-muslim-islamist-minorities-lgbt-christians-hardliners/.

Erlanger, Steve. "Sweden Was Long Seen as a 'Moral Superpower.' That May Be
Changing." *New York Times*, September 3, 2018. https://www.nytimes
.com/2018/09/03/world/europe/sweden-election-populism.html.

Evans, John H. "Where Is the Counterweight? Explorations of the Decline in
Mainline Protestant Participation in Public Debates over Values." In *Evan-*

gelicals and Democracy in America, edited by Steven Brint and Jean R. Schroedel, vol. 1, *Religion and Society*, 221–48. New York City: Russell Sage Foundation Press, 2009.

Everson v. Board of Education. 330 U.S. 1 (1947).

Ezrachi, Elan. "When Jewish Identity Meets a Modern Nation-State: A Challenge for Democracy." Unpublished manuscript provided to authors September 2018.

Farber, Seth. "Finding the Godliness in All Humanity." Unpublished manuscript provided to authors February 2019.

Feldman, Brian. "Megyn Kelly Assures Everyone That Santa Is White Even Though Santa Does Not Exist." *Atlantic*, December 12, 2013. https://www .theatlantic.com/culture/archive/2013/12/megyn-kelly-assures-everyone -santa-white-even-though-he-does-not-exist/356054/.

Field, Tiffany. "Problems in Infancy." In *Handbook of Clinical Psychology*, vol. 2, *Children*, edited by Michael Hersen and Alan M. Gross, 966–1011. Hoboken, NJ: John Wiley & Sons, 2008.

Fisher, Claude S., and Michael Hout. "Explaining Why More Americans Have No Religious Preference: Political Backlash and Generational Succession, 1987–2012." *Sociological Science* 1 (2014): 423–47. https://www.sociologi calscience.com/download/volume%201/october/SocSci_v1_423to447.pdf.

Flannery, Austin, and P. P. Northport. *Basic Sixteen Documents, Vatican II Constitutions, Decrees, Declarations*. Northport, NY: Costello Publishing, 1996.

Fleishman, Fenella, and Karen Phalet. "Religion and National Identification in Europe: Comparing Muslim Youth in Belgium, England, Germany, the Netherlands, and Sweden." *Journal of Cross-Cultural Psychology* 49, no. 1 (January 2018): 44–61.

"Flight Ban for Sea Rescuers Is an Amputation of Humanitarian Assistance." Evangelische Kirche im Rheinland, July 17, 2018. http://en.ekir.de/flight -ban-386.php.

Foster, Greg. *The Contested Public Square: The Crisis of Christianity and Politics*. Downers Grove, IL: IVP Academic, 2008.

Fourquet, Jérôme. *À la droite de Dieu: Le réveil identitaire des catholiques* [To the right of God: The identity awakening of Catholics]. Paris: Cerf, 2018.

———. *L'archipel français: Naissance d'une nation multiple et divisée* [The French archipelago: Birth of a multiple and divided nation]. Paris: Editions du Seuil, 2019.

Fox, Jonathan. *An Introduction to Religion and Politics*. New York: Routledge, 2015.

Frank, Arno. "God's Right Hand." *Der Spiegel*, September 14, 2017. http://www.spiegel.de/kultur/tv/wahre-christen-oder-boese-hetzer-doku-ueber-afd-und-katholische-kirche-a-1167482.html.

Frank, Thomas. *What's the Matter with Kansas? How Conservatives Won the Heart of America*. New York: Henry Holt, 2005.

Friedman, Howard. "2016 Republican Platform on Religious Liberty." *Religion Clause* (blog), July 19, 2016. http://religionclause.blogspot.com/2016/07/2016-republican-platform-on-religious.html.

Fukuyama, Francis. "The End of History?" *National Interest* 16, no. 3 (1989): 1–18. https://www.embl.de/aboutus/science_society/discussion/discussion_2006/ref1-22june06.pdf.

———. *Identity: The Demand for Dignity and the Politics of Resentment*. New York: Farrar, Straus and Giroux, 2018.

Gebhardt, R. "Eine 'Partei neuen Typs'? Die Alternative für Deutschland" [A new type of party? The AfD]. *Forschungsjournal Soziale Bewegungen* 26, no. 3 (2016): 86–91.

Gelman, Susan A. "Psychological Essentialism in Children." *Trends in Cognitive Sciences* 8, no. 9 (2004): 404–9.

General Social Survey. Chicago: NORC at the University of Chicago, 2014. http://www.norc.org/Research/Projects/Pages/general-social-survey.aspx.

Gerbner, Katharine. *Christian Slavery: Conversion and Race in the Protestant Atlantic World*. Philadelphia: University of Pennsylvania Press, 2018.

German Ecumenical Committee on Church Asylum. "Welcome: German Ecumenical Committee on Church Asylum." N.d. https://www.kirchenasyl.de/herzlich-willkommen/welcome/.

Gessen, Masha. "How Trump Uses 'Religious Liberty' to Attack L.G.B.T. Rights." *New Yorker*, October 11, 2017. https://www.newyorker.com/news/news-desk/how-trump-uses-religious-liberty-to-attack-lgbt-rights.

Gidda, Mirren. "Death in India: Hindu Vigilantes Are Attacking Muslims in the Name of Protecting Cows." *Newsweek*, October 12, 2017. https://www.newsweek.com/2017/10/20/hindu-vigilantes-attack-muslims-protect-cows-modi-683623.html.

Glatz, Carol. "'The Joy of the Gospel': Our Top Pics of Quotable Quotes." Catholic News Service, November 26, 2013. https://cnsblog.wordpress.com/2013/11/26/the-joy-of-the-gospel-our-top-picks-of-quotable-quotes/.

"God in the White House." WGBH Educational Foundation, October 11, 2010. https://www.pbs.org/wgbh/pages/frontline/godinamerica/god-in-the-white-house/.

Goldman, Russell. "Pastors Challenge Law, Endorse Candidates from Pulpit." ABC News, June 23, 2008. https://abcnews.go.com/Politics/Vote2008/story ?id=5198068&page=1.

Gollwitzer, Helmut. "A Sermon about *Kristallnacht*." In *Preaching in Hitler's Shadow: Sermons of Resistance in the Third Reich*, edited by Dean G. Stroud, 115–26. Grand Rapids, MI: Eerdmans, 2013.

Goodhart, David. *The Road to Somewhere: The Populist Revolt and the Future of Politics*. London: Penguin, 2017.

Goodnight, Ethan. "William Apess, Pequot Pastor: A Native American Revisioning of Christian Nationalism in the Early Republic." *Religions* 8, no. 2 (2017): 18–34.

Gorski, P. S. "Conservative Protestantism in the United States? Toward a Comparative and Historical Perspective." In *Evangelicals and Democracy in America*, edited by Steven Brint and Jean R. Schroedel, vol. 1, *Religion and Society*, 74–114. New York: Russell Sage Foundation Press, 2009.

Graf, Friedrich Wilhelm. *Der Protestantismus: Geschichte und Gegenwart* [Protestantism: History and Presence]. Munich: Beck, 2006.

Graham, Jesse, Jonathan Haidt, Sena Koleva, Matt Motyl, Ravi Iyer, Sean P. Wojcik, and Peter H. Ditto. "Moral Foundations Theory: The Pragmatic Validity of Moral Pluralism." Social Science Research Network, December 4, 2012. https://papers.ssrn.com/sol3/papers.cfm?abstract_id=218 4440.

Greek Orthodox Archdiocese of America. "Response to Racist Violence in Charlottesville, VA." 2017. https://www.goarch.org/-/response-to-racist -violence-in-charlottesville-va.

Green, Clifford. "Christus in Mundo, Christus Pro Mundo: Bonhoeffer's Foundations for a New Christian Paradigm." In *Bonhoeffer, Religion and Politics: Fourth International Bonhoeffer Colloquium*, edited by Christiane Tietz and Jens Zimmermann, 11–36. International Bonhoeffer Interpretations 4. Frankfurt am Main: Peter Lang, 2012.

Green, John C. "Exploring the Traditionalist Alliance: Evangelical Protestants, Religious Voters, and the Republican Presidential Vote." In *Evangelicals and Democracy in America*, edited by Steven Brint and Jean R. Schroedel, vol. 1, *Religion and Society*, 117–58. New York City: Russell Sage Foundation Press, 2009.

Green, Steven K. *Inventing a Christian America: The Myth of the Religious Founding*. Oxford: Oxford University Press, 2015.

———. *The Separation of Church and State in the United States*. Oxford: Oxford University Press, 2014.

Greenberg, Irving. *For the Sake of Heaven and Earth: The New Encounter between Judaism and Christianity.* Philadelphia: Jewish Publication Society, 2004.

———. "Seeking the Religious Roots of Pluralism: In the Image of God and Covenant." *Journal of Ecumenical Studies* 34, no. 3 (Summer 1997): 385–93.

Greenwald, Glenn. "Glenn Greenwald: I Was Assaulted Live on Air. This Is Bolsonaro's Brazil." *New York Times*, November 25, 2019. https://www
.nytimes.com/2019/11/25/opinion/glenn-greenwald-bolsonaro-brazi
l.html?action=click&module=MoreInSection&pgtype=Article&region
=Footer&contentCollection=Opinion.

Gregory, Andy. "Family Shielded from Deportation in Dutch Church for Three Months Finally Granted Asylum." *Independent,* January 31, 2019. https://www.independent.co.uk/news/world/dutch-church-family-de
portation-granted-asylum-tamrazyan-netherlands-bethel-a8754416.html.

Gregory XVI. *Mirari Vos.* Encyclical. 1832. Vatican website. http://w2.vatican
.va/content/gregorius-xvi/it/documents/encyclica-mirari-vos-15-augusti
-1832.html.

Griffith, R. Marie, and Melanie McAlister, eds. *Religion and Politics in the Contemporary United States.* Baltimore: Johns Hopkins University Press, 2008.

Gruber, Hubert. *Katholische Kirche und Nationalsozialismus, 1930–1945* [The Catholic Church and Nazism]. Paderborn: Schöningh, 2005.

Grudem, Wayne. *Politics according to the Bible: A Comprehensive Resource for Understanding Modern Political Issues in the Light of Scripture.* Grand Rapids, MI: Zondervan Academic, 2010.

Grynbaum, Michael M. "After Another Year of Trump Attacks, 'Ominous Signs' for the American Press." *New York Times*, December 30, 2019. https://www.nytimes.com/2019/12/30/business/media/trump-med
ia-2019.html.

Guerra, Darren. "Donald Trump and the Evangelical 'Crisis.'" *First Things,* January 5, 2018. https://www.firstthings.com/web-exclusives/2018/01
/donald-trump-and-the-evangelical-crisis.

Haidt, Jonathan. "Profiles in Evolutionary Moral Psychology: Jonathan Haidt." Interview by Michael Price. Evolution Institute, October 29, 2013. https://evolution-institute.org/profiles-in-evolutionary-moral-psychology
-jonathan-haidt/.

———. *The Righteous Mind: Why Good People Are Divided by Politics and Religion.* New York: Pantheon, 2012.

"Haifa Chief Rabbi at Vatican: Wartime Pope Let Jews Down." *Haaretz*, July 10, 2008.

Halasz, Stephanie, Nadine Schmidt, and Ivana Kottasová. "Two More Suspects Arrested after Far-Right Supporter Confesses to Killing German Pro-immigration Politician." CNN, June 27, 2019. https://www.cnn.com/2019 /06/26/europe/germany-lubcke-murder-confession-grm-intl/index.html.

Handelman, Susan A. *The Slayers of Moses*. Albany: State University of New York Press, 1982.

Harari, Yuval N. *Sapiens: A Brief History of Humankind*. New York: Harper Perennial, 2015.

———. "Nationalism vs. Globalism: The New Political Divide." TED Talk. February 2017. https://www.ted.com/talks/yuval_noah_harari_nationalism _vs_globalism_the_new_political_divide.

Harper, Lisa Sharon. *Evangelical Does Not Equal Republican—or Democrat*. New York: The New Press, 2008.

Hasit, Arie. "How Dare Rabbi Amar Call Conservative and Reform Jews Corrupt?" *Haaretz*, June 26, 2012. https://www.haaretz.com/jewish/who-are -you-calling-corrupt-rabbi-amar-1.5190848.

Hauschild, W. D. "Kontinuität im Wandel: Die Evangelische Kirche in Deutschland und die sog. 68er Bewegung" [Continuity and Change: The Evangelical Church in Germany]. In *1968 und die Kirchen*, ed. Bernd Hey and Volkmar Wittmütz, 35–54. Bielefeld: Verlag für Regionalgeschichte, 1969.

Hawley, George. *Making Sense of the Alt-Right*. New York: Columbia University Press, 2017.

Heimbach-Steins, Marianne, and Alexander Filipović. *Grundpositionen der Partei "Alternative Für Deutschland" und der Katholischen Soziallehre im Vergleich* [A comparison of the core positions of the AfD Party and the Catholic ministry]. Münster: WMU, 2017.

Heller, Nathan. "The Structure of Equality: A Philosopher Investigates What Makes Us Free." *New Yorker*, January 7, 2019. Available online as "The Philosopher Redefining Equality." https://www.newyorker.com/magazine /2019/01/07/the-philosopher-redefining-equality.

Helson, Harry, Robert R. Blake, and Jane Srygley Mouton. "An Experimental Investigation of the Effectiveness of the 'Big Lie' in Shifting Attitudes." *Journal of Social Psychology* 48 (1958): 51–60.

Henderson, Katharine. "Christianity as the Antidote to Christian Nationalism." Unpublished manuscript provided to authors February 2019.

———. "Attorney General Sessions Task Force Is a Tool for Division: Statement of Auburn Seminary President Katharine R. Henderson." Auburn

Seminary, July 31, 2018. https://auburnseminary.org/press/religious
-liberty-task-force-division/.

Heschel, Abraham J. *Who Is Man?* Stanford, CA: Stanford University Press,
1965.

Hjelm, Titus, ed. *Is God Back? Reconsidering the New Visibility of Religion.*
London: Bloomsbury T&T Clark, 2015.

Hochschild, Arlie. *Strangers in Their Own Land: Anger and Mourning on the
American Right.* New York: The New Press, 2016.

Hockenos, Paul. "Poland and the Uncontrollable Fury of Europe's Far Right."
Atlantic, November 15, 2017. https://www.theatlantic.com/international
/archive/2017/11/europe-far-right-populist-nazi-poland/524559/.

Höhne, Valerie, and Peter Wensierski. "Neue rechte Allianz: AfD auf dem
Kreuzzug." *Der Spiegel,* July 18, 2017. http://www.spiegel.de/spiegel
/fromme-christen-und-rechte-waehler-verbuenden-sich-im-widerstand
-a-1158077.html.

"Hungarian PM Sees Shift to Illiberal Christian Democracy in 2019 European
Vote." Reuters, July 28, 2018. https://uk.reuters.com/article/uk-hungary
-Orbán/hungarian-pm-sees-shift-to-illiberal-christian-democracy-in
-2019-european-vote-idUKKBN1KI0BY.

"Hurricane Gus Update: Church Politicking Scheme Is Category 4 Threat to
American Democracy." *Wall of Separation Blog,* September 26, 2008.
Americans United for Separation of Church and State. https://www.au.org
/blogs/wall-of-separation/hurricane-gus-update-church-politicking
-scheme-is-category-4-threat-to.

"An Ideal Place to Retire." BestPlaces. https://www.bestplaces.net/religion
/city/west_virginia/charleston.

Immerzeel, Tim, Eva Jaspers, and Marcel Lubbers. "Religion as Catalyst or
Restraint of Radical Right Voting?" *West European Politics* 36, no. 5 (2013):
946–68.

Immigration to the United States, 1789–1930 [digital collection of historical ma-
terials]. Harvard Library, Harvard University. http://ocp.hul.harvard.edu
/immigration/restrictionleague.html.

Isenberg, Nancy A. *White Trash: The 400-Year Untold History of Class in
America.* New York: Viking, 2016.

"Is Poland a Failing Democracy?" A symposium of leading thinkers, politicians, and policymakers. *Politico,* last updated January 26, 2016. https://
www.politico.eu/article/poland-democracy-failing-pis-law-and-justice
-media-rule-of-law/.

John Paul II. "Message for the 85th World Immigration Day." Vatican website, 1999. https://w2.vatican.va/content/john-paul-ii/en/messages/migration /documents/hf_jp-ii_mes_22021999_world-migration-day-1999.html.

Johnson, Mark. *Moral Imagination: Implications of Cognitive Science for Ethics.* Chicago: University of Chicago Press, 1993.

Johnson, William S. *A Time to Embrace: Same-Sex Relationships in Religion, Law, and Politics.* Grand Rapids, MI: Eerdmans, 2012.

Just, W. D. "The Rise and Features of Church Asylum in Germany: 'I Will Take Refuge in the Shadow of Thy Wings Until the Storms Are Past.'" In *Sanctuary Practices in International Perspectives: Migration, Citizenship and Social Movements*, edited by Randy K. Lippert and Sean Rehaag, 135–47. New York: Routledge, 2014.

Justice, Jessilyn, and Taylor Berglund. "Trump, Palin Challenge ORU Students to Launch 'Great Awakening.'" *Charisma News*, January 20, 2016. https:// www.charismanews.com/politics/54595-trump-palin-challenge-oru -students-to-launch-great-awakening.

Kaiser, Wolfram, and Helmut Wohnout, eds. *Political Catholicism in Europe, 1918–45.* Vol. 1. London: Routledge, 2004.

Kalyvas, Stathis N., and Kees van Kersbergen. "Christian Democracy." *Annual Review of Political Science* 13, no. 1 (2010): 183–209.

Kampeas, Ron. "Israeli 'Terror' Group Funded by David Friedman Blames Listing on 'Ignorance.'" *Forward*, May 14, 2018. https://forward.com /news/breaking-news/401010/leader-of-group-that-received-money -from-charity-headed-by-david-friedman/.

Kaplan, Esther. *With God on Their Side.* New York: The New Press, 2004.

"Katholiken-Präsident stuft AfD als rechtsradikal ein" [Catholic president classifies AfD as right-wing radical]. *Frankfurter Allgemeine Zeitung*, September 8, 2018. http://www.faz.net/aktuell/politik/inland/nach-chemnitz -katholiken-praesident-stuft-afd-als-rechtsradikal-ein-15777609.html.

Katz, Jacob. *Tradition and Crisis.* New York: New York University Press, 1993.

Kaufmann, Eric. "Immigration and White Identity in the West." *Foreign Affairs*, September 8, 2017. https://www.foreignaffairs.com/articles/united -states/2017-09-08/immigration-and-white-identity-west.

———. *Whiteshift: Populism, Immigration, and the Future of White Majorities.* London: Penguin, 2018.

"Kein religiöses Symbol?" [No religious symbols?]. *Bayerische Staatszeitung*, April 24, 2018. https://www.bayerische-staatszeitung.de/staatszeitung /politik/detailansicht-politik/artikel/kein-religioeses-symbol.html.

Kifner, John. "Zeal of Rabin's Assassin Linked to Rabbis of the Religious Right." *New York Times*, November 12, 1995. https://www.nytimes.com /1995/11/12/world/zeal-of-rabin-s-assassin-linked-to-rabbis-of-the-reli gious-right.html.

Kniss, Fred, and Paul D. Numrich. *Sacred Assemblies and Civic Engagement: How Religion Matters for America's Newest Immigrants*. Piscataway, NJ: Rutgers University Press, 2007.

Koch, Anne. "Introduction: Revisiting Civil Religion from an Aesthetic Point of View." *Journal of Religion in Europe* 10, no. 1–2 (2017): 1–15.

Kook, Abraham. *The Essential Writings of Abraham Isaac Kook*. Edited and translated by Ben Zion Bokser. Teaneck, NJ: Ben Yehuda Press, 2006.

Kraetzer, Ulrich. "AfD legt sich mit der evangelischen Kirche an." *Berliner Morgenpost*, October 29, 2016. https://www.morgenpost.de/berlin/article 208608251/AfD-legt-sich-mit-der-evangelischen-Kirche-an.html.

Krastev, Ivan. *After Europe*. Philadelphia: University of Pennsylvania Press, 2017.

Krause, Christian. "Christliche Symbole bei Pegida-Demo 'pervers.'" [Christian symbols by Pegida are perverse]. *Die Welt*, January 5, 2015. https:// www.welt.de/regionales/nrw/article136026490/Christliche-Symbole -bei-Pegida-Demo-pervers.html.

Krings, Günter. "Von strikter Trennung zu wohlwollender Neutralität—Staat und Kirche in Den Vereinigten Staaten und die gewandelte Auslegung der Religious Clauses der US-Verfassung" [From strict separation to benevolent neutrality: State and church in the United States and the changed interpretation of the Religion Clause in the US Constitution]. In *Zeitschrift für Evangelisches Kirchenrecht*, no. 45 (2000): 505–57.

Kubovich, Yaniv, and Noa Landau. "Elor Azaria, Israeli Soldier Convicted of Killing a Wounded Palestinian Terrorist, Set Free after Nine Months." *Haaretz*, August 5, 2018. https://www.haaretz.com/israel-news/.premium -hebron-shooter-elor-azaria-released-from-prison-after-nine-months -1.6070371.

Kushner, Lawrence. *Honey from the Rock*. Woodstock, VT: Jewish Lights, 1995.

Kuzmany, Stefan. "Mit Verachtung" [With contempt]. *Der Spiegel*, April 28, 2017. http://www.spiegel.de/kultur/tv/sandra-maischberger-ueber-popu listen-nur-verachtung-uebrig-a-1089692.html.

Ladd, Chris. "Pastors, Not Politicians, Turned Dixie Republican." *Forbes*, March 27, 2017. https://www.forbes.com/sites/chrisladd/2017/03/27/pas tors-not-politicians-turned-dixie-republican/#5c6e00b695fc.

Lam, Athena. "Religion in the EU: Only Germany Is Getting More Religious." Dalia Research, March 8, 2017. https://daliaresearch.com/religion-in-the -eu-young-germans-more-religious-than-old/.

Landres, J. Shawn, and Michael Berenbaum, eds. *After the Passion Is Gone: American Religious Consequences.* Walnut Creek, CA: AltaMira, 2005.

Larsen, Timothy. "No Christianity Please, We're Academics." *Inside Higher Ed*, June 30, 2010. https://www.insidehighered.com/views/2010/07/30/no -christianity-please-were-academics.

Laycock, Douglas, Anthony R. Picarello Jr., and Robin F. Wilson. *Same-Sex Marriage and Religious Liberty: Emerging Conflicts.* Lanham, MD: Rowman & Littlefield, 2008.

Lease, Mary Elizabeth. "History Is a Weapon." Speech to Women's Christian Temperance Union, 1890. http://www.historyisaweapon.org/defcon1/mary lease2.html.

Lees, Charles. "The 'Alternative for Germany' (AfD): The Rise of Right-Wing Populism at the Heart of Europe." *Politics* 38, no. 3 (2006): 295–310.

Leithart, Peter J. "A Better Christian Nationalism." *First Things*, June 29, 2018. https://www.firstthings.com/web-exclusives/2018/06/a-better-christian -nationalism.

Lemon v. Kurtzman. 403 U.S. 602 (1971).

Lepore, Jill. "In Every Dark Hour." *New Yorker*, February 3, 2020. https: //www.newyorker.com/magazine/2020/02/03/the-last-time-democracy -almost-died.

———. *These Truths.* New York: W.W. Norton, 2018.

Levinas, Emmanuel. *To Love the Torah More Than God.* Translated by Helen A. Stephenson and Richard Sugarman. Paris: Alban Michel, 1963.

Levitsky, Steven, and Daniel Ziblatt. *How Democracies Die.* New York: Crown, 2018.

"Lights Out in Dresden and Cologne against Pegida." *Der Spiegel*, January 5, 2015. http://www.spiegel.de/politik/deutschland/protest-gegen-pegida-licht -aus-in-dresden-und-koeln-a-1011387.html.

Lilla, Mark. *The Once and Future Liberal: After Identity Politics.* Oxford: Oxford University Press, 2018.

Linden, Ian. *Global Catholicism: Diversity and Change since Vatican II.* New York: Columbia University Press, 2009.

Lindner, Nadine. "Eine unheilige Allianz." Deutschlandfunk, June 12, 2019. https://www.deutschlandfunk.de/afd-kritisiert-ekd-eine-unheilige -allianz.886.de.html?dram:article_id=451091.

"Liturgy." In *Jewish Understandings of the Other: An Annotated Sourcebook*. Center for Christian-Jewish Learning, Boston College. http://www.bc.edu/research/cjl/metaelements/texts/cjrelations/resources/sourcebook/Aleynu.htm.

Livni, Ephrat. "Does Freedom of Religion Protect Americans Who Have a Religious Duty to Shelter Migrants?" Quartz, October 19, 2018. https://qz.com/1430347/does-us-freedom-of-religion-protect-christians-who-shelter-migrants/.

Lubbers, Marcel, and Peer Scheepers. "Explaining the Trend in Extreme Right-Wing Voting: Germany, 1989–1998." *European Sociological Review* 17, no. 4 (December 2001): 431–49.

Lugg, Catherine, and Malila Robinson. "Religion, Advocacy Coalitions, and the Politics of U.S. Public Schooling." *Educational Policy* 23, no. 1 (January 2009): 242–66.

MacIntyre, Alasdair. *After Virtue*. 2nd ed. Notre Dame, IN: University of Notre Dame Press, 1984.

Madison, James. The Federalist Papers, no. 10. http://avalon.law.yale.edu/18th_century/fed10.asp.

Magid, Jacob, et al. "Left-Wing Activists Injured in Reported Assault by Settlers." *Times of Israel*, August 25, 2018. https://www.timesofisrael.com/left-wing-activists-injured-in-reported-assault-by-settlers/.

"Marriage and Religious Freedom: Fundamental Goods That Stand or Fall Together." An open letter from interfaith leaders in the United States to all Americans opposing same-sex marriage. United States Conference of Catholic Bishops, January 12, 2012. http://www.usccb.org/issues-and-action/marriage-and-family/marriage/promotion-and-defense-of-marriage/upload/Executive-Summary-Marriage-and-Religious-Freedom-Letter-January-12-2012.pdf.

Marshal, Ellen Ott. *Christians in the Public Sphere: Faith That Transforms Politics*. Nashville: Abingdon, 2008.

Marzouki, Nadia, Duncan McDonnell, and Olivier Roy. *Saving the People: How Populists Hijack Religion*. London: Hurst, 2016.

Matt, Daniel Chanan, trans. *Zohar: The Book of Enlightenment*. New York: Paulist, 1983.

Maximus the Confessor. *The Four Hundred Chapters on Love*. In *Maximus the Confessor: Selected Writings*, 33–98.

———. *Maximus the Confessor: Selected Writings*. Translated and edited by George C. Berthold. New York: Paulist, 1985.

McCulloch, Tom. "The Nouvelle Droite in the 1980s and 1990s: Ideology and Entryism, the Relationship with the Front National." *French Politics* 4, no. 2 (August 2006): 158–78.

Menzel, Björn. "Schwarz-Rot-Dumpf" [Black-Red-Dull]. *Der Spiegel*, December 12, 2014. http://www.spiegel.de/politik/deutschland/anti-islam-demo-pegida-demonstranten-singen-stille-nacht-in-dresden-a-1010039.html.

Merolla, Jennifer, Jean Reith Schroedel, and Scott Waller. "Evangelical Strength and the Political Representation of Women and Gays." In *Evangelicals and Democracy in America*, edited by Steven Brint and Jean Schroedel, vol. 1, *Religion and Society*, 159–86. New York: Russell Sage Foundation Press, 2009.

Meyendorff, John. *Imperial Unity and Christian Divisions*. Yonkers, NY: St. Vladimir's Seminary Press, 1989.

Miles, Jack. *Religion as We Know It: An Origin Story*. New York: W. W. Norton, 2019.

Milgrom, Jacob. *Leviticus: A Book of Ritual and Ethics*. Minnesota: Fortress, 2004.

———. *Leviticus 1–16*. Anchor Bible. New York: Doubleday, 1991.

Miller, Donald E., and Tetsunao Yamamori. *Global Pentecostalism: The New Face of Christian Social Engagement*. Berkeley: University of California Press, 2007.

Milliner, Mathew. "Evangelicals in Exile." *First Things*, June 2, 2017. https://www.firstthings.com/web-exclusives/2017/02/evangelicals-in-exile.

Minkenberg, Michael. "Religion and the Radical Right." Chapter 9 in *The Oxford Handbook of the Radical Right*, edited by Jens Rydgren. Oxford: Oxford University Press, 2018.

Montgomery, Kathleen, and Ryan Winter. "Explaining the Religion Gap in Support for Radical Right Parties in Europe." *Politics and Religion* 8, no. 2 (June 2015): 379–403.

Montopoli, Brian. "Rick Perry Hosting Prayer Event for America 'in Crisis.'" CBS News, June 6, 2011. https://www.cbsnews.com/news/rick-perry-hosting-prayer-event-for-america-in-crisis/.

Morieson, Nicholas. "Are Contemporary Populist Movements Hijacking Religion?" *Journal of Religious and Political Practice* 3, no. 1–2 (2017): 88–95. https://doi.org/10.1080/20566093.2017.1292171.

———. "Religion and Identity at the 2017 Dutch Elections." E-International Relations, March 26, 2017.

Moskwa, Wojciech. "Poland's President Thanks Trump for Battling 'Fake News.'" *Bloomberg*, January 18, 2018. https://www.bloomberg.com/news/articles/2018-01-18/poland-s-president-thanks-trump-for-battling-fake-news.

Mudde, Cas, and Cristóbal Rovira Kaltwasser. *Populism: A Very Short Introduction*. Oxford University Press, 2017.

Mudler, John M. "The Moral World of John Foster Dulles." *Journal of Presbyterian History* 49, no. 2 (Summer 1971): 157–82.

Müller, Jan-Werner. "Towards a New History of Christian Democracy." *Journal of Political Ideologies* 18, no. 2 (2013): 243–55.

———. "What Happens When an Autocrat's Conservative Enablers Finally Turn on Him?" *Atlantic*, September 13, 2018. https://www.theatlantic.com/international/archive/2018/09/Orbán-hungary-europe-populism-illiberalism/570136/.

"The Munich AfD Attacks the Church." FOCUS Online, May 26, 2018. https://www.focus.de/regional/muenchen/parteien-afd-attackiert-kirche_id_5568159.html.

National Association of Evangelicals. "Evangelical Leaders Urge President Trump to Keep Families Together." June 1, 2018. https://www.nae.net/evangelical-leaders-urge-president-trump-keep-families-together/.

———. "Mission and Work." https://www.nae.net/about-nae/mission-and-work/.

———. "NAE Condemns White Supremacy." August 16, 2017. https://www.nae.net/nae-condemns-white-supremacy/.

National Council of Churches. "General Secretary Jim Winkler's Speech to Cairo Peace Conference." April 27, 2017. https://nationalcouncilofchurches.us/general-secretary-jim-winklers-speech-to-cairo-peace-conference/.

National Council of the Churches of Christ. "The Churches and Immigrationl [*sic*]." Statement adopted February 27, 1962. http://nationalcouncilofchurches.us/common-witness/1962/immigration.php.

———. "Immigrants, Refugees and Migrants" [policy statement]. Adopted May 14, 1981. http://nationalcouncilofchurches.us/common-witness/1981/immigration.php.

Nelson, Libby, and Kelly Swanson. "Full Transcript: Donald Trump's Press Conference Defending the Charlottesville Rally." Vox, August 15, 2017. https://www.vox.com/2017/8/15/16154028/trump-press-conference-transcript-charlottesville.

Neufert, Birgit. "Church Asylum." *Forced Migration Review* 48 (November 2014). https://www.fmreview.org/faith/neufert.

Newman, John Henry. *An Essay on the Development of Christian Doctrine.* Westminster, MD: Christian Classics Inc., 1968.

Newman, Stephen A. "From John F. Kennedy's 1960 Campaign Speech to Christian Supremacy: Religion in Modern Presidential Politics." *New York Law School Law Review* 53, no. 4 (2008–9): 691–733.

Norden, Günther van. *Der deutsche Protestantismus im Jahr der nationalsozialistischen Machtergreifung* [German Protestants in the year of Nazi control]. Gütersloh: Mohn, 1979.

Norris, Pippa, and Ronald Inglehart. *Cultural Backlash: Trump, Brexit, and Authoritarian Populism.* Cambridge University Press, 2019.

———. "Trump, Brexit, and the Rise of Populism: Economic Have-Nots and Cultural Backlash." Faculty Research Working Paper Series. Harvard Kennedy School, 2016.

Ochs, Peter. "The Jewish View of a Christian God." In *Christianity in Jewish Terms*, edited by Tikva Frymer-Kensky, David Novak, Peter Ochs, David Fox Sandmel, and Michael A. Signer. Boulder, CO: Westview, 2000.

Ojewska, Natalia. "Catholic Nationalism: The Church of the Far Right in Poland." Euronews, February 8, 2018. https://www.euronews.com/2018 /02/08/catholic-nationalism-the-church-of-the-far-right-in-poland.

Orth, Stefan, and Volker Resing. *AfD, Pegida & Co.: Angriff auf die Religion?* [AfD, Pegida and Co.: Attack on Religion?] Freiburg: Herder Verlag, 2017.

Pangritz, Andreas. "'To Fall within the Spokes of the Wheel': New-Old Observations concerning 'the Church and the Jewish Question.'" In *Dem Rad in die Speichen fallen: Das Politische in der Theologie Dietrich Bonhoeffers* [To fall into the spokes of the wheel: The political in the theology of Dietrich Bonhoeffer], edited by Kirsten Busch Nielsen, Ralf K. Wüstenberg, and Jens Zimmermann, 94–108. Gütersloh: Gütersloher Verlagshaus, 2013.

Park, Benjamin E. "The Revolutionary Roots of America's Religious Nationalism." *Religion and Politics*, March 20, 2018. https://religionandpolitics.org /2018/03/20/the-revolutionary-roots-of-americas-religious-nationalism/.

Pence, Mike. "Remarks by the Vice President on Healthcare and Tax Reform in Anderson, Indiana." September 22, 2017. American Presidency Project. https://www.presidency.ucsb.edu/node/331609.

Perrineau, Pascal. *La France au Front: Essai sur l'avenir du Front national* [France at the "Front": Essay on the future of the National Front]. Paris: Fayard, 2014.

Persico, Tomer. "The End Point of Zionism: Ethnocentrism and the Temple Mount." *Israel Studies Review* 32, no. 1 (Summer 2017): 104–22.

Pew Research Center. "As Election Nears, Voters Divided over Democracy and 'Respect': Trump Seen as Lacking Respect for Women, Minorities, Democracy." October 27, 2016. http://www.people-press.org/2016/10/27/as-election-nears-voters-divided-over-democracy-and-respect/.

———. "Being Christian in Western Europe." May 29, 2018. https://www.pewforum.org/2018/05/29/being-christian-in-western-europe/.

———. "Religious Belief and National Belonging in Central and Eastern Europe." May 10, 2017. http://www.pewforum.org/2017/05/10/religious-belief-and-national-belonging-in-central-and-eastern-europe/.

Pius X. *Pascendi Dominici Gregis*. Encyclical. 1907. Vatican website. http://w2.vatican.va/content/pius-x/en/encyclicals/documents/hf_p-x_enc_19070908_pascendi-dominici-gregis.html.

———. *Sacrorum Antistitum*. Decree at the Bishop's Ceremony. 1910. Vatican website. http://w2.vatican.va/content/pius-x/la/motu_proprio/documents/hf_p-x_motu-proprio_19100901_sacrorum-antistitum.html.

Plattner, Marc F. "Illiberal Democracy and the Struggle on the Right." *Journal of Democracy* 30, no. 1 (2019): 5–19.

Plecita, Klara. "The Importance of Christianity and Customs/Traditions for the National Identity of European Countries." Presentation to the Association for the Study of Nationalities Conference, New York, May 2019.

Pollack, Detlef, and Gergely Rosta. *Religion and Modernity: An International Comparison*. Oxford: Oxford University Press, 2017.

Porterfield, Amanda. "Religion's Role in Contestations over American Civility." Chapter 6 in Clayton and Elgar, *Civility and Democracy in America*.

Porter-Szűcs, Brian. "PiS in Their Own Words." Brian Porter-Szűcs, February 5, 2016. http://porterszucs.pl/2016/02/05/pis-in-their-own-words/.

Portier, Phillippe. "L'État et les religions en France: Une sociologie historique de la laïcité (Collection 'Histoire') [The state and religion in France: A historical sociology of secularism ('History' Collection)].'" Rennes: Série, 2016.

Prange, Astrid. "How the Catholic Church Ties in to Poland's Judicial Reform." Deutsche Welle, July 24, 2017. https://www.dw.com/en/how-the-catholic-church-ties-in-to-polands-judicial-reform/a-39809383.

Putnam, Robert D., and David E. Campbell. *American Grace: How Religion Divides and Unites Us*. New York: Simon & Schuster, 2010.

Püttmann, Andreas. *Ziviler Ungehorsam und christliche Bürgerloyalität: Konfession und Staatsgesinnung in der Demokratie des Grundgesetzes*. Paderborn: Schöningh, 1994.

―――. "AfD und Kirche: Abgrenzen statt annähern" [AfD and church: Differentiating instead of approximating]. *Die Zeit,* May 24, 2016. http://www.zeit.de/2016/22/afd-katholiken-ausgrenzung-ausschluss.

―――. *Gesellschaft ohne Gott: Risiken und Nebenwirkungen der Entchristlichung Deutschlands* [Society without God: Risks and side effects of the de-Christianization of Germany]. Asslar: Gerth Medien, 2010.

Quinnipiac University Poll. "U.S. Voters Dislike Trump Almost 2–1, Quinnipiac University National Poll Finds." Quinnipiac University, August 14, 2018. https://poll.qu.edu/national/release-detail?ReleaseID=2561.

Rambachan, Anantanand. "A Hindu Theological Critique of Hindutva." Unpublished manuscript provided to authors February 2019.

Rapp, Sandy. *God's Country: A Case against Theocracy.* New York: Routledge, 1991.

Rasor, Paul. *Reclaiming Prophetic Witness: Liberal Religion in the Public Square.* Boston: Skinner House Books, 2012.

Reagan, Ronald. "Remarks at the Annual Convention of the National Religious Broadcasters." February 9, 1982. American Presidency Project. https://www.presidency.ucsb.edu/node/244759.

Reese, Thomas. "Pollsters Confused about Catholic Voters." National Catholic Reporter, April 20, 2017. https://www.ncronline.org/blogs/faith-and-justice/pollsters-confused-about-catholic-voters.

Religion and the Founding of the American Republic: Religion and the New Republic. Exhibition. Library of Congress. https://www.loc.gov/exhibits/religion/rel07.html.

Religion Clause. "2016 Republican Platform on Religious Liberty." July 19, 2016. http://religionclause.blogspot.com/2016/07/2016-republican-platform-on-religious.html.

"Religion in Charleston, West Virginia." BestPlaces. https://www.bestplaces.net/religion/city/west_virginia/charleston.

"Religionszugehörigkeiten in Deutschland 2016" [Survey of 2016 German elections by religious affiliation]. Forschungsgruppe Weltanschauungen in Deutschland, July 4, 2017. https://fowid.de/meldung/religionszugehoerigkeiten-deutschland-2016.

Richie, Tony. "A Conservative Evangelical Response to Polarization in the United States." Unpublished manuscript provided to authors.

―――. "Neither Naïve nor Narrow: A Balanced Pentecostal Approach to Christian Theology of Religions." *Cyberjournal for Pentecostal-Charismatic Research,* no. 15 (2006). http://www.pctii.org/cyberj/cyberj15/richie.html.

———. "Pragmatism, Power, and Politics: A Pentecostal Conversation with President Obama's Favorite Theologian, Reinhold Niebuhr" *Pneuma* 32, no. 2 (Summer 2010): 241–60.

———. *Toward a Pentecostal Theology of Religions*. Cleveland, TN: CPT Press, 2013.

———. "What Kind of Spirit Are We Of? One Pentecostal's Approach to Interfaith Forgiveness and Interreligious Reconciliation." Presentation at the Global Congress on World Religions after 9/11, Montreal, September 12–15, 2006. http://pneumareview.com/what-kind-of-spirit-are-we-really-of -a-pentecostal-approach-to-interfaith-forgiveness-and-interreligious-rec onciliation/.

Ringshausen, Gerhard. *Widerstand und christlicher Glaube angesichts des Nationalsozialismus* [Resistance and Christian belief in light of Nazism]. Lüneburger theologische Beiträge 3. Berlin: Lit, 2008.

———. "Der Widerstand und die Kirchen" [Resistance and the churches]. In *Christen im Dritten Reich* [Christians in the Third Reich], edited by Philipp Thull, 21–30. Darmstadt: Wissenschaftliche Buchgesellschaft, 2014.

Ritter, Zacc. "How Much Does the World Trust Journalists?" *Gallup Blog*, December 27, 2019. https://news.gallup.com/opinion/gallup/272999/world -trust-journalists.aspx.

"'Rolle wie im Dritten Reich': AfD-Weidel erhebt schwere Vorwürfe gegen die Kirche" [AfD Plays a Role as in the Third Reich: AfD-Weidel raises serious allegations against the church]. FOCUS Online, December 25, 2017. https://www.focus.de/politik/deutschland/alice-weidel-afd-fraktion schefin-erhebt-schwere-vorwuerfe-gegen-die-kirche_id_8036449.html.

Roos, Lothar. "Die Schöpfung als Gabe Gottes und Aufgabe des Menschen" [Creation as a gift from God and task of human beings]. Krone-Seminar, during the week of Palm Sunday, 2010. http://www.unitas-ruhrania.org /images/content/100421_kroneseminar_2010.pdf.

———. "Katholische Soziallehre und Kultur der Entwicklung." In *Die Einheit der Kulturethik in Vielen Ethosformen*, edited by Werner Freistetter and Rudolf Weiler. Berlin: Duncker & Humblot, 1993.

Roy, Olivier. *L'Europe est-elle chrétienne?* [Is Europe Christian?] Paris: Seuil, 2019.

———. "The French National Front : From Christian Identity to Laïcité." Chapter 5 in Marzouki, McDonnell, and Roy, *Saving the People: How Populists Hijack Religion*.

————. "The Populist Paradox: How the Promotion of Christian Identity by European Populists Contributes to Secularization." Talk presented at the Contemporary Europe and European Union Study Groups, February 1, 2017. https://ces.fas.harvard.edu/events/2017/02/europe-religion -integration.

Rüther, Tobias. "Es Gibt zu wenige konservative Mitstreiter" [There are too few conservative comrades]. *Frankfurter Allgemeine Zeitung*, July 9, 2018. http://www.faz.net/social-media/instagram/andreas-puettmann-ueber -katholiken-gegen-populismus-15678858.html?premium.

Rydgren, Jens, ed. *Movements of Exclusion: Radical Right-Wing Populism in the Western World.* New York: Nova Publishers, 2005.

Saperstein, David. "The Use and Abuse of Jewish Tradition." In *CCAR Journal*, Spring 2008, 13–33.

Sarup, Madan. *Post-Structuralism and Postmodernism.* Athens: University of Georgia Press, 1993.

Sason, Talya. *Summary of the Opinion concerning Unauthorized Outposts.* Badil Resource Center for Palestinian Residency & Refugee Rights, n.d. file:///C:/Users/Owner/Downloads/SassonReportonSettlements-summary %20(1).pdf.

Scham, Paul. "'A Nation That Dwells Alone': Israeli Religious Nationalism in the 21st Century." *Israel Studies* 23, no. 3 (Fall 2018): 207–15.

Schlaich, Klaus, Martin Heckel, and Werner Heun. *Gesammelte Aufsätze: Kirche und Staat von der Reformation bis zum Grundgesetz* [Collected articles: Church and state from the Reformation up to the basic law] Jus ecclesiasticum 57. Tübingen: J. C. B. Mohr, 1997.

Searcey, Dionne. "The 72-Hour War over Christmas." *New York Times*, November 29, 2019. https://www.nytimes.com/2019/11/29/us/politics/christ mas-parade-charleston-wv.html.

Sekulow, Jay Alan. *Witnessing Their Faith: Religious Influence on Supreme Court Justices and Their Opinions.* Oxford: Rowman & Littlefield, 2006.

Shapiro, Marc B. "Islam and the Halakhah." *Judaism: A Quarterly Journal of Jewish Life and Thought* 42, no. 3 (Summer 1993): 332–43.

Shulman, Stephen. "Challenging the Civic/Ethnic and West/East Dichotomies in the Study of Nationalism." *Comparative Political Studies* 35, no. 5 (2002): 554–85.

Sider, Ronald J., and Knippers, Diane, eds. *Toward an Evangelical Public Policy.* Grand Rapids: Baker Books, 2005.

Silberstein, Laurence J., and Robert L. Cohn. *The Other in Jewish Thought and History: Constructions of Jewish Culture and Identity*. New York: New York University Press, 1994.

Smidt, Corwin E. *The Disappearing God Gap: Religion in the 2008 Election*. Oxford: Oxford University Press, 2010.

———. *Pews, Prayers, and Participation: Religion and Civic Responsibility in America*. Washington, DC: Georgetown University Press, 2008.

Smith, Gregory A. "Among White Evangelicals, Regular Churchgoers Are the Most Supportive of Trump." Pew Research Center, April 26, 2017. http://www.pewresearch.org/fact-tank/2017/04/26/among-white-evangelicals-regular-churchgoers-are-the-most-supportive-of-trump/.

Snyder, Timothy. *On Tyranny: Twenty Lessons from the Twentieth Century*. New York: Tim Duggan Books, 2017.

Southern Baptist Convention. "Resolution on Racism." Resolution adopted at the Annual Meeting of the Southern Baptist Convention, Las Vegas, June 1, 1989. https://www.sbc.net/resource-library/resolutions/resolution-on-racism-2/.

Stanley, Ben. "Defenders of the Cross: Populist Politics and Religion in Post-Communist Poland." Chapter 7 in Marzouki, McDonnell, and Roy, *Saving the People*.

Stanley, Jason. *How Fascism Works: The Politics of Us and Them*. New York: Random House, 2018.

Steppat, Timo, and Jens Giesel. "Spätentscheider verhindern das Schlimmste für CSU." [Late Voter Decision-Makers Prevent the Worst Results for the CSU]. *Frankfurter Allgemeine Zeitung*, October 15, 2018. http://www.faz.net/aktuell/politik/wahl-in-bayern/wahlanalyse-nach-der-landtagswahl-in-bayern-15829201.html.

Story, Joseph. "Joseph Story, Commentaries on the Constitution 3: §§1865–73." Document 69, under "Amendment I (Religion)." In vol. 5 of *The Founders' Constitution*, edited by Philip B. Kurland and Ralph Lerner. Chicago: University of Chicago Press, 1986. http://press-pubs.uchicago.edu/founders/documents/amendI_religions69.html. First published in *Commentaries on the Constitution*, by Joseph Story. Boston, 1833.

Strand, Paul. "Vice President Pence Blasts ABC's 'The View': Christianity Is Not a Mental Illness." CBN News, February 14, 2018. http://www1.cbn.com/cbnnews/politics/2018/february/vice-president-pence-blasts-abcs-the-view-christianity-is-not-a-mental-illness.

Strohm, Christoph. *Die Kirchen im Dritten Reich* [The church in the Third Reich]. Munich: C. H. Beck, 2011.

Sumiala, Johanna Maaria. "Introduction: Mediatization in Post-Secular Society—New Perspectives in the Study of Media, Religion and Politics." *Journal of Religion in Europe* 10, no. 4 (2017): 361–65.

Sweden. "Celebrations in the Countryside." Official website of Sweden and the Swedish Institute, last updated May 2, 2019. https://sweden.se/culture -traditions/easter/.

Sweetman, Brian. *Why Politics Needs Religion: The Place of Religious Arguments in the Public Square*. Downers Grove, IL: IVP Academic, 2006.

Swenson, Kyle. "Sessions Says the Bible Justifies Separating Immigrant Families." *Washington Post*, June 15, 2018. https://www.washingtonpost.com /news/morning-mix/wp/2018/06/15/sessions-says-the-bible-justifies-sepa rating-immigrant-families-the-verses-he-cited-are-infamous/?noredirect =on&utm_term=.0017cbea7777.

Taguieff, Pierre-André. *Sur la Nouvelle Droit* [About the New Right]. Paris: Descartes & Cie, 1994.

Tamir, Yuli. *Why Nationalism*. Princeton: Princeton University Press, 2019.

Tavard, George H. *Holy Writ or Holy Church: The Crisis of the Protestant Reformation*. New York: Harper and Brothers, 1959.

Tentang Wahid Foundation. "Tentang Wahid Foundation." http://wahidfounda tion.org/index.php/page/index/About-Us.

Thielmann, Wolfgang. *Alternative für Christen? Die AfD und Ihr Gespaltenes Verhältnis zur Religion* [An alternative for Christians? The AfD and its split relationship to religion]. Wupperthal: Neukirchener Verlag, 2017.

Thieme, Daniel, and Antonius Liedhegener, A. "'Linksaußen,' politische Mitte oder doch ganz anders? Die Positionierung der Evangelischen Kirche in Deutschland (EKD) im parteipolitischen Spektrum der postsäkularen Gesellschaft" (Left-wing, political center or something completely different? The positioning of the Evangelical Church in Germany (EKD) in the party-political spectrum of postsecular society). *Politische Vierteljahresschrift* 56, no. 2 (2015): 240–77.

Tibon, Amir. "'Racist and Reprehensible': AIPAC Slams Kahanist Party Backed by Netanyahu." *Haaretz*, February 20, 2019. https://www.haaretz .com/israel-news/elections/.premium-racist-and-reprehensible-aipac -slams-kahanist-party-backed-by-netanyahu-1.6959858.

Topolski, Anya. "A Genealogy of the 'Judeo-Christian' Signifier: A Tale of Europe's Identity Crisis." In *Is There a Judeo-Christian Tradition? A European Perspective*, edited by Emmanuel Nathan and Anya Topolski, 267–84. Berlin: de Gruyter, 2016.

Town of Greece v. Galloway. 572 U.S. 565 (2014).

Troeltsch, Ernst. *Die Soziallehren der christlichen Kirchen und Gruppen* [The social teachings of the Christian church and community]. Tübingen: J.C.B. Mohr, 1923.

Tucker, Gordon. "Can a People of the Book Also Be a People of God?" *Conservative Judaism* 60, no. 1–2 (Fall/Winter 2007–8): 4–25.

Tufecki, Zeynep. *Twitter and Tear Gas.* New Haven: Yale University Press, 2017.

Tversky, Amos, and Daniel Kahneman. "Judgment under Uncertainty." *Science*, n.s., 185, no. 4157 (September 27, 1974): 1124–31.

United Nations. Universal Declaration of Human Rights. United Nations, 2018. http://www.un.org/en/universal-declaration-human-rights/.

United States Conference of Catholic Bishops. "Brothers and Sisters to Us." Pastoral Letter on Racism. 1979. http://www.usccb.org/issues-and-action /cultural-diversity/african-american/brothers-and-sisters-to-us.cfm.

UVA Center for Politics. "New Poll: Some Americans Express Troubling Racial Attitudes Even as Majority Oppose White Supremacists." Sabato's Crystal Ball, UVA Center for Politics, September 14, 2017. http://www .centerforpolitics.org/crystalball/articles/new-poll-some-americans-express -troubling-racial-attitudes-even-as-majority-oppose-white-supremacists/.

Van Kessel, Stijn. "Using Faith to Exclude: The Role of Religion in Dutch Populism." In Marzouki, McDonnell, and Roy, *Saving the People*, 61–77.

Van Norden, Günther. *Der Deutsche Protestantismus im Jahr der nationalsozialistischen Machtergreifung* [German Protestantism in the year that the Nazis siezed power]. Gütersloh: Gütersloher Verlagshaus Mohn, 1979.

———. "Widerstand im Deutschen Protestantismus, 1933–1945" [Resistance in German Protestantism, 1933–1945]. In *Der deutsche Widerstand, 1933– 1945*, edited by Klaus-Jürgen Müller Höpfner, 108–34. Paderborn: Schöningh, 1986.

"Visit to the Idomeni Refugee Camp: Europe Must Not Accept These Conditions!" Evangelische Kirche im Rheinland, April 7, 2016. https://www .ekir.de/www/service/idomeni-english-19969.php.

Vorländer, Hans, Maik Herold, and Steven Schäller. *Wer geht zu PEGIDA und warum? Eine empirische Untersuchung von PEGIDA-Demonstranten in Dresden* [Who is going to PEGIDA and why? An empirical study of PEGIDA demonstrators in Dresden]. Schriften zur Verfassungs- *und Demokratieforschung* 1/2015. Dresden: ZVD, Zentrum für Verfassungs- und Demokratieforschung, 2015.

Wahid, Alissa. "My Islam, Your Islam, Our Islam." Unpublished manuscript provided to the authors February 2019.

Wallace, George. "Segregation Now, Segregation Forever." Inaugural speech Wallace gave as governor of Alabama, Montgomery, February 8, 1968. Black Past.org, January 22, 2013. http://www.blackpast.org/1963-george -wallace-segregation-now-segregation-forever.

Wallace v. Jaffree. 472 U.S. 38 (1985).

Wallis, Jim. *God's Politics: Why the Right Gets It Wrong and the Left Doesn't Get It.* San Francisco: Harper, 2005.

Walzer, Michael. *The Paradox of Liberation: Secular Revolutions and Religious Counterrevolutions.* New Haven: Yale University Press, 2015.

Ward, Alex. "Poll: 67% of Republicans Agree with How Trump Handled Charlottesville." Vox, Aug 17, 2017. https://www.vox.com/2017/8/17/161610 16/cbs-poll-charlottesville-republicans-55-percent-67-percent.

Weigel, George. "Pope John Paul II and the Dynamics of History." Templeton Lecture on Religion and World Affairs, presented at the Foreign Policy Research Institute, Philadelphia, May 2, 2000. Foreign Policy Research Institute. https://www.fpri.org/article/2000/05/pope-john-paul-ii-and-the -dynamics-of-history/.

Weiqian, Xia. "Christian Religiosity and Support for Populist Radical Right Parties in Europe." PhD diss., School of Social and Behavioral Sciences, Tilburg University. http://arno.uvt.nl/show.cgi?fid=144492.

Weir, Kristen. "What's at the Root of Racial Stereotyping?" *American Psychological Association* 48, no. 9 (October 2017): 56. http://www.apa.org/moni tor/2017/10/stereotyping.aspx.

Welna, David. "Some Gun Control Opponents Cite Fear of Government Tyranny." *It's All Politics*, April 8, 2013. NPR. https://www.npr.org /sections/itsallpolitics/2013/04/08/176350364/fears-of-government -tyranny-push-some-to-reject-gun-control.

"Wenn die Gottlosen für das christliche Abendland demonstrieren" [When the godless demonstrate for the Christian West]. *Der Tagesspiegel*, September 23, 2015. http://www.tagesspiegel.de/politik/pegida-und-das-chris tentum-wenn-die-gottlosen-fuer-das-christliche-abendland-demon strieren/12345386.html.

Whitehead, Andrew L., Samuel L. Perry, and Joseph O. Baker. "Make America Christian Again: Christian Nationalism and Voting for Donald Trump in the 2016 Presidential Election." *Sociology of Religion* 79, no. 2 (2018): 147–71.

Wike, Richard, Katie Simmons, Bruce Stokes, and Janell Fetterolf. "Globally, Broad Support for Representative and Direct Democracy." Pew Research Center, October 16, 2017. http://www.pewglobal.org/2017/10/16/globally -broad-support-for-representative-and-direct-democracy/.

Wilcox, W. Bradford. "How Focused on the Family? Evangelical Protestants, the Family, and Sexuality." In *Evangelicals and Democracy in America*, edited by Steven Brint and Jean R. Schroedel, vol. 1, *Religion and Society*, 251–75. New York: Russell Sage Foundation Press, 2009.

Willaime, Jean-Paul. *Lumières, Religions, Laïcité*. Under the direction of Louis Châtellier, Claude Langlois, and Jean-Paul Willaime. Paris: Riveneuve Editions, 2009.

Williams, Pamela Rose. "David Jeremiah Quotes: 23 Inspirational Sayings." What Christians Want to Know, 2013. https://www.whatchristianswantto know.com/david-jeremiah-quotes-23-inspirational-sayings/.

Williamson, Kevin D. "Chaos in the Family, Chaos in the State: The White Working Class's Dysfunction." *National Review*, March 17, 2016. https:// www.nationalreview.com/2016/03/donald-trump-white-working-class -dysfunction-real-opportunity-needed-not-trump/.

Willis, Cecil L. "Durkheim's Concept of *Anomie*: Some Observations." *Sociological Inquiry* 52, no. 2 (Spring 1982): 106–13. https://doi.org/10.1111/j .1475-682X.1982.tb01242.x.

Wilsey, John D. "Our Country Is Destined to Be the Great Nation of Futurity: John L. O'Sullivan's Manifest Destiny and Christian Nationalism, 1837– 1846." *Religions* 8, no. 4 (2017): 68. https://www.mdpi.com/2077-1444/8 /4/68/htm.

Winkler, Jim. "The Christian Call to Engage the World." Unpublished manuscript provided to authors February 2019.

Winthrop, John. *A Model of Christian Charity*. 1630. Reprinted in "April 7, 1630: Puritans Leave for Massachusetts." Mass Humanities. https://www .massmoments.org/moment-details/puritans-leave-for-massachusetts .html.

Wissenschaftszentrum Berlin. "Manifesto Project." https://manifesto-project .wzb.eu/.

World Council of Churches. "Xenophobia, Racism and Populist Nationalism in the Context of Global Migration." Message from the conference organized by Dicastery and Pontifico Council (Catholic) and the WCC, Geneva and Rome, September 18–20, 2018. https://www.oikoumene.org/en /resources/documents/message-from-the-conference-xenophobia-racism

-and-populist-nationalism-in-the-context-of-global-migration-19-septem
ber-2018/.

Wright, Jonathan R. C. Review of *Kirchen in der Nachkriegszeit: Vier zeitge-schichtliche Beiträge* [The church postwar: Four historical contributions], by Armin Boyens, Martin Greschat, Rudolf von Thadden, and Paolo Pombeni. *Journal of Ecclesiastical History* 32, no. 1 (1981): 124–25.

Yong, Amos. *In the Last Days of Caesar: Pentecostalism and Political Theology.* Grand Rapids, MI: Eerdmans, 2010.

Young, Neil J. Review of *Family Values and the Rise of the Christian Right*, by Seth Dowland. *Journal of American History* 103, no. 4 (2017): 1093–94.

Zander, Helmut. *Die Christen und die Friedensbewegungen in beiden deut-schen Staaten: Beiträge zu einem Vergleich für die Jahre 1978–1987* [Christians and the free church movements in both German states: Contributions to a comparison for the years 1978–1987]. Beiträge zur politischen Wissenschaft 54. Berlin: Duncker & Humblot, 1989.

Zauzmer, Julie, and Keith McMillan. "Sessions Cites Bible Passage Used to Defend Slavery in Defense of Separating Immigrant Families." *Washington Post*, July 15, 2018. https://www.washingtonpost.com/news/acts-of-faith /wp/2018/06/14/jeff-sessions-points-to-the-bible-in-defense-of-separating -immigrant-families/?arc404=true.

Zertal, Idith, and Akiva Eldar. *Lords of the Land: The War over Israel's Settle-ments in the Occupied Territories, 1967–2007.* Translated by Vivian Eden. New York: Nation Books, 2007.

Zeskind, Leonard. "Christian Coalition and Republican Party." First published in *Searchlight Magazine*, October 1993. Republished on LeonardZeskind .com. http://www.leonardzeskind.com/1993/09/30/searchlight-magazine -october-1993/.

Zieve, Tamara. "70% of European Jews Won't Go to Shul on High Holy Days despite Heightened Security." *Jerusalem Post*, September 20, 2016.

Zion, Noam. *Elu v'Elu: Two Schools of Halakha Face Off on Issues of Human Autonomy, Majority Rule and Divine Voice of Authority.* Jerusalem: Shalom Hartman Institute, 2008. http://www.hartmaninstitute.com/uploads /Holidays/Elu-02062008_0957_45.pdf.

Zylstra, Sarah Eekhoff. "Presbyterian Church in America Apologizes for Old and New Racism." *Christianity Today*, June 24, 2016. https://www.chris tianitytoday.com/news/2016/june/pca-apologizes-for-new-and-old -racism.html.

ABOUT THE AUTHORS

David Elcott has spent the last thirty-five years at the intersection of community building, the search for a theology of cross-boundary engagement, and interfaith and ethnic social justice organizing and activism. Trained in political psychology and Middle East affairs at Columbia University and Judaic studies at the American Jewish University, Dr. Elcott is the Taub Professor of Practice in Public Service and Leadership at the Robert F. Wagner School of Public Service at New York University and director of its specialization in advocacy and political action. Over the past four years, Dr. Elcott has worked to build a robust training program of community organizing and advocacy campaigns housed in Wagner and attended by students from across the university.

David has addressed a wide array of public policy issues, building interfaith and interethnic coalitions to address Middle East peace, immigration reform, civil liberties, and workers' rights. He has mediated conflicts between and among religious communities in the United States and around the world, finding collaborations and solutions on issues as diverse as posthumous Church of the Latter-Day Saints baptisms, financing the World Lutheran Federation's hospital in Jerusalem, prison reform and reentry for those once incarcerated, and Israeli-Palestinian issues. He led a major event at the Arizona-Mexico border and helped organize national demonstrations for immigration reform.

As a theologian, he has represented the Jewish community in dialogue with the Vatican, the World Council of Churches, and the National Council of Churches and in a range of academic settings. His book *A Sacred Journey: The Jewish Quest for a Perfect World* provides a Jewish theology for the twenty-first century.

His present research is focused in two areas: Dr. Elcott has published academic and popular studies on why Christians vote as they do and how religious leaders affect civil discourse and democracy; in so doing he has searched for pathways for constructive religious involvement in civic affairs. He has written numerous articles and monographs on power and war, increasing civic engagement, and cross-cultural pluralism.

C. Colt Anderson is the outgoing dean of the Graduate School of Religion at Fordham University. A church historian and theologian, he has focused his research on the intersection between three areas of concern: the communication of the gospel (evangelization), how to reform the church, and the importance of an eschatological perspective for Christian life. His publications have concentrated on ways to heal the growing divisions among members of the Catholic Church by drawing upon models of leadership from historical figures such as Gregory the Great, Peter Damian, Bernard of Clairvaux, Bonaventure, and others. Professor Anderson has focused his research on the origins of the Franciscan movement as a means to understand the important development of lay ministry in the church. He lectures nationally on issues related to spirituality, ecclesial reform, and evangelization. He is the recipient of a 2008 Catholic Press Association of the United States and Canada Book Award for history.

After spending several years as a scriptwriter and film producer, he has tried to find ways to recover the proper place of narrative in theology as a means to communicate the Catholic tradition to contemporary people.

Tobias Cremer is a Junior Research Fellow at Pembroke College, Oxford, and a PhD from the University of Cambridge whose doctoral research focused on the relationship between religion and the new wave of right-wing populism in Western Europe and North America. In particular, the project aims to understand the ways in which traditionally secularist right-wing populist parties are seeking to employ Christian symbols and language as cultural identity markers, and how believers and church authorities are reacting to such co-optation attempts. Prior to coming to Cambridge, Tobias was a McCloy Fellow at the Harvard Kennedy School, where he received a master's degree in public policy. He also holds a BA in politics, philosophy, and economics from the Paris Institute of Political Studies and an MPhil in politics and international studies from the University of Cambridge. He has gathered work experience in the German Parliament, in the German Federal Foreign Office, and in management consulting, and acted as an advisor to the German Foreign Office's strategic communication unit during his time at Harvard. He has authored studies on how the religious right highjacks nationalism and the role of the Protestant church during the Nazi era.

Volker Haarmann, an ordained minister of the Evangelical Church in the Rhineland, is the chief executive of its Department of Theology. The department that Rev. Dr. Haarmann manages is responsible for theological issues, ethical and systematic questions, denominational theology, evangelism, church music, worship, Christian-Jewish dialogue, ministry of preachers, Rhenish church history, and higher education. Volker studied in Tuebingen, where he received his PhD from the University of Tuebingen, and has also studied in Heidelberg, in Jerusalem, and at Harvard. He is the author and editor of many theological treatises, including *JHWH – Verehrer der Völker* (YHWH: Admirer of peoples).

INDEX

Alternatives for Germany (AfD)
  anti-Muslim attitudes, 52
  attacks on democratic institutions
    and values, 55
  and Christian identity, 45, 46, 47,
    56
  elections, 58–59, 124
  leaders, 57
  mission, 35–36
Anderson, Elizabeth, 2
Appiah, Kwame, 22
  habitus and essentialism, 25–26
Appleby, Scott, 13
Asad, Talal, 17
Avineri, Shlomo, 9

Bakshi, Rajni, viii, 22, 31
Bavaria, 59
  Christian symbols, 23–24
  elections and AfD, 58, 60
Berger, Peter, 27
Bible, 73, 77, 117, 146, 152, 162
  democratic values, 41, 125, 152

against idolatry, 11
purity and pollution, 12, 78, 79,
  119, 151
Bonhoeffer, Dietrich, 14, 29, 122, 163
  and asylum, 128, 130
  and Christians defending "the
    other," 123, 125
  the Church and the Jewish
    question, 126
  the Holocaust and Nazis, 123
  sanctorum communio, 125, 163
  three dimensions of Church
    resistance, 125–26
  Victoria Barnett explaining
    Bonhoeffer's courage, 122–23
Braunstein, Ruth, and Malaena
  Taylor, 32

Carse, James, and infinite games, 2–3
Casanova, Jose
  on anti-Muslim attacks, 56
  and the return of religion in
    politics, 29

Catholic Church, 23, 96, 111
anti-Muslim attitudes and the
Turks, 95, 98–99
Catholics and nationalism, 12, 16,
33, 48, 89, 92
conquest, Crusades, and inquisitions, 90, 96, 97–98, 102
and democracy, 48–50, 57, 60, 78
Donatism, 96
education and reform, 51, 91, 93,
95, 101, 106, 107, 111–12, 114
Gelasius and papal authority, 97
illiberal democracy, 90, 91, 93
immigration, 8, 94
modernism and religious freedom,
25, 78, 90, 92, 94, 100, 108–9, 113
and Nazism, 49
opposing nationalism, 91–93, 104
in the United States, 93–95
Vatican II, 92, 102–4, 109
See also Bavaria; Second Vatican
Council
Christianity
Christian supremacy, 72, 73,
120–21
and democracy and pluralism in
Europe, 30, 47, 49–50, 60, 122,
126, 130, 132
and democracy and pluralism in
the United States, 68, 69, 78
identity marker, 25, 29, 52, 55, 62
Nazism, 48, 123, 124–25
populist nationalism, 17, 35, 46, 52,
74, 76–77, 85
refugees and asylum, 126, 128–29,
131–32
white supremacy and anti-Muslim
attitudes, 14, 58, 62, 81–82, 98

Churches' Commission for Migrants
in Europe, 130
Council of Trent, authority of scripture and tradition, 104–7

de Gruchy, John, and the struggle for
democracy, 132
Derrida, Jacques, and the "other,"
143

Eatwell, Roger, and Matthew
Goodwin, 6
Elman, Miriam, 21
Evangelical Church in Germany
(EKD)
and colonialism, 118
and democracy, 49
and Muslims, 8
speaking out against AfD and
PEGIDA, 60
Stuttgart Declaration of Guilt, and
Grundgesetz, 49-50
Evangelicals
awakening in the U.S., 73, 76–77
challenge church-state separation,
12, 73, 76, 78–79
and illiberal democracy, 78, 123
missionary conversions, 118
and the Republican Party, 123,
143
against secularism, 12, 76
and white nationalism, 78–79, 80,
87
See also purity and pollution
Ezrachi, Elan, viii, 150

Farber, Seth, viii, 39, 139
Francis (pope), 16, 42

French Rassemblement National
(formerly Front National), 35,
60
and Jean-Marie Le Pen, 124
Fukuyama, Francis, 32

Gauland, Alexander, 124
Gelman, Susan, 26
Germany
and democracy, 2, 47, 48, 52–53,
60, 124, 129
illiberal populist nationalism, 38,
45, 52
Muslims and asylum, 7, 8, 56,
126–27
Nazism and the Holocaust, 48, 70,
122, 123, 124
and politics, 38, 47, 55, 60, 124
religion and liberal democracy, 48,
50, 60–61
and religious identity, 27, 34, 46,
53
Gollwitzer, Helmut, 123
Green, John, 125
Green, Steven, and the four pillars of
faith, 118
Greenberg, Irving, 144

Haidt, Jonathan, 157
Hariri, Yuval, 53, 157
Henderson, Katharine, viii, 14, 40,
84, 119
Hinduism, 22, 42
illiberal democracy, 6, 12, 31,
36
and Nerendra Modi, 31
Hjelm, Titus, 25
Hochschild, Arlie, 7

homosexuality, 12, 32, 95
homophobia, 120, 130, 151
See also LGBTQ community
Hungary
Christian nationalism, 45, 55, 61,
90, 93
Fidesz movement, 54, 123
and George Soros, 38
illiberal democracy, 5, 6, 34, 37, 40,
54, 93
and Viktor Orbán, 6, 35, 45, 54

idolatry, 30, 121
in Judaism, 137–39, 145–46, 152, 161
illiberal democracy, 4, 9, 11, 31, 46,
48, 149, 157
and Catholicism, 89, 92–93, 101,
110–11
and Christianity, 6, 27, 55, 65, 68,
78, 83, 85, 123, 130, 132
definition, 3, 5, 10, 17, 90, 95
and Judaism, 6, 137, 143
and populist nationalism, 32, 52,
83, 87, 94, 95, 100, 121, 149
and purity, 28, 157
and religious identity, 13–14, 22,
30, 40, 161
immigration, 7, 54, 60, 122, 127
and Christianity, 81, 93, 95, 99
and national identity, 35, 55, 58
support for, 61, 94, 131, 145
as threat, 6, 39, 53, 113
See also Evangelical Church in
Germany (EKD)
India and Hindu nationalism, 2, 6,
12, 31, 33
Indonesia and democracy, 6, 8, 10,
32, 33, 37

Israel, 10, 21, 139, 141, 150
  and illiberal democracy, 5, 13, 39,
    122, 142–43, 150
  and nationalism, 6, 32, 37, 140

Jackson, Andrew, and the wall of
    separation, 69
Jefferson, Thomas, and the wall of
    separation, 69, 70
Jews and Judaism, 8, 19, 22, 81, 85,
    135, 137, 140, 155
  and anti-Semitism, 98, 99, 113, 124,
    141
  Charlottesville, 26, 84, 120
  democracy and pluralism, 15,
    135–37, 144, 146–47, 149
  and identity, 28
  Jewish illiberal democracy, 12,
    37, 39, 137–39, 142, 143,
    150–51
  Noahide covenant, 145
  and the "other," 136, 137, 140–41,
    144, 151–52
  politics, 138, 144, 145, 149
  ultra-Orthodox, 141–42
  Washington speech at synagogue,
    66
John Paul II, 92
  caring for neighbor, 92
  opposing nationalism, 91
  See also Catholic Church

Kook, Abraham Isaac, 136, 139
Ku Klux Klan, 80
  Charlottesville, 74, 83
  and Christianity, 80
  Woodrow Wilson and Birth of a
    Nation, 81

Lepore, Jill, 4, 12
Levinas, Emmanuel, 154
Levitsky, Steven, and Daniel Ziblatt,
    36–37
LGBTQ community, 6, 7, 8, 15, 142
  and Christianity, 13, 74, 93, 94,
    112, 120
  and illiberal democracy, 95, 101
  See also marriage equality/same-
    sex marriage

Madison, James, and Federalist Paper
    No. 10, 38
marriage equality/same-sex marriage,
    67
  religious opposition, 94–95
  religious support, 8, 84, 85, 120
  USCCB, and "Marriage and
    Religious Freedom," 94
Maximus the Confessor, 109
Merkel, Angela, 47, 54, 127
Modi, Narendra, 31
Muslims, 5, 98, 101, 140, 141, 145,
    152
  anti-immigrant attitudes, 35, 39,
    83, 95, 113
  anti-Muslim attitudes, 6, 7, 25, 27,
    39, 56, 62, 83, 130, 144
  nationalism, 8, 26, 32, 150

National Council of Churches, 41,
    121, 129, 131
nationalism, 4, 8, 9, 90, 91, 104, 117,
    122, 161
  Catholic nationalism, 90, 95,
    111
  Christian nationalism, 71, 78, 80,
    82–83, 87, 118, 121, 123–24

and illiberal democracy, 40, 68, 90, 92, 93, 94, 111, 122, 149, 161
and liberal democracy, 41, 62, 160
and populism, 4, 14, 83, 122, 158, 161
and religious identity, 2, 5, 28, 33, 35–36, 46, 67, 91–92
New Sanctuary Movement, Charter of, 129

Orbán, Viktor, 6, 35, 45, 54

Patriotic Europeans Against the Islamisation of the Christian Occident (PEGIDA), 60
anti-Muslim attitudes, 62
and Christian nationalism, 45, 46, 56, 58, 62
and illiberal democracy, 56
Peace of Westphalia, 99
Pence, Mike, and speech to "pray for America," 79
Perry, Rick, call for prayer and healing, 79
Plecita, Klara, 17
Poland, 23, 61, 90, 93, 109
anti-immigrant attitudes, 7, 126
Catholic Law and Justice Party, 22, 54
and Christian nationalism, 55, 90, 93
and illiberal democracy, 5, 37, 40, 54
Marcin Dybowski, 99
"Pure Blood, Clear Mind!" banners, 93
populism, 2, 10, 11, 45, 122
and Christianity, 29, 32, 56, 59, 60, 85–86

definition, 3, 4, 54, 158
illiberal democracy, 35, 37, 46, 52, 54, 110, 160
immigration, 35, 55, 122, 126
and nationalism, 5, 11, 75, 83, 161
and politics, 55, 59
and religious identity, 6, 14, 46, 62, 158–59
Porterfield, Amanda, 71, 87
Protestant Reformation, 48, 99, 117, 118, 125
Protestants, 76, 96, 99, 104, 117, 130, 132
Christian nationalist identity, 10, 122–23, 124
and democracy, 122
and divine providence, 118
immigration and asylum, 80–81, 122, 128, 131
Manifest Destiny, 118–19
nationalism, 77, 78, 87, 119
Nazism and the Holocaust, 48, 49, 119, 122–23, 126, 129, 130, 132
politics, 48, 50, 59, 69, 85, 117, 120, 123, 144
and race, 77, 81, 119, 123
purity and pollution, 18, 28, 41
and Christian nationalism, 28, 67, 78, 80
definition, 6, 9, 31, 89
human evil and sin, 31, 76, 77–78, 142
politics, 82

Rambachan, Anantanand, 10, 36
Reagan, Ronald, and Christianity, 11, 73
Rekowski, Manfred, 131

Religious Freedom Restoration Act (1993), 72
religious identity, 3, 12, 22, 33–34, 62, 161, 163
 definition, 14, 16–18, 23, 28, 40
 and democracy, 9, 11, 32, 42, 86, 154
 and politics, 14, 34, 62
 and populist nationalism, 3, 22, 27–28, 78–79, 158, 161
Republican Party, 86
 and Christian nationalism, 74, 79, 82, 86–87
 and politics, 82, 84, 86
 and segregation and race, 83, 84
Richie, Tony, 30
Roos, Lothar, and "cultural-ethical triangle," 56

Saperstein, David, 15
Second Vatican Council, 106, 108
 Council of Trent, 104
 democracy and nationalism, 92, 101–2, 109, 111
 Dignitatis Humanae, 102, 103
 human rights, 110, 112–13
 religious liberty, 102, 103
Snyder, Timothy, 158
Story, Joseph, 72

Tamir, Yuli, 7–8
Trump, Donald, 7
 and anti-Muslim attitudes, 27, 28, 39, 145
 Charlottesville, 74, 84
 and Christian nationalism, 32, 68, 74, 79, 85–86, 87

and illiberal democracy, 27, 38, 40, 80, 83, 143
 and immigration, 35, 38, 129
 and politics, 7, 74, 86, 87, 94, 123, 144
Tucker, Gordon, 146–47

United Nations, and the Universal Declaration of Human Rights, 30, 99, 126
United States Constitution, and the Establishment Clause of the First Amendment, 65, 69, 72–73
United States Supreme Court, 39, 70, 86
 and Christianity, 72
 crosses on public land, 72
 on funding parochial schools, 70
 and Potter dissent, 72
 and prayer in school, 47, 70
 Town of Greece ruling, 72

Wahid, Alissa, viii, 8
Wallace, George, on segregation and God, 82
Walzer, Michael, 9
Whitehead, Andrew, Samuel Perry, and Joseph Baker, on Christian nationalism and Donald Trump, 66, 67, 78, 87
Wilders, Geert, 35, 45, 59
Winkler, Jim, 41, 121
Winthrop, John, and "City upon a Hill" declaration, 75

Zion, Noam, on God and rabbis, 148

9 780268 200602